# No Parent Left Behind

Navigating the Special Education Universe

## SUSAN M. BREFACH Ed.D.

### www.susanbrefach.com

ISBN: 1482030772
ISBN-13: 9781482030778
Library of Congress Control Number: 2013901344

CreateSpace Independent Publishing Platform
North Charleston, South Carolina

# DEDICATION

This book is dedicated to my husband, Don. Every person who reads this book and is better able to help a child should send him their mental thanks, for without his encouragement and support it would never have been written.

# ACKNOWLEDGEMENTS

I am indebted to each and every parent who entrusted their children to me over the past thirty-three years. I am awed by their love, their persistence, and their courage. Even when they were confused or frustrated, they did not waver in their commitment to help their children be successful.

I also need to acknowledge the wonderful, unique children who have marched bravely into my office and let me see the things they couldn't do. It takes great strength to let a stranger watch you struggle and fail, to share your feelings, to trust that this person will help you do the thing you want most—to learn and be successful. Thank you for letting me know you.

Throughout my career, I have observed many skilled, effective teachers and specialists in a wide variety of settings. I appreciate the opportunities I have had to see them at work, helping children to master curriculum and compensate for their learning problems. I have also been able to observe many fine school programs that provide excellent services to meet the needs of children. These teachers and programs have helped me understand and recognize effective practices in education and remedial services.

The illustrations and graphics in this book (and on my website) are the work of Michael Upright, who has been incredibly patient with my limited skills in the areas of technology and social media. I am grateful for his talent, advice and wonderful sense of humor.

A number of parents, educational advocates and attorneys have reviewed chapters of this book and provided many helpful comments and suggestions. I am grateful for their wise and relevant input.

I thank one parent in particular for suggesting the title for this book. It captures perfectly what I wanted to accomplish.

# HOW TO KNOW IF THIS BOOK IS FOR YOU

*"Parents have become so convinced that educators know what is best for children that they forget that **they** are the experts."*
*Marion Wright Edelman*

- This book is a **roadmap for parents of children with learning needs** who are concerned that their children may need more help in order to achieve success in school.

- It is a **tool kit** to help you help your children.

- My goal is to **educate** you in how the system works, and to **empower** you so that you can be an effective advocate for your children.

According to the National Center for Education statistics, about 13 percent of the students in public school—**about 6.5 million children**—received special education services during the 2009-2010 school year (Monitor on Psychology, American Psychological Association, September, 2012). This, of course, does not include children who attend private schools, or those whose parents have them tutored outside of school. It does not include children who have not yet been identified as having special needs, or those who have needs but do not yet receive special education services. The actual number of children in need is likely to be higher, possibly much higher. And all of these children have parents who care about them.

All over the country, there are children who are struggling with some aspect of school—struggling and sometimes failing. There are children who don't work up to their potential, whose gifts may be stifled or even ignored. Children who don't master the curriculum, and who can't perform at grade level.

Most parents know when their children are developing well and meeting with success. They have good instincts, and they've been watching their children since they were babies. They also know when their children are struggling, "going under" for the third time, or flat-out failing.

If you take only one piece of information from this book, I hope it will be the following: TRUST YOURSELF. **You know your child best**, better than any school employee or outside professional, regardless of their degrees and certifications. **If you think there's a problem with your child or the education they are being provided, you are most likely correct.**

In the past thirty-plus years, I have almost never seen a case in which the parent was wrong about a child's **need** for some kind of intervention. Parents might not know the fancy diagnostic labels, but they know when a child's development or performance is not at an age-appropriate level. Parents often tell me they suspect there is a problem, even if they don't know exactly what it is or what to do about it.

Parents whose children are struggling need to know three basic things:

- what specific **areas of need** their child has

- what specific **services** their child needs to be successful

- **what to do** to get those services provided

This book will help you understand both the educational system and the outside services that can be used to help your children learn. It will teach you what you need to know to help your child.

To use an analogy, congress sets the rules of the education game. Schools are where the game gets played out. My goal in writing this is to **level the playing field**. Once you know how the game is played, and who you need on your team, you have a much better chance of winning. In this case, "winning" means **helping your child to be successful** in school, and in life. For most parents, this is the primary goal—the end result that motivates them.

Which parents are most likely to benefit from this book? They are the parents of children with some type of special learning need or learning disability, as defined by state and federal laws[1]. These laws apply to children of average and above average ability as well as to children of below average ability.

The laws were designed to identify children who have specific disadvantages that interfere with learning.

What are these disadvantages? Essentially, they are differences in the wiring of the brain—neurological differences that affect the way a person's brain works. All behavior (including learning) is affected by how the brain works. Everything we think and do is the result of brain activity. It sounds so simple, but the connection between brain and behavior is absolute. Any child's difficulty with learning is due to his or her specific neurological development and performance. Even if you are told that the problem is "only anxiety", or nervousness, or "not being ready", or shyness—**it all comes from the brain.**

This means a child who is having difficulty can be diagnosed with any of a very long list of problems. The decision tree for determining "need" is discussed in the chapter on the Individualized Education Program and provided in the Appendix. It includes:

- specific learning disabilities (dyslexia, language-based learning disability, nonverbal learning disability, visual-spatial difficulties, problems with written language, math, sensory integration, etc.)

- attention deficit disorder

- lower cognitive ability (low intelligence)

- physical limitations

- medical problems (chronic conditions such as Crohn's disease, seizure disorders, etc)

- behavior problems

- mood disorders

- autism and related, milder developmental disorders

- a wide range of psychological issues.

People often wonder where these brain differences come from. There are many causes, and some will be discussed in the chapter on early development. The bottom line is, we all learn in slightly different ways. Based on my experience and observations, schools are designed to teach to the **average**—the average learner, of average intelligence, with an average temperament and language skill and social style. If you've spent any time in a school, you may have noticed this yourself—especially if your child falls **outside** the average.

Educators will mention "differentiation" or the importance of providing an individualized approach, but in my observations, I generally find that instruction is geared to the average in regular education classrooms.

---

1    The link to the federal law is included in the appendix, along with links to department of education sites for individual states

Children who learn differently—for whatever reason—may need a more adapted or specialized mode of instruction. Everyone knows people who "learn best by doing", or who need you to "draw them a picture" or "give them a map" so they'll understand, or even a lucky few who can remember anything they hear. We all have a preferred learning style. Fortunately, most of us can cope when information is not presented in the "best" way for us—it's how we survived in school, where our teachers differed from year to year.

Children with learning difficulties, however, require a **different type of instruction** from what is used in a typical classroom. They learn in ways that don't respond well to many teachers' typical teaching style. In order for them to fully understand and be able to use essential skills such as reading and arithmetic, **they need be taught a certain, specific way**.

For example, the language a teacher uses may need to be adapted or simplified.

Some children will need a sensible "visual" to help them make sense of a lecture.

Some children won't simply "pick up" social skills, or skills for organization and note-taking, or skills for written language, when they are merely presented as part of a regular school day.

Special education laws were designed to help these children. The idea was that children at risk for failure in the learning environment would be identified and provided with the types of instruction or accommodations that would **allow them to learn and be successful**. This has turned out to be easier in theory than in practice.

In fact, it's often not a problem to get your child to **qualify** for services. Schools are often in agreement with parents that **an obstacle to learning** exists. It's what happens afterward that determines whether your child will overcome or compensate for these learning difficulties—or whether they will struggle even more, fall farther behind, and ultimately fail.

So, is this book for you?

It is, if you have a child covered by federal law and:

- you aren't sure they are getting the help they need;

- you know they are not getting enough help, and don't know what to do about it;

- you don't even know the right questions to ask to understand your child's needs;

- you don't know if you can believe what the school tells you about your child's skills and performance;

- you feel overwhelmed at school meetings, with ten school personnel sitting around the table and only one of you;

- you don't know whether your child is making progress;

- you don't know what to expect from a Team Meeting, or how to interpret an Individualized Education Program or 504 Accommodation Plan;

- you don't understand what the testing results mean;

- you don't know what steps to take to begin getting services for your child;

- you don't know whether an outside evaluation is needed, and what it might tell you that a school evaluation will not;

- you aren't sure what an educational advocate could do for you, or whether you need to work with one

- you don't know when in this process you should consult an attorney, and what an attorney can do for you.

**Why should you listen to me?** For parents who truly need a book with this kind of information, there is still the question of who I am. What qualifies me to offer you advice, checklists, and opinions about the way education—and especially special education—works today?

I have been working as a psychologist for more than 30 years. I have worked in hospitals and mental health clinics, as well as in schools. I have had training in neuropsychology and am licensed as both a clinical psychologist and a school psychologist. I specialize in working with children and adolescents, and have seen more than 1600 clients for individual evaluations. I have spent years of my life (in terms of hours) in hundreds of school meetings and classroom observations, and in dozens of school systems. I have advocated for children's needs for over 30 years—in places ranging from the post-testing meeting with parents to a Special Education hearing. In some cases, my results have shown parents that their children were receiving the appropriate help, and were making good progress. In other cases, I have recommended additional services or programs to meet a child's needs. In all cases, to the best of my ability, I have provided information and support to parents, so they could be **effective advocates** for their children.

I see what I do as a blend of science and art. I use my knowledge base and my testing skills, but there are several additional, equally important aspects of what I do—the detective part of pulling the scores and behaviors and clues together, the art of integrating what I know and writing it well, and a willingness to advocate in the most truthful, effective way for necessary services. I have to accept the strengths and weaknesses of the education system as it currently exists, but I **don't** have to accept what is offered if it isn't right for the child. My moral center demands this level of commitment, and I feel passionately about making a difference in the lives of many children. This is our future—well educated, emotionally healthy children who will be fully functioning members of society.

**Children** are the **most important** members of the education system. Their success validates the work of everyone in the system. They are the reason I do the things I do, and my goal is simple. As it says on my website, my mission is "making school work for your child."

# TABLE OF CONTENTS

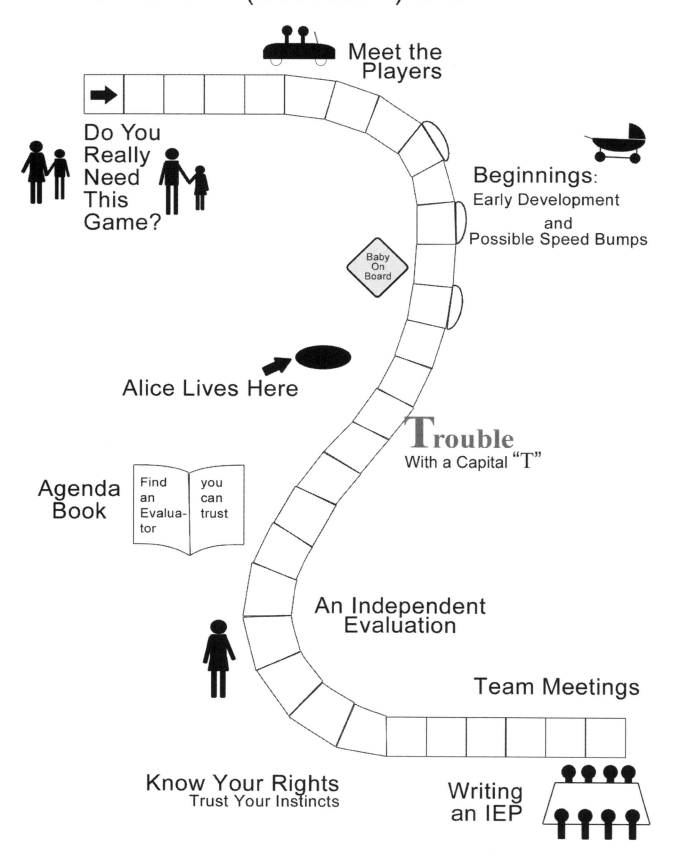

# ROADMAP

## The Game of (Education) Life

Meet the Players

Do You Really Need This Game?

Beginnings: Early Development and Possible Speed Bumps

Baby On Board

Alice Lives Here

Trouble With a Capital "T"

Agenda Book

Find an Evaluator you can trust

An Independent Evaluation

Team Meetings

Know Your Rights Trust Your Instincts

Writing an IEP

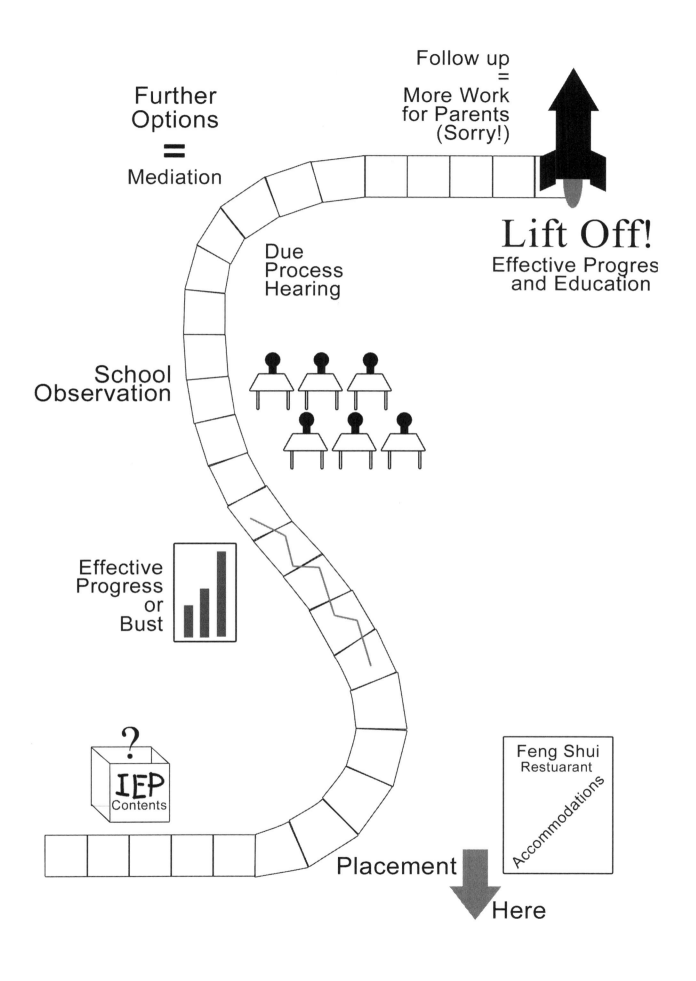

# CHAPTER 1

## SO, WHO ARE THESE CHILDREN?

*"I believe the children are our future; teach them well and*
*let them lead the way."*
*George Benson, The Greatest Love of All*

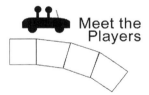 Meet the
Players

For you as parents, reading this book is not like reading a novel or the newspaper.

It can be interesting to put yourself in the shoes of another parent, or to read about the learning disabilities or social problems of someone else's child. There are plenty of books and magazine articles describing those journeys.

Most of all, I know you want to understand how to help **your child**. I know your concerns, and I promise that this book takes you through **all the steps,** from those first stirrings of concern to the point where you can step back and believe that your child is on his or her way to an independent, successful life.

The best way I know to show you this path is to follow some children through all or part of the process. By sharing the stories of children whom I have seen for testing—and especially those I have followed over time—I can illustrate different types of learning disabilities and how they "show up" at different ages. I can describe the steps I took in testing the children and working with their parents, the recommendations I made, and what happened over time.

That is probably one of your chief concerns. **What happens** to these children over time? Are most of them successful? Do they make effective progress? Do they have a good life, in school and beyond?

You ask—**Will my own child overcome his learning issues and be able to master the necessary skills to achieve success?**

I hear you. If you follow the steps in this book, if you get your child the help he or she needs to make effective progress, if you advocate for them and monitor their growth—then the chances of a successful outcome are **much** better. I want to **show** through example, rather than merely **telling** you what to do. To this end, I say, "**Imagine** that this is your child. **Follow** the steps, and **match** the symptoms I describe with the interventions we put in place. **Remember** what worked, so you can be sure to get **appropriate services** to meet your own child's needs."

There are no guarantees when you are raising a child—it's not like buying a refrigerator. All I know is that I believe parents truly do the best they can. I'm not doing experiments with the children I test, so I can't give you a "success rate" or tell you what "percent" will learn to read at grade level, for example. What I **can** say is that most of the children referred to me are having a very tough time. When I am able to get them effective academic instruction, and follow their progress through re-testing, and help their parents advocate for their needs, they do well—they learn to read, they make friends, they graduate from high school and often go on to college. No guarantees. But without the help described in this book, I doubt any of them would have done as well.

# Early Identification/Evaluation

Let me describe a few "beginnings", so you can see some of the patterns that I see when children first show up in my office. I will also share the interventions I helped them receive, so they could be more successful.

The first three children were either at-risk in infancy or early childhood, or were identified as having special needs before beginning school. Children with these profiles make up about a quarter of my practice.

#

**Adam**[2] was 8 years old, still in first grade, and not really reading. He was slow to develop language skills, and didn't say single words until age 2. In preschool, it often seemed as though

---

2    For all cases in this book, the name and any identifying information have been changed to assure the privacy of the child and family. In some cases, the child referenced may be an individual case history, and in others a

he was not paying attention. He was usually one of the last to clean up or sit on the rug for circle time, because he watched the other children to see what he should be doing.

Adam started kindergarten late, just after his 6th birthday. His parents hoped it would give him a chance to "catch up". By the end of the year, he still did not recognize all upper and lower case letters reliably. He had only a few letter-sound associations. He still wrote only his first name, in upper case letters. The teacher recommended that he repeat the year, which he did.

At the beginning of first grade, the school tested Adam. He got help with reading and written language from a teacher with special education certification, in a small group setting, but still spent most of his day in the regular classroom, where he was confused by instructions and the language-heavy math curriculum.

Adam was a good-natured boy who wanted to please. He was well-behaved all day in school, but fell apart at home as soon as it was time to do homework. He would cry, saying he didn't know what to do. With a parent sitting beside him, it took more than an hour to do ten minutes' worth of writing and math. He was unable to read well enough to do any reading at home.

I first saw Adam for testing at the end of first grade. After observing his classes, it was clear he needed more language-based instruction, but it took 2 years of meetings, and documenting his lack of progress, before the school agreed to a more appropriate setting at another school in the district. There, much more of his day was adapted, and he was given an individual reading tutorial as well as more speech/language instruction. He is making slow, steady progress, but I am continuing to work with his parents to ensure this continues.

#

**Ann** was also completing first grade when first seen for testing, and although she was very bright, this had not been a successful year. As I say in many Team meetings and parent conferences, the **two main goals for first grade** are to learn to read and to "buy into the system". This means that a child needs to finish the work she is given, listen to and follow instructions, control her behavior, and deal with daily routines.

Ann had not been successful at any of these tasks. Reading was still mostly guess-work, and math made even less sense to her. For much of the year, she had worked on the classroom floor or underneath a table—when she worked at all.

Ann had always struggled with what could be called "cognitive regulation". She was very poor at "filtering out" distractions in her environment, or deciding what was important to attend to and what she should ignore. She had been diagnosed with a sensory integration disorder as a toddler. As a result, the visual, auditory and tactile stimuli of preschool or a

---

composite of two or more cases. Every child discussed in this book displays a pattern of difficulties that I have seen many times.

regular classroom were overwhelming to her. She also had poor pencil control and some motor planning weaknesses.

Ann also had great difficulty paying attention. She was bouncy, fidgety, very talkative, and unable to work independently for even a brief time. She required a great deal of structure from an adult to start or complete a task, both in school and at home. Her active mind was always darting from one thought to another. She was distracted by things around her and by her own internal sensations and thoughts.

Given her problems managing both input and output, it was not surprising that academic learning had not kept pace with expectations. Ann received help in school, in class and in a small group, but her attention was an issue. She was also tutored privately by a reading specialist, and received sensory integration therapy. Even with this help, both Ann's parents and her teachers realized that she wasn't meeting grade-level expectations—and she was only in first grade.

After I completed testing, we all agreed that it made more sense for her to transfer from her private school to the public one, where she was able to receive much more small-group and individual instruction. I also strongly suggested that medication be considered for her, to address attention and mood issues. Her private services were continued. The last time I re-evaluated Ann, she had moved up to middle school and was still placed in two small special education classes, with support for the other two. She was much calmer, more focused, and more productive—and her academic skills were close to grade level.

#

**Rory** was a premature baby, born three months early. His developmental milestones were delayed for walking and talking. He was extremely active and distractible, without much inhibition or regulation of his responses. With a summer birthday, he started kindergarten as a young five year old, although his "true" due date of October would have meant he missed the cutoff and got an additional year of preschool. It would definitely have helped.

Rory had received early intervention services since his first birthday, with parents "topping up" these services with additional speech and language and sensory integration therapies. He showed clear signs of a sensory integration disorder, as well as difficulties with articulation, motor planning, gross motor coordination, and fine motor control (printing and copying).

I saw Rory for testing near the end of Kindergarten. During that year, his mother had worked with him an average of two hours per day, in late afternoon and early evening. He continued to receive his "outside" therapies (paid for by parents), as well as limited speech services and reading help in school. Because his town had only half-day kindergarten, there wasn't time to offer more services, or to address his motor and sensory weaknesses. He was having difficulty learning letter names, letter-sound combinations, and skills for analyzing words on a sound-by-sound basis. His printing was very awkward, with large, poorly formed letters. His parents were concerned about possible learning disabilities.

Rory's schedule was packed with extra help, and he was still struggling. His pediatrician felt he should repeat the year, and my testing showed he was not ready for the demands of first grade. Although he was very bright, with a good vocabulary, he was significantly below age level in his academic skills, speech, attention span and activity level. The school, however, said he was "making adequate progress" and needed to "move on".

In this case, the parents had few options. Rory was certainly at risk, but had not yet "failed", and he was not three years below grade level (one criterion for a more specialized program)—though it was hard to see how he could have managed this when he was only in kindergarten. The school system actually did not have the type of classroom I wanted for this child, or the sensory integration services. The parents decided to sell their home and move to another town, where they thought Rory had a better chance of an appropriate placement and more remedial services.

# Identification in Late Elementary/Middle School

Some children manage to cope with early developmental expectations without too much difficulty. Parents report that they were "easy" babies who talked and walked on schedule. In preschool, their teachers said they were "doing fine". They were able to make social connections and learned some early pre-academic skills, although usually with greater than average effort.

Although they managed to "keep their heads above water" for years, eventually these children were "not waving but drowning" as expectations changed or increased. Usually, things started getting tense as they failed to develop smooth, automatic skills in upper elementary school—grades 4 and 5. They still read with difficulty, had poor memories, were disorganized and inattentive, didn't make friends, didn't write much, couldn't solve word problems in math—any of a dozen or so skill areas that were necessary for success in learning, behavior, or social development. Often, their self esteem has also begun to "take a hit". These children comprise about half of my practice.

#

**Michelle** was ten years old when I first saw her for testing. She was in fourth grade, but still reading at approximately a first grade level. The letter-sound system had never made much sense to her, and she was still unable to accurately isolate and sequence the individual sounds in a syllable or a word. In part, this was because she didn't really hear or analyze them correctly. Her auditory processing skills and auditory memory span were extremely limited, according to an audiology exam.

Michelle attended a private school, although the class size was about the same as in public school. There were very limited academic support services available. Michelle went to the public school several days a week, before school started, for remedial help. To my dismay, this had not included direct instruction in the skills she didn't have—how to analyze and sequence the sounds that make up words.

In class, Michelle always seemed to be "in her own world". Often, she was not able to "make sense" of what the teacher was saying, or she did it much more slowly than her classmates. Her teachers described her as "spacey" and "easily distracted".

There was an aide for the whole class, who ended up sitting with Michelle for most of the day, focusing her and explaining what she was expected to do. Without this help, Michelle would not have been able to do any of the work; with the aide doing the reading, interpreting, and writing for her, she managed to do a small percentage, but didn't seem to remember much. At home, a parent sat with her while she struggled to complete homework.

Michelle was sweet and good natured, a skillful skier and soccer player, and a very hard worker when she understood what to do and was able to do it. Math made more sense to her, as long as she didn't have to remember math facts independently. She had always struggled with activities such as girl scouts, where she missed social cues and couldn't follow directions well. The other girls tended to leave her out of their plans, and didn't call for play dates.

During my first evaluation, Michelle commented to me that she thought she might just "quit school", and go to work with her father at a local utility company. At age 10! I could hear the sadness and discouragement in her voice. Instead, I fought to get her placed in a private school for children with dyslexia and language-based learning disabilities. It took a year before a place was available, and we went right to the door of the hearing officer before a settlement was reached.

The good news was that she was up and dressed each morning (on her own!), eagerly waiting for the cab to take her to school. I watched her work unbelievably hard in her tutorial sessions and her classes. However, even in this setting, she struggled with reading, memory, and making friends. She had to learn all kinds of strategies to compensate for the ways in which her brain didn't "work". But Michelle made good use of her years in this school. Last year, she graduated and went to a small college with good academic support, planning to become a nurse.

#

In early elementary grades, **Hannah** had such severe sensory integration sensitivities and problems with mood regulation that she spent most of the time hiding under her desk, or in a corner of the classroom. She ran away from class on many occasions, and had explosive tantrums where she threw things and hit her teachers. She was mostly too overwhelmed by the amount of input to function.

The school finally agreed to place her in a private therapeutic day program, and even here she struggled. She was so easily frustrated that she often couldn't complete work that she was capable of. In therapy sessions at school, her thinking was disorganized and off-topic.

She had trouble with the normal give-and-take of a conversation. She imagined dangers in the classroom and persecution by her classmates. Her program provided some help with sensory integration skills, but this was the heart of her problem, and her progress was slow.

Hannah had difficulty "making sense" of much of what she saw. She couldn't complete puzzles, copy block patterns with even four blocks, or draw simple visual designs. Her drawing and printing skills were years below age level. Tasks that involved sequencing, directionality, or visual-spatial analysis were extremely difficult. As a result, she had trouble with rote learning such as making change, telling time, or remembering the months of the year. Gym classes and playground times were very challenging, as might be expected.

I saw Hannah for testing in mid fifth grade. In addition to her sensory, academic, and motor planning problems, she had difficulty keeping friends and handling social situations. She had a very small peer group and only one outside activity. Her parents were especially concerned because Hannah's program only enrolled children to the end of fifth grade. The public school wanted her to return to a sprawling middle school of 800 students, possibly with an aide for part of the day. They said she had made progress, and they would be able to meet her substantial academic needs with a daily period in a learning center with 8-12 other students.

Hannah needed to continue in the kind of small, highly structured, supportive, and specialized placement she'd had for the past three years. Even in this setting, she had barely been able to make "effective progress". She was too young for a boarding program, and there were few local options. We finally placed her in another therapeutic program, and as part of the agreement with the school system, parents paid for outside sensory integration therapy and a language pragmatics class (to help with her social functioning). Hannah continued to improve, and actually made a small group of friends at this new school, where she remained through high school.

#

**Lucas** was adopted as an infant, from a troubled family with a significant history of impulsive behaviors, attention deficit disorder and learning problems. As a young child, he had poor language skills, a short attention span, and behaved in ways that endangered his safety. His adoptive parents had worked very hard to be flexible and consistent with him, to develop his social and athletic strengths, and to help with schoolwork. As a result, he was moderately successful within the structure of elementary school.

In middle school, however, Lucas had tremendous trouble staying focused long enough to complete tasks, even while working in his classes. He struggled to communicate verbally, and often gave up on assignments that required logical thinking or a sequence of steps. As much as possible, he avoided reading and writing.

A major problem for Lucas involved mood control and regulation. In addition to his attention deficit, he was easily irritated and frustrated, and had explosive outbursts at home and in school. He was often depressed and withdrawn, and would then refuse to do any work.

At times, he would put his head on his desk and just "check out" for the whole class period. Various medications had been tried with limited success, so he had good days and bad ones. His symptoms were not under control.

Lucas presented a complex profile, with problems in his family history, his biochemistry, his learning, and his behavioral control. At times, he was simply unable to cope with increased expectations. When I first saw him for testing, his academic skills were 3 to 4 years below grade level. He needed very specific accommodations and remedial help in order to address his emotional, behavioral and academic difficulties.

Unfortunately, these were not available in the public school he attended. Lucas was placed in a class for children with behavior problems, which meant that this active, restless and socially sensitive boy was in a single room for most of the school day, separated from nearly the entire school, including his teammates (he was an excellent athlete). He was miserable and becoming more reactive as a result. The program included consequences for inappropriate behaviors, but no real therapy or training to improve Lucas' self-control and self-awareness. No one addressed his poor organizational skills or even his long-standing language needs. As a result, he had fewer skills to help him negotiate verbally and manage a more grade-appropriate work load. The program did not allow him to have the experience of changing classes, using a locker, working with different teachers and their styles, or taking elective classes.

I include Lucas to show how hard it can be to find a place for a young adolescent with several areas of need, none of which had been addressed appropriately. The public school program was inadequate in academic and social areas, and was too restrictive. However, his behavior and his moods meant we couldn't place him in a school for children with language-based learning disabilities, though he needed that type of instruction. Programs for children with emotional/behavioral problems did not provide enough remedial instruction to improve his academic skills, and in two cases his skills were too low for him to have an academic peer group. One program for adolescents with attention deficit disorder and mild learning needs couldn't deal with his outbursts or provide on-site therapy. What we had to "settle" for was less than Lucas needed. Had I been able to work with the family 5 years sooner, we might have obtained a far more appropriate placement.

# High School and Beyond

I never know whether to consider it "good luck" or "bad luck" when a child makes it all the way to high school before being seen in my office. On the one hand, I know they are persistent, hard working, and probably have a lot of family support. Some are not too far below grade level in their skills. On the other hand, things have often gone too far by the time an adolescent "crashes and burns". The program they are in often cannot be modified enough for success, and something very different may be needed to provide enough emotional support as well as intensive remedial help for the few remaining years of school.

#

**Sarah** was fourteen, completing ninth grade, when I first evaluated her. Although she had always struggled academically, she managed to make it through middle school with many hours per week of outside tutoring and in-school support. Her first year of high school turned out to be more than she could cope with, both academically and socially.

At home, she was often moody, angry and depressed. She began to swear at her parents when they tried to help her with school work. She seemed discouraged and gave up quickly on most assignments. She had never been able to read grade level textbooks or novels independently, but now it took hours for her mother to read everything to her—when Sarah would even allow her to do so.

Sarah had chronic ear infections beginning when she was an infant, with three sets of ear tubes put in before her tonsils and adenoids were removed at age seven. She always struggled to hear the final sounds in words, and had specific word retrieval problems as well. She reversed letters when writing, read some words backwards or substituted a word that "looked" similar, and mixed up the order of letters when spelling words. She was diagnosed with dyslexia in elementary school.

Testing showed that Sarah was extremely bright, but in school her performance was barely average. Even in math, where her skills were advanced, she was often unable to figure out how to solve the word problems. During lectures, she couldn't analyze what the teacher was saying quickly enough to take complete notes; she missed information or wrote the wrong words. The other students teased her about being "slow", because she needed information repeated on so many occasions. Because of her problems with language processing, memory, and reading, her foreign language classes in middle school had been a disaster.

Sarah was emotionally fragile and withdrawn during testing, becoming tearful while doing academic tasks. The public high school did not have the types of language-based classes or the specialized remedial instruction she needed, and she was no longer able to simply "tough it out". With the help of an attorney, her parents and I were able to place her in a private program for children with dyslexia. She learned strategies to improve her reading and compensate for her learning problems, graduated and went to college with an updated accommodation plan.

#

**Evan** was in seventh grade, but was reading four grade levels lower than this. The school said they helped him with all his work, and so it "wasn't really a problem". His mother noted that he was unable do any of his homework independently, even though it was "modified".

She sat beside him each night, helping him do homework for hours. By the time I saw him for testing, he didn't want her to help him anymore—he wanted to be able to do it himself.

Evan struggled in school beginning in kindergarten, in spite of his above-average intelligence. He took several years to learn all the letter-sounds and develop a sight word vocabulary. His reading was hesitant, slow, and often inaccurate. His writing showed better potential in his choice of vocabulary—but almost all the words were misspelled, and often they weren't even phonetically "sensible". In math, he struggled to remember facts and the correct sequence of steps to solve arithmetic problems.

Evan's classes were considered to be co-taught, with a special education teacher in the room along with a regular teacher. The special education teacher took notes during classes, and "checked in" with a number of students, including Evan. He generally received the same handouts and class assignments as his peers. He had a daily period of academic support in a small group.

Evan also had migraine headaches. These occurred three or four times per week, requiring prescription medication. He'd had them for several years—except in the summers, when he had a different schedule. He would get up at six a.m. and travel for forty-five minutes to go to a private school that offered an intensive, remedial summer school program, with classes of eight students as well as an individual reading tutorial, designed specifically for children with dyslexia. Six weeks, five days per week in summer school—and no headaches, because he actually understood what to do and was successful in this setting.

Evan's mother paid for the summer program for several years, but it was like a blood transfusion—the effects lasted only a short time. The public school was already providing as much support as they had, and Evan was still popping pills for his headaches. After some fairly heated meetings with school personnel (and again, an attorney) we placed him in the private school full-time, where he repeated seventh grade, went on to graduate at the top of his high school class, and attended a small college with a strong academic support program.

#

**Joseph** made it all the way to senior year in high school, though I'm not sure how he managed to stay "under the radar" for so many years. By report, he always struggled with academic learning. He had a number of significant illnesses during childhood, and missed a lot of school some years, but even when he attended regularly he showed clear signs of dyslexia and language learning disabilities. He was easily confused by lectures or more complex spoken language; he would "lose" information from short-term memory, and he had trouble memorizing material for tests. Often, he couldn't find the words or facts he needed, and would stick with simple sentences when speaking and writing. His math skills were better, though he often had trouble interpreting and solving word problems.

Because of these learning problems, Joseph never acquired the "habits of mind"—the logical, sequential thinking skills—that were essential for success in high school. In middle school, when other kids picked these up, he was trying to handle the reading and the work load. He was not taught directly how to work in an organized way on a task from beginning to end, how to plan his work load and monitor the amount of work he had, how to "break down" a larger assignment into smaller steps, or how to use active strategies for problem solving.

As a result, he was poorly equipped to handle the expectations of high school, both in terms of reading skill and in his general approach to tasks. His writing showed signs of good intelligence and creativity, but spelling, vocabulary and technical details were often incorrect. He was placed in an academic support class each day, where he tried to do some homework but didn't get help with the skills he lacked. In classes, an aide took notes, but Joseph was overwhelmed by the amount of language, the pace, and the reading level. He simply got too little attention, and not enough remedial help.

When I saw him for testing, he had gotten to a point of simply giving up, due to lack of confidence in himself and his skills. He just wanted to "get out and be done", but he still did not have most usable skills for learning and working. His parents didn't want him limited to unskilled jobs, but he was not ready at all for college, even if he would have considered going.

We found several post-high school programs that were designed to improve academic skills through intensive individual remediation. These programs also taught the executive functioning skills that would help a teen to be successful in planning, organizing, and monitoring his performance on more complicated tasks. Most of these programs were expensive, and the best ones were two-year programs. Joseph and his parents found one that met his needs and their budget, and he reluctantly agreed to try. Although he dropped out twice, he finally improved his skills enough to allow him to transfer to a technical school, where he got training for a job in the computer industry.

# 

Of course, these few children represent the "tip of the iceberg" in terms of the various **types** of problems and possible **outcomes** for children with learning, behavioral, or emotional problems. They give you just a small idea of how difficult it can be to get the right program or remedial instruction for a child—even with help. In many cases, there **isn't** an appropriate program. Either the child has an unusual combination of needs, or the program is too far away, or the peer group isn't a good "fit", or there's some other limitation. We'll have to accept a smaller amount of specialized instruction or the parents will have to add outside services. It can take years to get an appropriate placement, and sometimes we won't be successful.

I estimate I've seen more than 1600 children and young adults since I began testing—one of them probably very similar to yours. Each one was unique, and I remember a startling number of them as individuals. In many cases, now that I have a certain reputation for helping with complex cases, the children are referred to me. Often, they arrive "at the end of their rope"—exhausted, discouraged, falling apart emotionally, and far behind their peers in terms of academic skills.

Some of these children have complex diagnostic profiles, and I'm not surprised they haven't been well diagnosed or adequately serviced. Some are painfully dyslexic or learning disabled; others have serious cognitive and emotional problems; some are so poorly regulated I wonder how they, and their parents, get through the day. Other cases are straightforward. It's absolutely clear what the children need, and I am angry that they haven't gotten it.

For each of them, there are parents who do the best they can, and school systems hoping what they have on hand will work.

Maybe you saw your child in one of these brief descriptions, or maybe you said, "Well, sort of, but not quite." That's okay. If you see even part of your child's problem, chances are this book has information you can use. There will be many other children whose needs will be discussed in the following chapters. In any case, it's the process of **identifying needs** and **following the path to get services** that is most important.

Children learn in different ways and at different rates. Usually, this isn't a problem, as long as they reach certain milestones by certain times.

When they don't, parents often find themselves in a bind. Do they go with their gut, telling them something is wrong? Or do they trust the school, telling them their child will catch up and everything will be fine?

Remember- **You as parents know your child best**. Never, ever ignore your gut instincts.

With every child I see, the parents have been watching and wondering for years. These children didn't just suddenly drop out of the sky one day and land in a family or a school in 2nd or 6th or 9th grade.

Parents have been asking questions, often since infancy or the toddler years. They have often had outside evaluations done—in some cases, multiple evaluations, by multiple professionals. Some of these kids come in with binders the size of the Boston yellow pages, literally hundreds of pages of reports, educational plans and progress notes, samples of class work and homework assignments, standardized test scores—and they aren't even in middle school!

Parents have often sat in dozens of school meetings. They have puzzled over the disconnect between their knowledge of their child and the school's description of how well the child was doing with the help that was being offered. They were quite sure, in spite of what they heard, that their child couldn't do grade level work, or work independently, or read effectively, or follow lectures, or organize their papers the way their peers did.

Even though many parents knew for years that there was a problem, they didn't know how to get **enough of the right kind of help** to allow their children to succeed.

Each child I see has a different level of intelligence, from below average to highly gifted. Some are so socially adept and charming, I'd gladly spend all day chatting with them, while others are silent and withdrawn, or fall along the autistic spectrum and struggle to read any social cues or even to make simple conversation.

Language skills vary over such a wide range. There are times I find myself speaking more slowly and deliberately, and in a louder voice, as though the child had a hearing impairment. I simplify questions and repeat them, when it's clear the child has mis-interpreted what I asked. Some children's memory spans allow them to remember only three or four "bits" of information, much less than the testing situation requires.

For other children, language is their strength, but the simpler four-block puzzles bring them to a screeching halt. They turn themselves sideways out of their chairs to try to "make sense" of what I want them to draw. They start over on paper and pencil tasks—often, multiple times. They choose answers that are rotated or slanted in a different direction from the correct one, and they can't tell a story in the proper sequence (I will sometimes ask about a movie they've recently seen, or even something as simple as "tell me how to make a peanut butter and jelly sandwich").

Some are **so embarrassed by their academic limitations**, they can barely get through this part of the evaluation. One fifth grader, who was bright and sensitive, hid his face with one hand while working with me, humiliated and near tears because of his inability to spell or read words. Younger ones try to distract me; older ones just give up or get surly. **Better to be bad than stupid**, they think.

The ones who are emotionally fragile come into the waiting room practically flashing with warning lights, like little bombs primed and ready to go off. You can see the anxiety in their parents' faces—*will my child make it through this?* It's incredibly stressful for both of them. There are those who won't make eye contact, some who don't talk for the first hour or so (which makes doing the verbal subtests of the WISC-IV a challenge). Others cry or have tantrums, or throw up. Most need more than one session, and as much gentleness and flexibility as I can find.

One school-phobic teen needed **8 sessions**—including the first three, when he wouldn't even get out of the car, and the fourth, where we worked in the waiting room. We would start to work, and at a certain point, sometimes after only twenty minutes, he'd say "I have to leave", and that would be it. He'd been out of school for most of a year. In another case, I was horrified to realize the teen was actively hallucinating in my office—while the school was telling his mother he was holding his own and basically doing fine.

There are times when it is extremely difficult to sit with a child who is so obviously struggling and in pain. Most are achingly aware of what they cannot do. I wonder, "Isn't anyone paying attention to this child? How can school personnel miss what's going on? How can they **not know** how low these skills are, or what an emotional wreck he is?"

I am always astonished at the work ethic of these children. Often, they have experienced chronic frustration or failure in school, and **still** they "knock themselves out" for me. Most adults in the same situation would tell me to leave them alone! Instead, these children push themselves to do their best; they wrack their brains for answers; they eat their snacks and settle back in without whining for more time off.

They leave the testing session and no matter how awful it was, they often tell their parents it was good or at least "fine", that it "wasn't so hard", that they'd even come back. I'm touched by their ability to find something good to say about such a stressful experience. Parents tell me they nearly all fall asleep in the car on the way home—even the teenagers.

It is a matter of pride to me that my scores are **accurate**. I **don't** give children the answers, ever. And my scores aren't **lower** because I ask them to do too much, either. I am testing what a child can do on nationally-normed tests, **completely independently**.

Some public school coordinators may try to discredit my work, when it is in conflict with their own findings, but I am confident of my accuracy. The majority of children I see have moderate to severe disabilities and/or have reached a point where remediation and help should have begun years before.

**Accuracy** is particularly important to most parents, because my scores represent a child's **real levels of skill**—what they can do if they go to a restaurant and have to read the menu, or need to make change at the mall, or want to read a sports magazine or apply for a job or send a thank-you note. I've had parents tell me their children couldn't send a text message because their spelling was so bad—even allowing for abbreviations, no one could understand what they had written.

**These are the things that worry parents**. The school tells them one thing; they see another. Most parents realize that it doesn't matter what the school says their child can do. To be honest, it doesn't matter what **I tell them** he or she can do. The only thing that matters is whether their child is an independent learner and can be successful, first in the grade they're in and then in the real world.

How do I see my role in working most effectively with parents and school systems? Let me give you an analogy. Some of you may have heard of the Horse Whisperer, a man who was able to connect with horses on a very deep level, and then train them or help them overcome certain behaviors. Many more of you may have seen or read about Cesar Millan, the Dog Whisperer, who does the same thing with dogs, and who has his own TV show and has written several books. He has built his reputation on his incredible instincts, his effective communication skills, and his ability to shape behaviors for positive results.

I read an article he wrote a couple of years ago about what dogs could teach us about life. I was struck by the fact that it was all equally true for parents trying to deal with their child's school and the special education system. I thought, "that's me. I'm the Special Education Whisperer".

Don't laugh or feel insulted!

Isn't that what you want your independent psychologist to be able to do—communicate effectively and get a positive result for your child? I thought so.

These are Mr. Millan's 8 ideas, and my explanation of how I use them, and help parents use them, to help their children succeed:

1. *Live in the moment*. When you suspect there's a problem, deal with that one issue before moving on or getting distracted by other concerns. It's easy for a parent, who has a full plate of work, homecare, childcare, adult relationships, and personal items, to get distracted from a specific concern about a child. Keep the focus on your area of concern until there are concrete steps being taken to address it—schedule a consulta-

tion or an evaluation, talk with your child's teacher or tutor, go online to find information about your concerns, etc. If necessary, post your concern on the bathroom mirror, or on Facebook—your family and friends will keep asking you about it, helping you to maintain focus.

2. *Nurture a balanced life.* It is just as important to keep reminding yourself and your child of his strengths and gifts and positive personal traits as it is to address the areas of need. Every person needs to know, in their gut, that they are worthy. That they do some things really well. That there are people who love and value them. When I did therapy, I would sometimes tell children that we were going to write down 25 wonderful things about them. Initially, they would give me a strange look and say there weren't 25 things, but as I started listing the ones I could think of, they would always join in with their own ideas. Often, we'd get beyond 25. The best part was, the child would just **glow** with pleasure while we did this exercise. It was an amazing self-esteem booster. Yes, your child may have a number of significant learning problems, or emotional, social, developmental, or physical challenges. One of the most important roles you will play as they move through childhood will be to remind them, and yourself, of their special strengths and areas of competence. These must be nurtured, just as the other areas must be improved. Without these strengths, your child won't make it through.

3. *Trust your instincts.* This is one of my mantras. You will see it throughout this book. **You are the expert on your child.** You know your child better than anyone else. Always trust your gut, voice your questions, hunt for answers, and don't give up.

4. *Be direct and consistent in your communication.* Good relationships—with children, teachers, school personnel, therapists—begin with clear and consistent communication. You can't help your child unless you make sure his teachers and other personnel know exactly what he needs, and what you expect them to do to help him achieve his goals. This will be important as your child moves through the educational system. You will be monitoring progress towards goals, modifying those goals, addressing new needs as they show up. All of it will hinge on frequent, honest, and direct communication between you and the service providers. However, I must warn you not to assume that school personnel will be your **friends.** This is not their role, or yours. You must focus on getting the help your child needs to succeed, which is **not** the same as trying to "be a nice person" or "soothe" the feelings of teachers or other adults at school.

5. *Learn to listen.* The other side of the coin. You need to listen carefully to what teachers and school personnel are saying (or not saying), though that doesn't mean you will always agree with them. It really helps to have a "translator" in the form of a skilled professional who listens with you, since "edu-speak" is sometimes hard to decode. Once you understand what is being said, you and your professional can decide what needs to happen to **make things work for your child.** Remember, you can't fix the school's problems—and those problems are not a reason to offer your child a level of service that will not allow her to make effective progress.

6. *Don't hold grudges.* It is important to deal with conflicts early, before they get out of control. However, when a child has been struggling for years and is clearly not making progress, it's difficult to stay calm and centered and positive. Many parents have cried in my office, and in meetings. I may not be hopeful about the program being offered. There are times I am furious about what a child has had to deal with. But again, I have to stay in the moment, and help the parents do so as well. We move forward, starting from the time I begin working with the child. Being angry just wastes energy. An attorney may focus on what has been done (or not done) in the past, but I try to get forward momentum going, with the best possible services for a child from this point on.

7. *Live with purpose.* Another easy one, since parents looking at this book are probably doing so with a purpose already in mind. They have concerns, and want the school to address them. They want to succeed in helping their child be successful. I feel the same way. My purpose is to make sure that the children I work with will get the skills they need to master curriculum and be fully prepared for work and life. There are financial constraints, teacher limitations, and curriculum problems in every school system. **They are not my problem and they aren't yours, either.** My mission is making school work for **this particular child, your child,** now and in the future.

8. *Celebrate every day.* Yes, the Game of (Education) Life is a long and winding road, with speed bumps and pitfalls and detours all over the place. There are no guarantees of success in this game. Mr. Millan says dogs behave as though every walk is the best walk, every meal is the best meal, and every game is the best game. It will help both you and your child to find something each day that "went well" for your child. Something to celebrate—not with a big party, but with quiet pleasure. The consistency is actually more important than the size of the fuss. If there is always something to notice or praise, your child will begin looking for things to bring home and share with you, and will begin thinking about the quality of his work or the effort he puts in. That sort of attitude can snowball. It also can help cushion the not-so-good days, if you display reminders of skills that are growing stronger and performance that is improving.

So, these are some of the beliefs and strategies that I bring when I start working with a family and school system. My results may not always be as good as Mr. Millan's, but then again, the Special Education Whisperer is working with people, not dogs! I can say that I use these strategies consistently, find them helpful, and recommend them to parents.

However, even when I channel all the optimism of a golden retriever, I find that many cases have gotten more stressful and frustrating over the past 30 years. Problems that I used to help solve in Team meetings now get bogged down and often require more time, money, meetings and arguments than before.

Admittedly, I see a select group of children, but there is a distressing pattern that I see more and more often:

- Nearly every child I see is below where they need to be in one or often many areas

- They are not independent learners with academic and thinking skills that put them "on top" of grade level tasks

- In many cases, the older ones do not have the skills they need to be successful in today's world of work

- Their parents know it, the kids often know it too, but the schools keep telling them they're doing fine, or at least "all right"

- Given the current state of school funding, with budget constraints and unfunded mandates, school districts are becoming more aggressive about fighting the provision of adequate services to children who qualify, or even denying services altogether

There have been some really bad situations where, sitting in a school meeting, I couldn't imagine we were all talking about the same child. In my darker moments, I've been afraid that the child could have been lying on the classroom floor (with his arms and legs in the air like a dead bug), and the school would still have assured us that he was happy, and learning, and perfectly fine. This is amusing, but also sad—because I've seen the results when schools can't acknowledge the extent of a child's problems.

In my practice, I can help a certain number of children per year, while still maintaining the absolute focus of my testing, observing, and writing—and, most important, the **art** that goes into producing each individual portrait. I can help a certain number of parents get the services their children need.

I decided that you and other parents might benefit from something similar. You don't just step onto the playing field and know what to do to win a complex game, whether it's football or soccer or school. Just like your children, **you need information, strategies, and a game plan** from beginning to end. You need an understanding of the rules of the game and how it is played, so you can be effective and successful.

If you are anything like the thousands of parents I have worked with, I know you will do **whatever it takes** to meet your children's needs. I know how important a goal this is. And I am going to help you.

# CHAPTER 2

# WHERE IT STARTS

*"You did what you knew how to do,
and when you knew better, you did better."*
*Maya Angelou*

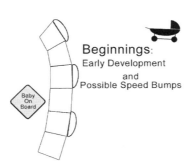

Beginnings:
Early Development
and
Possible Speed Bumps

Atsome point, a parent will become aware that there is a problem with some aspect of their child's development.

In parent conferences, they say to me:

- We knew when he was a baby there was something wrong- he was fussy and irritable all the time

- He didn't talk as early as his brothers

- Her speech was so hard to understand

- He never crawled and he walked late; he still can't kick or catch a ball

- She never stopped moving or talking, and she didn't need much sleep

- He could pay attention to TV or a video game, but he'd get bored by most other activities

- Everything bugged him- the way his clothes fit, the taste and texture of foods, taking a bath, noisy places, even being too close to other kids

- When she got to preschool, she only did parallel play; she didn't make friends or get invited for play dates

- He never chose to draw or use scissors, and he'd switch hands when using a pencil

- In kindergarten, she couldn't pay attention at circle time

- We'd show him letters, but he wasn't interested—not even for his name

- She couldn't remember her address or phone number or birthday

At some point, the red flag (or flags) goes up, and parents begin to ask questions of the people who deal with their children, whom they hope will have some answers.

It's important for parents to understand the general course of child development from infancy to the beginning of kindergarten—what a child should be able to do in different areas, such as language, motor skills, sensory integration, social abilities, and attention. There are many books available on this topic, and it is not the purpose of this book to offer a complete exploration of child development. I will address several areas that are important for parents of children with some type of learning difficulty—where these problems might come from, some common signs of a possible learning disability, a guideline for "how soon" a parent should be concerned—but please know that the authors listed in the Appendix have far more relevant experience and will provide you with much more detail about specific problems. I will focus mostly on issues that affect a child's readiness for early learning and school-related tasks.

The authors I list have been respected experts in their fields for many years. They are wise people who write clearly and are not trying to be "trendy" or to scare parents. Their books are designed to be read and used. New books on child development are always being written, some of which will contain updated research, but a lot of child development is not "new". I think it is more important for a parent to understand the basic time-lines for developmental milestones, and what you should be looking for as your child grows.

One question parents often ask is "what caused this problem?" It is a reasonable question, but with a few exceptions there isn't a good answer. We still know relatively little about how the brain works. Learning disabilities are subtle, mild problems with brain functioning that most likely involve several interacting neurological processes. They don't show up on a CT (computerized tomography) scan or an MRI (magnetic resonance imaging) scan, both of which look at physical features of the brain. There is research being done to identify the parts of the brain that become "active" when a certain task is being done (such as paying attention, flexible thinking or dealing with anxiety) and a recent article in The Lancet seems to have identified some genetic markers for Attention Deficit Disorder, but these are still very preliminary findings.

The chances are that your pediatrician or any specialist you consult will not find a clear "cause" of your child's learning disability, emotional problem, or social difficulty. Even if there **is** an abnormality on an EEG, as is true for a small percentage of the children I test, these abnormalities don't correlate with any specific type of learning disability.

In fact, when I went back through the records of children I had seen in the past few years who had **abnormal EEGs**, I found one child with severe cognitive limitations, one with mild limitations, one with an active seizure disorder and severe language-based learning disabilities, one with seizures and a nonverbal learning disability, one with attention deficit hyperactivity disorder, and one with an anxiety disorder. Clearly, if you were trying to make a connection between brainwaves and behavior, these EEGs would not be much help!

Certainly, there are **risk factors** for learning and behavior problems in children: alcohol or drug use in pregnancy, premature birth and low birth weight, being part of a multiple birth group (triplets, etc.), trauma during childbirth such as prolonged labor or oxygen deprivation, head injuries, high fevers, chromosomal abnormalities, the age of one or both parents (both eggs and sperm from older parents have been associated with a greater number of mutations that might affect development of the fetus), poor nutrition during pregnancy or infancy, and many other factors. While these **may** be correlated with later learning problems, it is far from a one-to-one relationship. Plenty of children with these risk factors have no learning difficulties whatsoever.

A higher than expected number of the children I see are adopted, but I don't know what the connection might be, and often there is very little information about family history or risk factors during pregnancy or infancy. Chronic ear infections that cause short-term hearing loss are associated with language and learning problems, but not in all children. Left-handedness that is not found in other family members may indicate some kind of prenatal neurological problem, but not always. Even adding these all together, they "explain" only a small number of the cases I see in my practice, and there is no good correlation between a certain risk factor and a certain type of learning problem.

Some family histories seem to show a relationship, but again it may not be a real cause-and-effect relationship. Dyslexia, speech and language problems, attention deficit disorder, anxiety and depression, among others, may appear in several generations or in siblings and first cousins. I've tested children from four different families, each with at least three generations of severe dyslexics, but in most cases we don't find such a clear family trend.

Problems with mood control and regulation may be evident from early childhood, often in combination with reduced attention and impulsivity. These mood problems are often part of a more complex profile that includes learning disabilities. These children are often very challenging to treat.

Of course, there are medical problems that often affect a child's ability to learn in school, and these are recognized as qualifying a child for special education services. Seizures, tic disorders, autoimmune diseases, lyme disease, and birth defects are just a few examples, but again these tend to occur **with** learning problems. They have not been proved to **cause** specific learning disabilities.

One exception may be lyme disease. There have been studies showing deficits in short and longer-term memory and information retrieval, which do have a significant impact on academic performance. I have seen these problems in the children with lyme whom I've evaluated, and according to parents they showed up after the child was infected, not before.

In most cases, parents haven't "done" anything to cause their child's difficulties. He or she simply "showed up" this way, due to some minor error in neurological development (remember, it all begins with the brain). So, the best thing to do is be "tuned in" to your child and pick up on signs of a problem as early as possible.

Some kids "hit the wall", as I describe it, in kindergarten; some make it to 4th or 6th grades—or even to the beginning of high school. At some point, however, there will be a big enough **disconnect** between what is **expected** and what a child can really, truly **do on his or her own**, to cause a parent to notice. In the previous chapter, I provided examples of children who fell within 3 different broad timeframes (early childhood, upper elementary-middle, and high school), along with their struggles to be successful learners.

In some cases, school personnel may be the first to mention a problem, though I urge parents not to rely on getting this feedback. Your child is part of a group in school, ranging from 15-30 children, and things are easily missed. That said, parents may **not** be aware of certain problems if they mostly occur in school. A child's behavior in school may be **very different** from that at home, for several reasons.

Difficulty making friends or sharing with peers, problems sitting still or following directions, or an inability to finish tasks, may not be an issue at home if there are no siblings and a parent is "accommodating". The same is true for pencil skills, puzzles, following sequences, memory, or pre-reading skills—a parent may not notice the child's lack of skill if the child simply avoids those tasks.

There **are** some common "speed bump" times:

- In preschool, when children need to use language to communicate clearly, when they need basic gross motor coordination on a playground, and adaptive fine motor skills for cutting and drawing in class, when they are expected to play in a cooperative way, to help clean up, to sit and listen to a story.

- In kindergarten, when they need to be able to pay attention for more than a few minutes, to follow directions and filter out unnecessary distractions, to line up quietly and transition to other parts of the school for activities. They will, of course, need all the skills from pre-school as well. In this grade, children also begin to recognize and copy letters, numbers, and sight words.

- In first grade, when the abstract nature of the letter system must begin making sense on a more automatic level, and children need to learn letter sounds and how to combine those sounds in ways that make words. In addition, all of the social, fine and gross motor, and attentional skills from kindergarten are expected in first grade. Children are expected to display greater emotional and behavioral self-control. There are **two**

**main tasks** in first grade (as any teacher who is being truthful will agree)—to learn to read and to "buy into the system". This second one means learning to listen to instructions, start and complete the work that is given, then sit and wait for the next set of instructions or piece of paper to do. Both of these tasks are essential for future grades.

- In fourth grade, which is the beginning of upper elementary school, children need to be able to extract information from print more independently, and put their thoughts and their knowledge into written form with greater detail and some degree of technical accuracy. They need to solve a wider range of problems with less direct instruction and fewer explicit rules, not only in academic areas but in terms of social skills. They are expected to be "over the hump" in terms of learning to read; they now "read to learn" more often. The four arithmetic operations should be in use, with growing mastery of math facts.

- For **girls** in fourth grade, there is the additional expectation of being able to handle the complex language and social interactions needed to keep up with, and be accepted by, their female peers. Girls with language-based learning disabilities, or communication disorders, often find themselves "shut out" of peer groups, and "left behind" by other girls, because they can't keep up with the speed of conversations. They may spend more time with male peers or become more isolated. They also have greater difficulty following instructions and lectures in class, as these become more complex and are repeated less often.

- In sixth grade, when the complexity of the whole system increases. Now, children are often expected to change classes multiple times per day, to adapt to the different learning styles of several (or many) teachers, to organize and remember a lot more information on a daily basis, to keep track of many papers and handouts from different classes, and to deal with assignments from different classes that are due at different times and often are very different from each other in format or expectations. The need for "executive functioning" skills becomes important. Being able to process information quickly and accurately is necessary to take good notes, and work pace becomes an issue. Some children struggle to finish tests in the time allowed. In addition, social stresses, physical and hormonal changes, and extracurricular activities add to the mix.

- In ninth grade, when the changes from middle school expectations to high school expectations hit a child on the head like a dropped piano. It's everything that was expected in sixth grade, only faster and more of it. There are lectures that last the whole period now. In some school systems, block scheduling means that some classes last for an hour and a half. There is much less "hand-holding". There is the expectation of more or less adult reading comprehension and written language skills. In addition, there are the all-important "executive functions" that allow a child to keep track of multiple assignments and ever-changing demands. The need to analyze more abstract or figurative language can be a problem in classes as well as socially. Slower workers, or those easily distracted, can fall behind in as little as a week. Schools expect teens to advocate for themselves if there is a problem, but often the teens are not self-observing enough to do this, assuming the teachers are available when a teen comes calling.

- After the first half of high school, when standardized testing, SATs, and college applications set up expectations for planning, performance, and independent work that many teens are simply not ready to take on. I see lots of teens between the ages of 16 and 20 who are not, or were not, ready to be fully independent learners. With diminishing structure from school and home (and almost none once they reach college), teens with weak attention, organization, or academic skills cannot keep up acceptable levels of performance. Every year, I tell parents, "it's cheaper to flunk high school than college", meaning that parents should see what a teen can do **on his own** during the last year of high school, so extra help can be gotten or extra time allowed before college. I also tell them, "unless you have $1800.00 per week to **throw away** (private college tuition of $55,000 or more, divided by roughly 32 weeks of class), you'd better make sure your child is **ready to go to college**". Many parents (and teens) have a hard time hearing this message, and sometimes I don't see them until they've already "crashed and burned", but this speed bump is very significant in terms of preparing to be a fully functioning and independent adult.

Many children are referred to me when they can't get over a certain "speed bump". This is not a concept I have seen in books on child development, but for me it is a useful visual aid when thinking about a child's performance compared to what I have found to be "average" expectations.

Of the experts I cite in the Appendix, several are most helpful for child development in the early years. Dr. T. Berry Brazleton, a pediatrician who worked in Boston for many years, did a great deal of research on styles of temperament that are noticeable in infancy and persist into childhood. His books are calm and informative without being overwhelming. These temperamental features will affect a child's learning and success in school, even when there is not a learning difficulty.

Dr. Penelope Leach is another pediatrician, from Britain this time, whose book on early development is comprehensive, pragmatic and very useful. She provides a clear, detailed discussion of areas of development (language, eating, social skills, motor skills, etc.) and how to help a child master the necessary skills if he or she is having difficulty.

If you and your child are having a particularly tough time getting through the day, due to differences in personal style, Dr. Stanley Turecki's book on difficult children may be helpful. He addresses the needs of children who are inflexible, over-reactive, too sensitive, or demanding, helping parents identify the areas of friction and then learn to interact with their children in ways that reduce stress and increase adaptive functioning.

The books in the "What to expect" series provide further details for early development, but there seem to be fewer books written to help parents understand and meet the needs of their school age children. This is surprising to me, since so many children struggle with one or more expectations of school. Many teachers have a good idea of what your child should be able to do when entering a certain grade, but the information rarely seems to be available in an organized format. However, I have seen some school websites that have lists of core competencies. There are also trade books dealing with a grade-level "comprehensive curriculum" available at large bookstores, and these can give a parent a "lower limit" idea of what a child should have mastered as they finish a grade (or what they will probably be expected to learn as they enter a grade).

In each of these books, there are checklists and age-appropriate milestones or expectations. These can give parents a sense of where their child falls on the spectrum of "normal". Often, this is a starting point, and once an area of concern has been identified, there are books that focus on your areas of concern in greater depth.

Dr. Melvin Levine is the author of numerous books on learning styles in children, including ones designed to help children understand their learning disabilities or attention deficit problems, and come up with strategies to improve their performance. In one book, he describes a major task of childhood as "managing the flow of expectations". To me, this is a very helpful way of thinking about what a child needs to be able to do to be successful. These expectations change as a child moves from pre-school through high school. Every child's development is unique, and there will always be areas where a child is somewhat behind or ahead of expectations, but parents need to know what things will be expected of their child at different ages and stages.

Dr. Levine writes about the skill areas that need to improve over time, including language skills, memory, social skills, attention, organization, and multi-processing. These are essential in order for children to manage expectations in school and in life, and will need to be monitored carefully by parents if a child is coping with learning issues or attention deficits. His books are sometimes written for parents, and sometimes for middle and high school students, but in either case they are both practical and hopeful.

For example, in one article he lists "signs of trouble" in the lower elementary grades, including: delayed decoding abilities for reading, trouble following directions, slow recall of facts, slow acquisition of new skills, poor spelling, impulsivity or lack of planning, careless errors, an unstable pencil grip, trouble with letter formation, poor grasp of math concepts, organizational problems, and trouble learning about time (temporal-sequential disorganization).

Whatever your child's age, school "mission statements" (often found on an individual school's website, or one for the entire school system) will say they **prepare the children** for what will be expected of them. In my experience, even children with no areas of weakness sometimes find themselves poorly-prepared for what a teacher may want, so each **transition time** is a possible swamp where they can get stuck, or fall behind. For the kids who really aren't ready, these "check points" can become concrete "road barricades".

Here are some of the possible problem areas that parents mention to me, when we discuss early development:

- Activity level, both at home and in school; a tendency to respond impulsively, or to be much more active and restless than peers

- Ability to maintain attention when listening and concentration when working, for an age-appropriate amount of time

- Expressive language skills; articulation; and the ability to communicate thoughts and ideas accurately

- Understanding and processing (making "sense" of) language that they hear

- Auditory discrimination (confusing ending sounds in words, or entire words, resulting in comprehension errors and early reading errors)

- Fine motor skills for manipulating items; paper and pencil skills; hand preference; adequacy of pencil grip

- Visual-spatial skills, such as the ability to look at a pattern, design, or picture and copy it, using a pencil, blocks, tiles, or some other "piece" of the "whole"

- Skills for sequencing and ordering items; remembering sequences such as the days of the week or months of the year; being able to understand and/or create a sequence of steps or events (a math problem with several steps, or a group of pictures that tell a story)

- Confusion of directionality; understanding whether a pattern or picture needs to be oriented in a certain way in order to be accurate (which way a particular letter "faces"); counting from left to right; mixed hand dominance; being able to quickly label left and right on himself; knowing which way to turn when walking a familiar path

- Developmental delays in self-help or interpersonal skills, including bathing, dressing, buttoning and tying, waiting one's turn, avoiding dangers, remembering safety rules and rules of the house

- Motor planning and gross motor coordination; delay in learning to do certain motor tasks such as standing on one foot, kicking a ball, riding a tricycle, hopping; problems playing early team sports or games

- Lack of expected social skills; poor eye contact; difficulty starting a conversation with the appropriate "lead in", or maintaining "give and take" in a conversation; difficulty sharing or ending a play date

- Problems with regulation (temperamental difficulties, poor self-control, behaving in age-appropriate ways, emotional outbursts)

- Sensory sensitivity to some aspects of the environment—food textures and tastes, the fit and softness of clothing or being irritated by tags or waistbands or seams in socks; noises, both loud and/or sudden; smells; changes in schedule or plans

- Early learning—being able to learn and remember letter-names, letter/ sound relationships, math concepts, beginning "number sense" such as the sequential nature of numerals; rote information such as ones birthday, the days of the week, phone number, etc.

What is it reasonable to expect from a child of a certain age, in these and other areas? When is a child considered "within the normal range", and when is he or she "behind" or "ahead", above or below the average? Again, I refer you to the books by pediatricians and educators that summarize and give rough age levels.

Parents often bring up the question of whether the expectations are equally valid for boys and girls. In other words, can we explain the difficulty a boy may be having by the fact that boys are simply "less mature" or "less ready" at any given age?

In my opinion, the research here is far from definitive. There is still debate about male/female differences in language, social skills, activity levels, learning styles, and general readiness—whether in fact there **are** any absolute differences, and what these might be.

Any parent with more than one child, even if they are identical twins, will tell you their children are different in a variety of ways. Not just that their boys are different from their girls, but that their boys differ from one another, too. Saying that boys and girls "learn differently" is not very useful, since every child is unique. I'm not sure I believe in any generalizations, even though we all can come up with anecdotes showing that boys are often more active or that girls frequently like dolls more than boys do.

Let me offer a few observations (simplified, of course) from my own family situation. I bought my firstborn, a boy, a full play kitchen and an anatomically-correct boy baby doll ("girl stuff"). He used them only when he had a female friend over to play. He preferred legos, blocks and the Brio train set ("boy stuff"). However, he engaged in imaginative, cooperative play ("girl stuff") as often as my second child, a girl. She used the kitchen, but preferred stuffed animals to dolls, and actually had more male friends than female ones throughout early childhood and elementary school. She was a tomboy, far more athletic (and coordinated) than my son. My third child, a boy, absorbed video game skills from his brother and imaginative play skills from his sister. He was athletic **and** an artist, a dancer **and** a fencer, who loved to build with tools **and** had social skills that drew peers of both genders like a magnet.

So, what conclusions could I draw about gender differences? Not many, I think.

My first boy was born 3 ½ weeks early (risk factor), was left handed (risk factor), and was somewhat inattentive as well as physically awkward as a young child (both risk factors). He struggled with fine motor skills and was only writing upper case letters when he entered first grade (another risk factor). A professional looking at those factors might have predicted some learning difficulties. Yet he was an accelerated learner for whom everything academic was effortless.

My full-term, right handed daughter, with advanced fine and gross motor skills, and the same type of logical, mathematical mind as her brother, would have been considered a perfect candidate for early academic success. The only risk factor was her history of chronic ear infections throughout childhood, which we treated with three sets of ear tubes. There is absolutely no family history of learning problems, and yet she struggled with mild dyslexia, and with weaknesses in auditory processing, word retrieval, and spelling.

Boys and girls **are** probably different, since they have different chromosomes and thus different genetic material. There may well be absolute differences that will be proven by research and have an impact on academic teaching. The current generalizations do not, I believe, apply across the board, to **all** boys or **all** girls, and so parents need to beware of putting too much faith in them.

Another issue that parents raise is one of "developmental readiness"—basically, maturity. School personnel will often tell parents that the reason their child is having difficulty with learning is due to **developmental factors**, and that he or she will "grow out of" these learning problems. Parents come to me for a second opinion, asking "Is this true? Is my child simply immature?"

In a few cases, this proves to be true, but in my experience the problems are nearly always due to **neurological factors**, and these **will not go away** just because the child gets older. It takes skilled testing to tell the difference, but a good neuropsychologist will be able to diagnose a learning disability vs. just taking longer to mature or "be ready" (more about finding an appropriate clinician in a later chapter).

If there is really a learning disability (or a language or fine motor or sensory disorder), then only **appropriate remedial instruction** will help a child to compensate, by helping them develop **alternate neurological pathways** to master that particular skill. Extra birthdays will do nothing, other than increasing a child's frustration and diminishing his or her self-esteem.

The one thing I have noticed, that I think applies to kindergarten through the first few grades, is a **style of teaching** and a **choice of tasks** that may tend to favor girls. Teachers at these grade levels have certain expectations that children simply have to deal with.

I tell parents that "schools are designed **by** women **for** little girls", meaning that there is often more emphasis on fine motor tasks (coloring, cutting, printing) and on self control (sitting in chairs, raising hands, waiting), and less emphasis on gross motor or kinesthetic tasks (physical play, moving around the room, use of manipulatives such as sandpaper letters or attribute blocks for math, rhythm or clapping to learn rote material).

Some boys will have more difficulty complying with these expectations—but then, so will some girls. The social and interactional expectations put in place by these (mostly female) teachers may be a problem for either boys or girls, since temperament and social style **do not** sort by gender.

Developmental progress is tricky because it is often uneven, and is not predictable based solely on whether your child is male or female.

The important thing, again, is to **trust yourself.** If you think there is a problem, observe, read, ask questions, and ask for the types of accommodations or services that will help your child to be successful.

Please realize that none of these age-level or grade-level "expectations" that you read about are designed to torture you or your child. What the schools are expecting is actually **an average, appropriate developmental sequence** for quite a few children—though, to be honest, **many fewer children** than the schools would like you to believe. If you looked at **all** the children in a district and followed them from kindergarten through high school graduation, I believe fully half of them would have been "out of the normal range" in one or more areas at some time during those 13 years.

If you add up all the areas that need to be mastered—cognitive, academic, social, physical, and emotional—it makes sense that many children will hit a snag somewhere. To me, this raises questions about factors such as class size in elementary school, academic standards, instructional methods, teacher preparation, the length of the school day and year, and how academic learning is measured.

For some kids, of course, these expectations are no problem. Some of the cakes come out of the oven just fine, regardless of the recipe used or the age of the ingredients or the skill of the bakers. Then the bakers say, "See, no problems here. We know what we're doing."

In my opinion, success is often more the result of luck than skill. Standard school programs and teaching methods are a good fit, or at least a "good enough" fit, for a certain percentage of children. It's the **other** children, who don't fit the standard "cake pan", who need more specialized instruction and extra help to get where they need to be. And **you, as their parents**, need a **recipe** with **better instructions**, so you can do your best to help them reach the end of this educational journey with **all the necessary skills** for a successful adult life.

## CHAPTER 3

# THE WAY THINGS WORK IN THE GAME OF (EDUCATION) LIFE

*"Cheshire-Puss", Alice began, rather timidly, "Would you tell me, please, which way I
ought to go from here?"
"That depends a great deal on where you want to get to," said the Cat.
"I don't much care where-" said Alice.
"Then it doesn't matter which way you go," said the Cat.
"—so long as I get <u>somewhere</u>", Alice added as an explanation.
"Oh, you're sure to do that," said the Cat, "if you only walk long enough."
Lewis Carroll: <u>Alice's Adventures in Wonderland</u>*

Most parents, when they send their children off to kindergarten, realize that they're giving up control of these precious little beings for the day. They know that for about six and a half hours a day, five days a week, one hundred eighty days a year, someone else is going to be in charge.

Most parents are okay with this. They see it as a **partnership**, and they are generally eager to do their part. They make sure their children have sneakers, pencils, vaccinations. They give them breakfast and send in boxes of Kleenex for the classroom. They look in their backpacks for notices, and supervise nightly homework.

In exchange, they expect their children to be taught the academic skills they need to be independent learners—readers, writers, mathematicians, and thinkers. If their child is as bright as most of his or her peers, they expect him or her to perform at least at "grade level".

When **something isn't working**, and their child is struggling or miserable, failing to make progress or just plain failing, they expect their "partner" to **fix it** so it works.

Unfortunately, this is where parents may encounter a problem.

In the real world, where mothers and fathers have to earn a living, a worker is expected to actually produce something that "works". If you don't cut hair the way your customers like it, you don't get more customers. If you don't actually fix their cars, they don't return with more business. The coffee is expected to be made correctly, the computer code is expected to work, bank deposits are expected to be put in the right accounts, and customer questions actually answered so the customer is satisfied. If your experiments don't work, you don't get more grant money.

Now, it's true that sometimes it takes a long time for people to finally decide that the cars aren't made well enough or the donuts are just too unhealthy. But eventually, dissatisfied people take their business elsewhere—because they can. **They have options**.

For the little **consumers of education**, the options are far more limited. They can't demand something different or vote with their feet—they can't vote at all. And they aren't able to simply opt out or stay home. They are legally required to go to school.

For the **parents** of these consumers, who can and do vote, the options aren't much better. Most of them work all day, and can't home school their children even if they have the necessary skills. Private schools are expensive, out of reach for most parents. In my opinion, many of these schools have learned that they can charge a lot of money for slightly smaller classes and a bit more flexibility, while offering essentially the same product. Plus, most have only limited services for children who are struggling with learning.

Meeting with school personnel to ask them to do something different and more effective—something that "works"—is not the simple process than many parents assume it will be. In my experience, parents of children with special learning needs will face a rocky road of frustration, confusion, delays, and often inadequate changes to their child's program. They can certainly succeed in getting what their child needs, but it will take persistence, and the kind of practical information presented in this book. In most cases, parents will also be **more successful** if they work with a trained professional who can advocate for the appropriate services.

Now, you might ask, **why is this system the way it is?** Why is it so hard to get the type of help that will result in true, measurable, effective progress for your child? More important, why does the system stay this way, even though many professionals in education, public policy, and psychology agree that it often doesn't "work"?

If you don't care about the "why", but just want to get to the next step, that's ok. You can go to the next chapter, about independent evaluations.

Some of what I am going to tell you here may sound critical. As I was writing this, I realized I **do** have feelings about why the education system is the way it is, but I have these feelings **because of the children involved.** I've already got my education, and my children are out of school. I've got nothing to gain by rocking the boat or criticizing school systems. My only motivation is to push the discussion towards positive "**action items**" or changes to the system that would result in **a better education for children with special needs**—and for all the others.

In fact, I have a lot of **positive ideas** to offer. I've seen great teachers in public schools, great classrooms, great principals and programs. I believe we need **more** of all of these, and we need them **now.**

The future of education is on the line—and with it, the future of our whole country. Having been "in the trenches" for 30 years, I can share what I've seen and experienced, but I'm like the Red Cross; I'm not "for" either side. I'm not an advocate for teachers **or** for administrators, superintendents, schools of education, school boards or taxpayers. I am on the side of the **children**, who don't have any power and who can't change the system. I want you as parents to be my **allies** in getting the help your children need. I can't do it alone.

Education is currently a "hot" topic in America, and every week there is another article describing our declining test scores, the bleak high school graduation rates for poor and minority students, our falling competitiveness with other countries. There are also stacks of articles about teaching methods, classroom configurations, and other ways to improve the quality of education and the level of skills our children need to have when they graduate high school. I have spent years thinking about ways of "reforming" education so it works better, but that is the subject of another book.

Remember The Game of Life? It's an old board game (I know, I'm showing my age, here) in which players spin the wheel and move a car around the board, adding markers for a spouse and children, dealing with life's ups and downs, trying to achieve success and financial rewards, until they get to the end of life. So, just think of your situation as The Game of Education Life, with one twist—once your child has some kind of special need, you may very well fall through a black hole into something resembling Alice's Wonderland. Here, you may find, **the rules of the real world don't apply**.

There's a scene in the book in which the Red Queen proclaims at the end of a chaotic game, "All shall have prizes"—even though it is clear to Alice that no one has won or deserves a prize. I often feel this way about the educational system in America today. Those who receive "prizes"—whether this is a high salary for an administrator, tenure for a teacher, or promotion for a student—often have not "earned" these rewards. They do not demonstrate the necessary skills. They haven't achieved the goals they were expected to achieve. So why do they get a prize? It may be the current "reality", but it doesn't make much sense. It also **does not serve** our children's need to be well-educated.

The basic format of this book addresses the questions that would be asked by anyone who finds himself in a tight situation—including parents of children with any type of special need: How did we get here? What problems are we facing? How do we get out?

Line yourself up at the start of our Special Education game board. As parents, you suspect (or know) that there is a problem with your child's learning, even if you don't know all the details yet. You need facts about the reality of the situation, if you are going to try to get truly effective services for your child. You need to understand the obstacles you are likely to face, as well as your rights and those of your child. You need to know who will help you.

One of the key issues affecting the **quality of education** our children receive, in my opinion, is whether individuals are held accountable for the outcomes of decisions they make. Let me explain. Over the years, I have noticed that there are rarely any logical consequences for decisions made by school personnel, such as curriculum choices that turn out to be ineffective or hiring teachers whose students don't make effective progress. Often, the people who are part of a school system are protected by contracts or tenure, and thus they don't face any real consequences if the outcomes of their decisions aren't positive. This would include school administrators who make staffing decisions, school boards who set policy, teachers' unions who defend ineffective or damaging teachers, and districts or states that decide on the standardized testing to be used.

At times, I have felt as though I were in some "Wonderland" where logical thinking wasn't even helpful. A sense of **responsibility** for the outcome is a necessary component of any change or improvement in our system of education. When there is no accountability, no one has to take any responsibility. And if no one is responsible, then **nothing has to change.** This does not serve the needs of your children.

I have had interesting discussions with people in education about this idea, but from what I read every week, the possibilities for **real change** do not seem very promising—the amount of "pushback" from certain interest groups seems to equal the amount of "push forward" by those who want to change the system. At least, after years of dodging the truth, accountability is finally being **discussed** on a national basis. In a few states, laws are being enacted that allow (or mandate) the use of student-progress data to help make teacher evaluations or tenure decisions. These laws are described as "revolutionary", though to many people they seem like common sense.

When you have a child with special needs, a lack of responsibility for educational outcomes (or "accountability") becomes a significant stumbling block that can prevent you from getting the help your child needs. That's because you can't compare your child to the norm, the average, the other kids in the class. **Your child** needs **different things** to make effective progress:

- simpler language

- more individual instruction

- a smaller class size

- a different reading or math program

- social skills training

- opportunities to work with specialists in areas of difficulty

- additional time for processing or working

- fewer distractions

- help with organization

- more frequent breaks

- psychological support

You need to be able to reach an agreement with school personnel that one or more adults will be **providing these interventions** (or whatever ones are needed) for your child, that you will be able to **see improvement**, and that **these interventions will be changed** when what's being done isn't working. Believe me, this is even harder than it sounds.

Responsible actions that are **measurable** begin with teachers. There need to be honest, reliable ways to measure the **how well** a teacher does his or her job. Arne Duncan, Education Secretary in the Obama administration, notes, "In other fields, we talk about success constantly, with statistics and other measures to prove it. Why in education are we scared to talk about what success looks like?"

Good question. **Every other professional** has to be able to **demonstrate** that what they actually do makes a positive and significant difference—to their customers, the goods or services they produce, the "bottom line" of their company.

It is time for teachers to demonstrate their effectiveness in concrete ways that can be measured and seen. Let me share two studies that have looked at this issue of teacher effectiveness. This is a real "hot button" issue in education, judging from the resistance of teachers' unions. To me, it is something that could **greatly enhance respect** for good teachers, and serve as a **baseline** for more **professional treatment** of them.

The Bill and Melinda Gates Foundation, which has spent over $4 billion on education projects over the past decade, has published the results of a study that found that **two questions** could predict how much children actually learn in a classroom: "Does your teacher use class time well?" and "When you're confused, does your teacher help you get straightened out?"

I had a hard time believing that such simple questions would correlate with effective learning. Then I read an article by Dr. R. Barker Bausell, a professor emeritus from the University of Maryland (New York Times, May 1, 2011) titled "A New Measure for Classroom Quality". Dr. Bausell described a direct, objective measure to assess teachers: measuring the amount of time a teacher actually spent delivering relevant instruction. He cited studies from 30 years ago that measured the amount of time teachers spent presenting instruction that matched the prescribed curriculum, **at a level the students could understand based on previous instruction** (meaning, at the level of their current mastery). Some teachers could apparently deliver as much as **14 more weeks** of relevant instruction during a school year, compared to others, through a combination of sticking to the curriculum, maintaining discipline, and minimizing non-instructional activities.

Think about it. Fourteen more weeks! At no additional cost to the taxpayer, and without adding to the school day or year! That's an entire year of additional instruction by the time a child reaches upper elementary school! I can only imagine how thrilled most teachers would be to have their students learning that much more each year. The question is, why isn't this being done in schools right now?

Based on just these two articles and the simple methods they describe, it would seem that evaluating teacher effectiveness might be done cheaply and easily, if there were the will to do so. This still leaves the problem of **evaluating students**, which currently is neither cheap nor easy—not to mention the concerns about accuracy. True accountability requires that we know:

· **how much** material a child is actually exposed to in a year;

· how much of this material a child has **mastered**; and

· how well the material has been retained and can be used to support the next year's teaching.

As all parents of children with special learning needs **know,** this is where it can really seem as though you've fallen "down the rabbit hole".

Is it possible to accurately evaluate your child's progress, using **just the information** provided by schools? In my opinion, if you have any concerns about that progress, the answer is no.

When I look at student reports and get that "Wonderland" feeling, I usually find that the scores or grades or whatever are not sufficient or accurate enough to determine whether a child is making **effective progress** and developing true **mastery.** Parents tell me the same things. They struggle to analyze the information they get and understand what it means in terms of their child's **real learning.** Within our educational system as it is currently run, I do not see a requirement for either **mastery** or **accountability** for an individual child.

Start with the grades students receive. At the present time, there is not an objective standard for academic mastery of material. In other words, different schools use different methods of evaluating student performance. Parents often tell me they do not know whether their child can successfully do grade level work, based on report cards. I can understand that teachers may not want to discourage children who are struggling. They may believe (or hope) that a child's difficulties are due to "developmental" factors. For whatever reason, children's report cards frequently do not reflect actual skill levels.

Many parents who come to see me bring report cards that show their child making the "honor roll", even when they tell me their child reads two or three years below grade level. They tell me their child is being given (or has been given) a "D-" grade rather than an "F", sometimes in several courses, so they won't have to repeat a year. I tell parents I don't need or want to see the report cards. Report cards can say **anything,** but I have no way of knowing how true the information is.

What about all the standardized testing that schools are required to do, you may ask? Surely that is objective, and truthful. Sadly, I do not believe this is so. Parents report that their children describe being "coached" to the correct answers for standardized test questions. Children who still fail are allowed to take these tests multiple times with increasing assistance so they can "pass" and be given a high school diploma. They are offered an increasing number of "prep" or "coaching" classes that teach only the material on the tests—often using exact questions and formats from previous test years.

Parents tell me they feel these techniques are dishonest. They prevent parents from knowing their child's actual academic performance levels. It is another way in which an unwillingness to face consequences affects the quality of education provided to students.

I don't believe these group tests are as **accurate** as the ones that are administered individually. However, I am **much** more concerned about the number of students who are apparently "coached" to take these tests, and about the effect of pressuring teachers to "teach to the tests". As a result, for many students it may not be possible to tell if the test scores are an accurate indicator of **student achievement**, mastery of **course curriculum,** or even whether children have acquired **specific skills** at a certain grade level.

Teachers tend to dislike standardized testing for a number of reasons, some of which I agree with. I've read articles quoting teachers who say the testing produces a culture of "sameness" or "conformity" rather than creativity. I would actually welcome greater "sameness" if the darn scores were **higher.** Since a significant percentage of students **don't** do well, I suspect the opposition to standardized testing is at least partly because the tests **expose the problems with mastery and effective learning in children.**

This is particularly true for children with learning disabilities, emotional issues, developmental delays, or other problems that interfere with effective learning in the first place.

To be honest, I think the focus on standardized testing is unhelpful to students **and** teachers. It can take over the curriculum and it sucks time from actual teaching. At the same time, it doesn't tell you who's having difficulty until the end of the school year, which leaves no time for additional help. I'm also quite sure the tests do not provide accurate measures of **grade level skills.**

However, I know there isn't time to evaluate each child individually. I'd encourage greater honesty from teachers, most of whom probably do know which kids are "on top of things" and which ones are "behind the curve." In Finland, to cite one example from a system that gets high marks for student achievement, teachers are given much more responsibility to ensure that children are making effective progress, and to work with the children who aren't. They are treated as professionals whose "work" (helping students master skills) is expected to be of high caliber (ie, effective). Individual teachers have a fair amount of freedom to choose how to teach and how to test, but their students are **expected to learn.**

Recently, I evaluated a young man, age 19, of average intelligence, with no significant academic learning disability. His reading skills clustered at a sixth grade level—and the school system admitted he had not passed the Massachusetts **assessment** test (at about an eighth grade level of difficulty). To my horror, his math skills were between a third and fourth grade level (yes, you read that correctly)—but the school system stated that the boy had passed the (eighth grade level of difficulty) assessment test in math! They insisted he had done so on his own, with only the accommodations permitted by his education plan. I said I couldn't see how this was possible. They wanted to give him a diploma and get him out of the system, but fortunately his parents did not agree.

This young man did not have **effective skills for independent living**, and it wasn't because he lacked the necessary intelligence. In my opinion, the school system had not kept their end of the bargain, to set up a program that would allow him to make "effective progress" in either regular **or** special education courses.

When I attend Team meetings or review "student evaluation" forms from the school psychologist or other clinicians (after I've completed my testing), the information from teachers is almost always positive. Since these students have been referred for testing **because of evident difficulties or concerns,** how can everything be fine? It doesn't make sense, and reinforces my feeling of being caught in "Wonderland".

Another area of concern is student promotions. In most schools, children move on from grade to grade, whether they have made sufficient progress or not. This is "social promotion", and most parents are aware that schools will do everything in their power to keep from retaining a child. I've worked with parents who **begged** schools to let their child repeat a grade—in several cases, the child himself said he wanted to do this, since he didn't feel "ready" for the next grade—but were told no. It was "up to the principal", who didn't agree. One parent had to threaten a lawsuit to get "permission".

Why would a school do this, even when everyone knows a child is struggling and can't do the work? Because there is no requirement for **mastery of grade level material**—really, truly at grade level—before one is allowed to move on.

Ironically, there are also times when a child in the first few grades is "kept back" for "developmental reasons", when the child actually **needs** special education services rather than just the same curriculum repeated for another year.

The end result of either scenario denies some children an appropriate education.

For children with special needs, the whole issue of **grade level performance** is often put aside once they are provided with an IEP, never to be raised again (until I raise it!). Many children with a specific learning need or other problem are capable of grade level performance—**if** they get diagnosed early enough, are provided with the right services in the right amounts, and **if** there is enough flexibility and accommodation in their programs to keep those "goal posts" moving forward as progress is made. Not as easy as it sounds!

One last look at standardized testing. Ten years ago, there was an attempt to address the issue of education reform through the No Child Left Behind act. The intent was good, but the implementation was flawed. One of the biggest problems, in my opinion, was that the standards of performance were not rigorous enough, and could be lowered by the states to ensure that more students "passed". At the same time, consequences affected entire schools, even when this was not justified. The law has often been perceived as unfair. The mandated testing takes obscene amounts of time, and—most important to you as parents and to me—the children with special needs are often "dragged along" and given too much help so they get the "right" answers, without enough emphasis on **real, independent mastery**.

Being held responsible for the outcomes of educational decisions should apply to both **teachers and students**. This responsibility should be addressed through evaluations that are honest, focused, and considered accurate by teachers, parents, and independent professionals. **No one** is served when we aren't honest about how effectively children are learning.

On to a second major reason for a lack of **true reform** in education—**money.**

I believe that schools actually **don't have enough money** to provide sufficient, appropriate services to meet all of the needs for all of the children. There are two main reasons for this, and only one is the fault of the school system itself. The state and Federal governments double-bind them, **mandating testing and programs**, but not providing **the necessary funding** to pay for them. This is a **political issue**, and one of these days I hope we as citizens will tell our elected officials that we won't pretend anymore that this system of payment works. It doesn't work, it isn't fair, and it means that many things schools would like to do—for regular **and** special education—cannot be done.

It is my belief that this also represents an **ethical** failing on the part of many people, including ordinary citizens who may not even have children in the public schools. Recently, the superintendent of schools in a local town wrote an article criticizing the movie *Waiting for Superman*. His "dislike" was laid out in very "black and white" terms that were fairly extreme as well as inaccurate, without appropriate "balance". He claimed, for example, that the movie was telling people "charter schools are the answer to all our problems", when that wasn't true, and was far from the "point" of the film.

In my opinion, this man represented a well-educated and therefore privileged member of society. Rather than "bashing" schools that were actually doing a good job, he should have been using his position of power to speak out against the numerous inadequacies of our current system, and particularly the inequality of what is available to most poor and minority students. He has a **responsibility not** to defend the status quo, but to advocate for those who **can not get** a decent education.

That said, schools **also don't have enough money** because they choose to do things in ways that don't make best use of the funds they do have. They make decisions that waste money, end up costing more in the long run, or that don't make good use of resources they already have available.

- School systems don't make enough use of **technology**, which could be a tremendous asset in advancing mastery as well as stretching the dollars. Most school districts have enough computers in classrooms or central locations. The software is available **right now** to let students practice skills, to increase student mastery, to support comprehension and teach factual material, to help with organization and planning.

Use of technology would allow individualization of instruction at **every grade level**. It would allow advanced students to explore areas of interest and further develop their skills. It would allow struggling students to practice as much as they needed to solidify basic skills. The software is commercially available and reasonably priced. As I write this, thousands of effective lectures are available on You-Tube, and at websites such as Ed-X, the collaboration between MIT and Harvard University that puts college courses on line for anyone to access. I am sure there are, and will be, many more examples of technology that could be used for education. However, schools have to choose to use it, to maximize both learning and use of time for students.

- School systems spend money developing partial programs for children with learning disabilities (which I don't consider adequate) but don't "go the distance" to provide a complete program (which I could then recommend to parents). They say it's because they don't believe in complete programs for ideological reasons—that "inclusion" is "better for the child". Depending on the child's needs, this may not be true. They say they are required to provide "a free and appropriate education", but again, if a child has significant needs, the most "appropriate" setting may well be small language-based classes (which I will discuss in greater detail in a later chapter) for all academic subjects. Whatever they use for justification, the bottom line is that they will often have to pay a great deal more money for private out-of-district placements because they have **chosen** to not provide the right services in-house.

- Schools don't use students as mentors or tutors, when this could be useful as early as third grade (in fact, the Department of Education's Institute for Education Sciences site lists "peer tutoring" as a method that has been shown in research studies to significantly improve reading skills). This method also improves social skills and provides benefits for both children, helping them feel more independent and successful. It allows the needier student to practice, and often results in more collaboration, since children with learning problems may have strengths in other areas that they will share with their "tutor".

- School systems spend money on expensive "new" materials that don't seem to work any better than older ones, from what I can tell. In some cases, these materials are actually **worse,** if you look at results (more about that later). If you think about it, basic reading and arithmetic **haven't changed much** in the past couple of hundred years.

- Schools are constrained by the contracts they have negotiated with teachers' unions, which force them to retain and pay staff **even when those staff are so deficient they cannot be allowed in a classroom**, (as in New York City, which in the past spent $30 million **each year** on these personnel). They are forced to lay off newer, less expensive teachers even when these people have superior skills (such as being nominated for "teacher of the year"), thus spending more on teaching salaries. They are bound by **seniority rules** and **tenure,** which can prevent them from choosing the best staff to work with their students.

- Schools are often funded through property taxes, which citizens have chosen to keep so low that the percent increase permitted each year does not even keep up with increases in fuel costs, food, textbooks, or insurance premiums, much less allow for capital improvements or salaries that would attract more people to teaching.

- Finally, schools spend way too much time and money on standardized testing that often isn't needed, or that isn't particularly helpful in reaching the most important goal—producing competent learners and thinkers with the necessary skills for success in the 21$^{st}$ century marketplace.

I've heard people complain about the quality of education and the poor showing of our students in international test results, though I rarely hear from people who want the cost of education to increase. I think to some extent you get what you pay for. Dave Eggers and Ninive Calegari write (New York Times, May 1, 2012), "For those who say, 'How do we pay for this?'- well, how are we paying for three concurrent wars?...How did we pay for the interstate highway system...or the equally ambitious project of sending Americans to the moon? We had the vision and we had the will and we found a way."

At the same time, I believe it is reasonable to expect to get value for our money. And especially for children with special needs, the services have to be **sufficient to meet the needs.** I am well aware that budgets for special education services have gotten larger each year, sometimes even "squeezing out" services for regular education students. I believe it is possible to use **mastery-based education** and several other techniques to enable school systems to provide quality services for **all students, without** busting the budget.

Besides the unwillingness or inability of schools to make good use of the resources they already **have,** there is a final reason for the lack of true reform in education—the tendency of school systems to discourage any disagreement with "official" policy or programs. In such a system, it becomes difficult or even uncomfortable for individuals to disagree or express an opinion at odds with the way things are usually done.

In most school systems, there is a certain social "culture" or set of beliefs that I have encountered over many years of meetings and discussions. The basic beliefs include assertions such as: all the teachers are fully qualified, all the teachers are doing the right thing, all of the methods they choose are the best ones, and all the children are learning what they need to learn.

Sounds a bit unreal, doesn't it? If you're the parent of a child who is struggling or failing, you know there's a problem with this set of beliefs. But when I find myself in "Wonderland", even the teachers who see a problem with a child or a recommendation will generally not say anything. To disagree with the culture is not permitted.

Why, you might wonder, will teachers not speak up, when they have tenure and can't be fired for anything less than a felony? I'm not sure, except that it's hard to work closely with the same people every day and feel as though you've upset the group. Most teachers I've met (or read about) have strong needs for affiliation, consensus, and group acceptance. "Rocking the boat", by speaking out honestly, threatens the whole atmosphere or environment at a school, and makes people uncomfortable. It is difficult to go against the tide in such a system. Having worked briefly in a public school, I know this from direct experience.

Regardless of the reason, this type of thinking is a very real problem in school systems. It influences the decision to refer a child for testing, or even to acknowledge that a child is struggling. Once there has been an evaluation, it prevents teachers or specialists from suggesting certain services or programs, much less admitting that they might not have the type of help a child needs.

It also prevents school systems from honestly evaluating the relative skills of their teaching staff. **Everyone knows** all teachers are not created equal, any more than all doctors or car mechanics or members of any other profession are equal. The difference, of course, is that you have word of mouth, Angie's List, Consumer Reports, and countless other ways of comparing and choosing in other areas. With teachers, there is little or no choice.

"Our very best teachers ought to be treated much, much better than they are today," says Joe Williams, the executive director of Democrats for Education Reform (quoted in the New York Times, August 2012). "But in order to get there, we need to be able to say out loud that some teachers are better than others."

It may sound reasonable to you and me, but it clashes dramatically with the accepted "culture" among some school personnel.

This type of thinking causes administrators to insist that a teacher with 20 or more students will be able to implement more than a dozen accommodations for a single student **while simultaneously teaching the rest of the class**—because that's what the child's Individualized Education Plan says should be happening. In a recent article, a teacher acknowledged that even though she was supposed to provide "diversified instruction" for individual students, it wasn't going to happen when she had 20 other children to teach at the same time. I don't find this shocking—it's simply the truth. A "culture of agreement" makes for report cards you can't believe, and unrealistic, consistently positive "progress reports".

The gears of the system are jammed by this set of beliefs, resulting in a lack of flexibility and honesty, as well as a lack of creative and rational thinking. It can cause teachers and their unions to "dig in their heels" over issues such as tenure and the length of a school day, while more important issues are not addressed.

It is crazy-making sometimes, listening to school employees tie themselves in knots trying to justify a service or program that isn't working, or that can't possibly work based on the testing—**just because it's available**. Sometimes, a school system's own reports, from their own teachers, will **support my recommendations**, and they'll still insist on something different.

Many parents have told me that a teacher pulled them aside and privately admitted that a child was not receiving appropriate services, was not making progress, did not belong in the group they were in—that the child needed more, sometimes **much more**. However, the teacher made it clear that he or she could not say this in public, in a team meeting.

I have sat in team meetings where a teacher **has** spoken out—often, agreeing with my findings. In every case, the team leader or special education director glared at her and shut her down—sometimes "nicely", by saying there were other opinions, and sometimes not so nicely. In any case, that teacher's input was not asked for during the remainder of the meeting.

Schools will often try to stonewall parents, hoping they will give up and accept what is being offered. A lot of times, I'm afraid it works.

Several years ago, I tested two similar middle school students, whom I'll call Jake and Karen, from two different school systems. Both children were thirteen years old. Both were severely depressed, with volatile moods, an inability to concentrate or complete tasks in school, and frequent school avoidance (meaning, they often didn't get there in the morning). Teacher reports documented their emotional fragility and explosive outbursts. Neither one could make it through a full class, much less a full day. They got next to nothing done in school and were extremely difficult to manage at home.

In both cases, the schools resisted placement in therapeutic programs, arguing that there wasn't enough "information" to justify the placements (even after they had my full testing report). They wanted the parents to agree to a short-term diagnostic setting. In my experience, the people at these two diagnostic placements almost always recommended returning a child to the public school, in the same type of program that had already failed.

Fortunately, Karen's parents refused to back down, and she was placed appropriately in a small, private, very therapeutic school. She adjusted to the more structured and psychologically supportive setting, was able to attend school more regularly, and began actually doing some school work. Her moods remained volatile for several years, even with medication, but the program was designed to be helpful when she couldn't cope, and gradually she began to feel better about herself. Fortunately, there weren't any real learning issues. Once her anxiety decreased and she could concentrate, her school performance became more appropriate.

In the other case, the school stalled and put up roadblocks, saying they would provide the right services but essentially working to delay and "wear the parent down". They placed Jake in a program that was part of their own system, but not therapeutic enough. There were too few consequences for inappropriate behaviors, and he continued to spiral out of control. His learning disabilities and limited attention span were not addressed. Within a year, Jake needed a residential placement, costing the district **much** more money than if they'd agreed to a private day placement in the first place.

As someone who has experienced how the system works, I think it is imperative for me to take the risk of challenging the school "culture" when necessary—and then offering as many **positive action items** as I can think of to improve the situation. I am not interested in merely whining about what isn't working. The only thing that matters is talking about what **does** work and **will** work, based on my own experience and that of other professionals. My goal is to make sure that your children get the education they need for a successful future.

The process described in this book—getting a skilled, accurate and independent evaluation, following up with the school, using professionals to help you advocate for services your child needs—is **the best way to monitor your child's growth in academic skills and other areas of functioning** (such as emotional and social skills, fine motor, organization, or language skills).

In most cases, in most schools, neither teachers nor children face real consequences if children do not make a year's progress in **real, measurable, independent skill levels** in one year.

Only the parents, pulling their hair out as they try to figure out homework that their child can't read or understand—only **they** are saying, "my child is not performing at grade level, because he can't do the work or read a grade level book."

I am concerned about the performance of all the students in this country; I don't believe we can afford to "waste" any of them. However, in this book I am focusing on my area of expertise—children with learning disabilities and other problems that interfere with learning. These children are **doubly handicapped** and thus **doubly at risk**—as a result of their own neurology **and** some of the policies of the current education establishment.

Remember- **You as parents know your child best.** You are almost certainly right if you believe your child is performing below the level of the other children in his or her grade. If that is not acceptable to you, then you need to advocate for the interventions that will help your child perform at a better level.

Schools districts are evaluated as "wholes"—in other words, did the district as a whole meet the state standards in reading or math or science. The scores are broken out by grade, and sometimes by gender or ethnicity. It's easy to lose individual children this way; they may pull down the average a bit, but if the whole district gets "over the bar", it's less likely a regulator will say, "but what about this one?"

You, of course, are concerned about "this one", **your own child.** You want to be sure that he or she is fully prepared to be successful in the world. When that doesn't seem to be happening, it's up to parents to arm themselves with knowledge and determination. I just don't think it's a good idea to rely solely on the school to alert you to a problem—or to suggest an appropriate strategy to correct it. Schools are dealing with their own problems, and pulling each child up to grade level is **not** the standard they are setting for themselves.

The current educational system often seems to be trying desperately to avoid making changes that I believe would work and result in **all** students making more **effective progress**. At the same time, they will embrace "new and spiffy" materials or teaching methods that don't seem to make a significant difference. Until education reform—no matter who designs it or which political party promotes it—truly deals with the issues of **measured outcomes, money, and school "culture"**, there will be no meaningful changes in what your children experience each day. No guarantee of meaningful progress or improvement.

Any new program that proposes reform without tackling the three "elephants in the room", cannot possibly work. The folks behind such a program are simply re-shuffling the same deck of cards, without adding any new ones. They are merely "re-arranging the deck chairs on the Titanic", as the saying goes.

For the foreseeable future, **you as parents** will need to make sure you know where the lifeboats on the Titanic are located, and how to launch one. You'll need to do your best to get on one of those lifeboats with your child, and then get the interventions your child needs to stay afloat and be successful in the ocean of education.

# CHAPTER 4

# WHY AN INDEPENDENT EVALUATION?

*"That which can be measured, can be managed."*
*Peter Drucker*


*"Fortune favors the prepared mind."*
*Louis Pasteur*

W hy would you want an independent evaluation?

When you think about it, the more important question is, why **wouldn't** you want an independent evaluation? This again is an issue of money, **your money**, whether it is your tax dollars or your out of pocket expenses. Most people planning to spend a large chunk of money on a purchase do some research first, whether they are buying a car, a television set—heck, even a coffee maker. Comparison shopping keeps outfits like Consumer Reports in business, and I have no idea how many comparison sites are on the internet.

When people read Consumer Reports, they know that organization has "no skin in the game". Consumer Reports doesn't give a hoot whose car or coffee maker or running shoe is the best; their job is to provide the objective results of how these items did on their tests. They figure you're smart enough to draw your own conclusions.

It's the same with an evaluation. If you choose an appropriate person (more on that later), you should expect that he or she will be **an independent agent**, with no loyalties to the place they work (such as a school system), no financial incentive to emphasize certain tests or maximize test scores, no motivation to recommend programs that "happen" to be available at your child's school. With no skin in the game, they can "call 'em like they are", not as someone else would like them to be.

Having your child evaluated is a big deal. It involves a lot of the child's time and energy, often some of your time, and a fair amount of money. If done right, it is the equivalent of going into a hospital for a complete diagnostic workup—pricey and time consuming, but incredibly helpful if there is a problem. So, you want to do it right—the first time, which means some "comparison shopping" to find the best person for your family.

I will walk you through the steps of finding the best clinician or option—what you look for, the questions you ask, the services you should expect, and what type of final product you want to receive.

Believe me, you don't want to put your child through this multiple times to get it right. Kids get really sick of being tested. It can be a challenge to sweet-talk some hyperactive 8 year old or thoroughly out-of-patience 14 year old into sitting through another morning or day of frustrating testing, because the first ordeal wasn't done well. I've had attorneys call me up and say, "I know so-and-so just tested the kid a month ago, but their results aren't complete (or accurate, or objective, or detailed enough), so I need you to do it again." Then it's my problem to persuade this poor child that I really will be the last one to work them over—for awhile, at least.

If your child has a substantial learning problem or a complex diagnostic profile, he or she is going to need regular re-evaluations to monitor progress and make sure that the placement or services are really appropriate. By law, schools must re-evaluate every 3 years. Many of the children I see come back yearly for the first several years, until I am confident things are going well. Sometimes, when there is disagreement with a school system, updates are needed at the beginning or end of a school year so that I can help parents get the right services for their child. No parent wants to put a child through this stuff any more often than necessary.

Plus, some of the tests can't be repeated for at least six months, and if they are tests that give important information, you're out of luck. When you finally get to the right clinician, he or she will have more limited options.

The Wechsler Intelligence Test for Children (WISC-IV), for example, is such a rich source of information for me that in many cases, I have my answers after administering that one test. I could stop there, but of course I don't, because no good clinician relies on only a single source of data. And I can't use a WISC-IV administered by someone else. I have to have my own data, my own interactions with this child, to integrate into my diagnostic picture, or risk having the results be less reliable.

How a child reacts to the test questions or the testing situation itself is often as important as the answers they give. By age six or seven, a child is expected to adapt to the test situation, most of the time, since this tells me a lot about how well the child will adapt to classroom expectations. If I'm the one who has to do the adapting, that's significant. The WISC-IV, like many parts of school, requires persistence, flexibility, and good listening. Does the child have these traits? How often do I need to repeat a question, or pause between phrases, or emphasize key words?

I once tested a 13-year old girl named Stacy who had significant language-based learning problems. She was already in a specialized school placement, but the teachers were frustrated with her "inattention". When I worked with Stacy, I noticed that she often did not respond to a question within a few seconds, as most children did. At first, I assumed she hadn't heard me or wasn't listening, and I repeated the questions or prompted her in some way. But that didn't seem to help her provide the answer. She'd previously scored quite low on the verbal subtests, and I thought I knew why. I was wrong.

When I asked a question and then simply shut up, Stacy would sit there, sometimes for more than a minute. She seemed to be in her own world, not paying attention. Then, amazingly, the answer would be given. Stacy's ability to process what she heard and retrieve the information she needed was incredibly slow—and if you interrupted her, she lost her train of thought completely. Once I explained this to her teachers, they started giving her a much longer time to respond, and she began showing them how much she'd actually been able to learn in their classes.

Information about a child's pace or learning style is a critical part of understanding how a child thinks or works. Any ten children with the exact same IQ scores can have ten different learning styles. Most children are flexible, but kids with learning difficulties are less so. I need to know **how they got to** that IQ score, so I can provide the most useful recommendations.

This is particularly important since **IQ tests measure a lot more** than raw intelligence. By the time most children are seen for testing, they've been in school for at least a few years. The tests are designed in part to measure what they've learned, and how well they've mastered the "method"—the best ways to respond to a standardized test.

This means the child has learned the skills of accurate listening, of being able to give a "standard" and complete response, or being able to solve certain "types" of problems. The tests measure a lot more than just the innate ability a child showed up with. I need to get a sense of how much "horsepower" was there to begin with, as well as how effectively they've been learning to "show what they know". This can be a complex mixture.

A child who works more slowly than average can be given extra time on some tasks, but will be penalized on others. The non-verbal tasks are often timed, and in keeping with the American obsession with speed, there are "bonus points" for rapid work. In the real world, of course, it's rarely an issue as long as one gets the right answer. In the "school and testing" world, however, kids who process, retrieve, or assemble parts at a slower pace will get lower scores. It's important to separate that out from raw intelligence or ability.

Other kids have plenty of "horsepower" but limited "brakes and steering". They make mistakes or respond impulsively, don't plan, miss details, fumble with the blocks, take several tries before putting something correctly in place.

I need to **see** it all, if I'm going to **make sense** of it all.

If somebody else mixes the ingredients and I bake the cake, I can never be confident of the result, because I didn't do all the work. The same thing goes for testing. I'll use an alternate test if I have to, but I'd rather be able to use all the tools I need, not just some of them. Any detective would tell you the same. In fact, any woodworker or car mechanic would tell you the same.

As the parent, you want to make the **best choice** possible the first time, for lots of reasons. Sometimes a school will tell you it doesn't really matter, that all clinicians are basically created equal. If that were true, I'd be out of a job—and we wouldn't have 9 million brands of cereal or donuts out there in the marketplace.

So here you are, knowing your child needs an evaluation, wanting to do this right—and probably feeling pretty overwhelmed by now. Where do you start?

Remember: **You know your child best**. This goes for picking a clinician, too. If you feel comfortable, understood, and respected when you talk on the phone, you're probably on the right track. If you get clear answers to your initial questions about what skill areas are included in the testing, what the report will include, the timetable and costs, this is probably a person you can work with and trust. You also need to be asking what they will do, and why, and what their relevant experience is, to be sure this is the person with the best skills to give you the answers you need.

The best place to start would be with a personal recommendation. In many cases, you will know a parent whose child has similar issues (or an equally complex set of issues), who has gone to a particular clinician for an evaluation and been very happy with the results. About half the children I see are referred to me in this way (or, they are re-evaluations, which is a similar vote of confidence). Sometimes a private tutor, or a friend or relative who works in special education, will be able to provide a recommendation, based on previous experience with this person.

Private schools are another possible source. They see a lot of reports on children they are considering for admission; they know which reports are helpful and accurate, and which are not. They may well have a list of names. If you go to a talk about special education services that is given by a parenting organization, the PTA, the Federation for Children with Special Needs (in Massachusetts), a public or private school, or some similar group, the speaker may have professionals whom he or she has worked with and been happy with.

I do not, in general, recommend asking the public school or contacting your insurance company, though in fairness I have gotten some referrals this way. In both cases, you have no way to know that you are getting the best person for your needs. It's like pulling a name out of a hat, if you're lucky.

Schools will rarely recommend a clinician who has disagreed with them often in the past. It's self-preservation. Why would they ask for trouble? There are clinicians who tend to request services the school already has, or who use tests that produce inflated or superficial results (more about this later). These people are less trouble, and more "cooperative", from the school's point of view. However, you can see why they might not be best from your point of view.

With an insurance company, it's pretty much like buying eggs—if a clinician makes it into the carton, they are assumed to be adequately trained and reasonably close to where you live. In some cases, they have agreed to take the reimbursement the insurance company offers (more about that later). However, there is no way for you to know what quality of product this person will provide. Remember, you are looking for someone who is in many ways an artist, a clinician with both talent and skill, who will produce a unique and very useful report for each child they test. The insurance company can't tell a Michelangelo from a no-talent hack; it's not their job.

Now, we come to hospitals and clinics that have clinicians who specialize in what you need—psychology or neuropsychology, learning disabilities, language and speech problems, sensory integration, etc. This is where it gets tricky. If you are seeking an independent evaluation, there are several things you need your clinician to be willing, and able, to do.

Besides being skilled, talented, and experienced, they must be willing to tell you the truth, and to tell the school system the truth—**especially** if nobody particularly wants to hear it. They have to be willing to disagree in a meeting with 10 or more educational professionals, to keep disagreeing if necessary, and to stick with you until your child gets something as close to what he or she needs as possible.

If a clinician works for a hospital (and I have), there is little or no time in their schedule for attending school meetings, doing school observations, or advocating for what a child needs. It is simply not part of their schedule.

With a clinic or a group practice (where I have also worked), there may be a referral system in place, in which the clinic gets testing referrals from schools. Telling a school what they don't want to hear, and being a pain in the behind about it if need be, is a good way to get fewer referrals.

As the kids say, "Well, duh!". Parents are bringing their child to this clinician because they **already have some concerns** or disagreements with the school. Otherwise, they wouldn't be looking for an independent evaluation. So, an independent evaluator who isn't able to "go to bat" for your child is probably not the best person for you to choose.

If the evaluator isn't comfortable supporting you all the way to the end of the process—or doesn't have experience doing this—for whatever reason, they should be willing to refer you to someone who is. They may be well-qualified and do fine work, and be helpful in certain types of cases, but they're not the one you will want to work with if you suspect there will be a conflict with your child's school about the types of instruction your child needs.

This is definitely a case of "let the buyer beware". Parents should not assume, but should ask some direct questions before making an appointment. How many referrals does the clinician get from schools or insurance companies, and how many from other sources? How often do they provide follow-up services? Will the clinician go to meetings or observe a program? What about providing expert testimony (for example, at a mediation session)?

These follow-up services are generally billed on an hourly basis. Parents should ask about the hourly rate. The most important question, however, is this—if the child needs services that the school doesn't have, or won't agree to provide, will the clinician advocate for your child?

This means he or she agrees to travel with you down a road that may well be long, frustrating, and disagreeable. There are many steps that a parent can take, beyond a Team meeting, when the "fit" between child and school does not seem to be working. These steps take time and cost money, but the biggest problem for a parent is having the clinician say, after the testing is done, "nope, won't go there."

Yes, you can hire an advocate to do the arguing. Some of them are excellent, dedicated people who know about alternative programs and are forceful in arguing for a child's needs. But if things aren't resolved and it comes to a hearing or settlement conference at your state's version of the Bureau of Special Education Appeals, you're going to need an attorney and (in most cases) a psychologist. You'll have the most clout and the best chance of success if the psychologist is the same one who did the testing, and if he or she has observed both the proposed and desired programs, and is seen as objective (more about those things later).

For the record, I do get hired and paid by school systems to evaluate children and programs. Sometimes this is a "second opinion" evaluation, requested by the parents, and the school is not exactly enthusiastic. But other times, they are looking for my expertise—and my reputation. I always make it very clear that I will be objective, that **I am first and only an advocate for the child, regardless of who is paying**. When this is okay with them, we can proceed. In some cases, it works out just fine.

Several years ago, I was contacted by the Special Education Director of a large regional middle/high school. The parents of a 9th grader had been unhappy with the services provided at the middle school, and were asking for a private placement for high school. At a mediation session, both sides agreed to have a neutral third party come in to observe the program proposed by the public school, and make recommendations for placement for this girl.

The director offered my name as someone who would be unbiased, commenting that I had "usually been on the opposite side of the table" from the public school. This was true. I did not test the girl, but I reviewed the extensive records and observed classes and extra-help remedial sessions. I had several recommendations to focus the tutorials on certain skills that were weak, and to improve school/home communication, but for the most part I felt the program met the girl's needs well, and actually provided some necessary remedial services that would not have been part of the private program. It also allowed her to stay with her friends and participate in sports, both of which were important to her.

The important thing to note here is that if I had come to a different conclusion, I would have said so, and then helped the parents obtain an alternate placement for their daughter—in spite of the fact that the public school paid for my evaluation and professional opinion.

Once you have the name of a psychologist who comes with a strong recommendation, you still have to do your "comparison shopping" to be sure this person is a good fit for your child. The clinician—not a secretary or triage person—should be willing to talk with you by phone, for a few minutes at least.

What are their qualifications? At the very least, are they a licensed clinical psychologist in your state? What is their clinical background and experience? Did they have training in neuropsychology or school psychology? The first is important, the second useful but not essential. How many years have they been doing testing? What kinds of problems do they specialize in? They should mention the areas that match your concerns—attention deficit, dyslexia, developmental delays, mood problems, a specific academic weakness, etc.

Can they administer a full range of tests in these areas: intelligence, neuropsychology, academics, and social/emotional functioning? In general, a clinician will never do every possible test for every possible problem in every area—the child would be on his next birthday by the time they finished. Clinicians should get a sense from you of the areas of concern, and should let you know if they can do in-depth testing in those areas. It's not necessary to do time-intensive psychological testing such as the Rorschach with children who don't have a problem with emotional functioning (more about this later), though a screening for self-esteem and social competence is important.

Just to clear up any confusion—a **psychologist** and a **psychiatrist** have different training, and generally do different things. Psychologists have a doctor's degree from a university. They receive training in therapy, evaluations, and research, among other areas. They are not medical doctors and do not usually prescribe medication (though some psychologists can receive training and certification in this area). The psychologists you are looking for will be specialists in testing children and adolescents, and in helping you get the services your child needs.

Psychiatrists and neurologists are medical doctors and are not trained to provide these types of evaluations. You may need the services of either or both of them, but not right now.

Some clinicians see very few school-age children; be sure to ask, especially if your child is very young (4-6 years) or an older adolescent (16-19 years). There are certain tests and ways of writing reports that are most useful for these age groups, for example. There needs to be a developmental focus for young children. With teens who are applying to colleges, the tests and recommendations need to be specific, so they can get accommodations if necessary. You want to make sure the person sees children like yours.

For example, I do not generally see children younger than age 4, or those who are non-verbal or severely autistic. There are certain tests designed for these populations, such as the Bayley Scales or the Brigance for toddlers, and the Leiter Non-Verbal Test of Intelligence. I don't have these tests, since I rarely need them. I am not set up to do a full diagnostic play assessment, although I would want to do so with these children. These are children whom I worked with in a hospital setting, as part of a multi-disciplinary assessment, and I still think this is the best option, even though the advocacy may turn out to be a more difficult issue.

If it seems that the clinician has the right skills and training, then you talk about scheduling, fees, and availability. A full neuropsychological evaluation will vary in cost, depending on a number of factors, including where you live and the reputation of the evaluator. You're looking for a licensed psychologist, whose hourly rates will probably vary from $150-$250 per hour, if not more. Some will charge by the hour or the test; some charge a set fee for a full evaluation. Some accept insurance for part or all of the fee; some do not. Parents may wonder how to get the most value for their money, especially since they will almost certainly be paying some or possibly all of the charges out of pocket.

I could probably write another chapter just dealing with the issue of costs, insurance companies and their limitations, and school system reimbursements. There are an incredible number of variables and possible problems to frustrate and confuse parents.

To cite just one example, insurance companies don't pay for tests to diagnose problems with school performance or learning difficulties. Their view is that academic functioning should be evaluated by school systems. The fact that a parent may be seeking an independent or "second" opinion is not their concern. Another variable is the fact that, in my experience, a parent cannot simply decide based on cost. The most expensive evaluation is not necessarily going to be the best one for a parent's needs.

My professional advice is that parents need to talk with one or more professionals who have been recommended by someone whose judgment they trust. If the clinician seems to meet their needs, and they can afford the fee (to pay for whatever the insurance company or the school won't cover, even if it's the entire amount), then they should go with this person. A top-notch evaluation is worth a great deal to a family, though of course there will be times when price is a deciding factor. A parent may need to explore several options before finding a good clinician whose fee is within the family budget. I have spent time on the phone with a parent who could not afford to use my services, explaining about other options and what steps to take to end up with a valid report and necessary follow-up services. In some cases, this will take longer or involve hiring a separate advocate. I will address this issue again in the chapter on steps to take after the evaluation is done.

The actual **testing** should, in my opinion, take less than a day. If I can't tell you what's going on with your child in 4-5 hours, I should get a different job. Occasionally, a child is so anxious, inattentive, or emotionally stressed that I can't finish in 4 hours and need a second brief session to complete testing. This is the exception, not the rule.

There should be a **feedback session** with parents within a week or two, to discuss results and recommendations. The **written report** can take 4-8 weeks, depending on the time of year. In the spring, when my caseload swells and there are more school meetings and observations, it is more difficult to get those reports out, but parents are entitled to a reasonable turnaround time. If you weren't anxious to get this process moving along, and didn't have real concerns about your child, you wouldn't be in the evaluator's office at all.

I have a strong opinion about the information I am given about a child before the testing session. Essentially, I want to know as little as possible beyond their name and date of birth. Parents are hiring me for my expertise and diagnostic skills, not my ability to read someone else's report and agree with it. I like to see a child "cold", gather my data and my clinical impressions, put together a diagnostic picture, decide what services I think a child needs. Then, I will look at what's been done before, what other people thought, and what the school is offering.

**This is an important difference in how I work,** compared to many other psychologists. I am considered by hearing officers and attorneys to be an "objective evaluator". It is the best compliment I could have from these people, in addition to being considered "accurate". Parents tell me that I have accurately described their child in terms of his strengths and weaknesses, his personality, and his levels of performance. This is very important to me, since **you as parents know your child best**.

These traits are hopefully the same ones you will find in your independent evaluator.

So, you know what you need—an independent evaluation—and why you need it—to be sure you get an objective and expert evaluation of your child. You now know how to look for the person you want, and the questions to ask that person before you schedule the appointment. Let's look at the component parts of an independent evaluation, to help you understand what should be in there, and why.

# CHAPTER 5

# THE INDEPENDENT EVALUATION

*"Underlying all assessments are a respect for children and their families, and a desire to help children. A thorough assessment should allow us to learn something about the child that we could not learn from simply talking to others about the child, observing the child, or reviewing the child's records."*
*Jerome Sattler, professor and researcher*

An Independent
Evaluation

My first clinical placement, as a second year master's student, was at a large semi-urban comprehensive mental health center that specialized in working with children and families. It was affiliated with a community health center. The staff were psychologists and social workers, and trainees from both disciplines were taught together. We received hours of clinical training seminars each week, as well as supervision for every type of service we offered (individual therapy, group therapy with young children or parents, etc.). Guest speakers came often, and staff gave presentations of patients with interesting profiles.

We all did "intake evaluations"—two-hour sessions with potential new patients. We then interviewed their parents or guardians. We didn't do testing, just in-depth clinical interviews that were then organized, analyzed, and written up with diagnostic impressions and recommendations. We presented these to a group of staff, who asked questions and made case assignments.

Without any data from testing, I learned to be an acute observer, noting how the child interacted with me, and with the toys and games in the room. I looked for personal style, coping strategies, signs of intelligence, language and fine motor skills, attention span. Like a good detective, I continue to rely on these skills, more than thirty years later.

My second placement was at a large urban multi-disciplinary children's hospital, that offered, among many other things, a 4 ½ day inpatient diagnostic evaluation. I worked as an intern for two years, while also taking classes for my doctorate, and stayed as a junior staff member for a number of years.

The inpatient evaluation teams saw 5 or 6 children a week. Each child would be examined by a very experienced neurologist and several neurology residents. They would be seen by a team of professionals in other disciplines—a psychologist, an audiologist, a speech and language pathologist, a reading specialist, and occupational and physical therapists. A social worker would interview the family and summarize background information, a full medical workup was done, and the nursing and behavioral staff lived with them on the unit the rest of the time.

Here, the psychologists did testing, as part of the team. Interns such as myself were each assigned to a senior psychologist, and together they were responsible for one child per week. On Friday mornings, there would be a case conference, where everyone who had worked with the child presented their findings, with the neurologist running the show.

At first, my supervisor did the presenting—and most of the testing—but clearly he had watched too many episodes of M*A*S*H. His idea of supervision was somewhere between battlefield triage and the medical model of "watch one, do one, teach one". In fact, the neurology residents were there from the beginning, sitting in the testing room to learn about what we were doing, so it was hard to hide any big blunders.

I had very little actual testing experience when I began in September. For a number of months, my supervisor sat in the room while I worked, but he basically threw me in and sat there with a hook, ready to fish me out if necessary. He expected me to swim, so I did. Once, after about a month, we were assigned a five year old.

"Have you given the WPPSI (the preschool Wechsler intelligence test, for 4-6 ½ year olds)?"

No, I had not.

"That's okay," he told me. "I'll go up to the unit and get the kid. You read the manual."

I did, and he helped and made sure it was done right, but I learned by doing.

The testing schedule was intense. I had time on Tuesday and Wednesday, and could generally "steal" a little extra time if I got in a bind, but the kids were scheduled as tightly as CEOs. I couldn't be wasting time, fumbling around, "missing" the main points of this child's diagnosis, letting them play or argue with me when I needed them to work. My day was as full as theirs.

The case conferences were equally scary. I had to be fully "on top" of my data, clear and concise, and ready for whatever oddball question the neurologist or a resident might throw out. When my supervisor moved out of state after seven months, they gave me another one, but the department head told me she hoped I had "absorbed enough of Dr. X" to pretty much do the evaluation on my own.

I put myself under tremendous pressure to get it right. I talked to the medical residents; they didn't know anything about psychological testing, and I didn't know much about neurology. I let them handle the tests and watch me work, and they told me things about how the brain worked.

The (mostly) women in the other disciplines were incredibly generous with their time and expertise. They explained what they did and why, they let me see their materials and tests, and when I could find the time, they let me watch. I also began reading all the records on each child, and spending time on the unit with each one.

To be honest, the other psychology interns in my group thought I was "under-supervised", and they were mystified by all the extra work I took on. I think I got sensible advice, a ton of information, and invaluable experience that has continued to serve me well.

I'm telling you all this so you as parents can understand why I do things the way I do, and what my training was like. The choices I make when I work with a child are not **arbitrary** or casual. When I discuss what a neuropsychological evaluation **should include**, or why I think a certain test is important, you'll know where I'm coming from. As I said in Chapter 1, I believe "all behavior is mediated by the brain". Everything we do is the result of something that happens in our brains, and is then expressed in a behavior. I think about that functioning, and how well it is working, as I do my testing.

You might agree or disagree with my analysis of the way school systems work, or why I think an independent evaluation is something every child is entitled to. That's fine. You're comparison shopping as you read this. But my opinions are the result of my training; there are no "hidden fees" or "fine print".

I know there are many excellent clinicians across the country who can and do evaluate children with skill and accuracy. I've met some of them and read their reports. I believe you as parents will be able to tell by how clear, complete and well-organized those reports are. A good evaluation will "hit all the bases" of cognitive, academic and emotional performance. When you read the report, you will know that the evaluator really "saw" and understood your child. The report and recommendations will "make sense" to you.

Years ago, I was told by my supervisor, over and over, "If your primary customer doesn't understand what you've written, you've wasted your time." And who is my primary customer? **The parents**, of course. When the music stops, the parent is the one left holding the hot potato. Parents have to be able to read a report and understand what is going on with their child, and why, and what the evaluator thinks should be done about it. No jargon, no fancy medical terms without explanation, no psycho-babble or confusing references to "ego functions" or "object relations".

Let me briefly summarize a few of the component skills that a well-trained neuropsychologist will bring to his or her work with your family. This will give you an idea some of the "ingredients" that go into crafting a useful report. Remember, too, that the evaluator should present a "complete package" with qualities of experience, flexibility and competence right from the beginning, when they talk with you on the phone. You should see these traits in the way they interact with your child, the types of recommendations that are made, and the way they work at a Team meeting.

First, a good clinician will take exhaustive **notes** while working with a child, often writing while they work independently or during breaks, trying to notice every detail, every aspect of their performance, every comment that reveals their self-concept or their attitude towards academics. When I'm done with a testing session, I'm as tired as the child. I've been totally focused on them for hours. I know how important it is that I don't miss a single thing that could help me pull together an accurate diagnostic picture. Even more important, if I miss some area of weakness or vulnerability, I might not recommend the appropriate services to address that need.

It's important to do the testing right **the first time**. An evaluator may do more testing than is absolutely needed, but hopefully they will not do less. Many kids come from a good distance away, and when they're gone, they're gone. An evaluator needs to be efficient, smooth with their materials, familiar with the tests. There's a rhythm to this, and if you use it, the child is less stressed and is able to complete more work in less time.

Second, a good clinician will be **flexible** and easy to work with, ready for any type of child who shows up—since they frequently do. One week at the hospital, my patient was an angelic-looking, placid, smiley three year old who was completely unresponsive to any and all of my tests. No clear autistic behaviors, but no play skills, no eye contact, no language. Getting a score of any kind for that case conference took three times the usual effort.

Another week, we were told that the 7 ½ year old girl was profoundly retarded. I sat her in my lap and put out the first item blocks for the Leiter, a non-verbal intelligence test that began at an extremely low level. After an hour, when she was still responding correctly, I hauled out the non-verbal parts of the Wechsler Intelligence Scale for Children, and watched in amazement as she scored in the average range! That afternoon, there was a note in my mailbox from the audiologist on the team. It turned out, the child was actually profoundly deaf. The audiologist sewed up a little vest with pockets for two enormous batteries, gave the child hearing aids—and her face lit up like a plugged-in Christmas tree. I did an awful lot of pantomime that week, but her intellectual abilities were solid and she was a quick, eager learner.

The hospital where I trained and worked saw recently-adopted 12 year olds with hardly any English, children with head injuries and seizure disorders, children with dysfunctional families and out of control behaviors, and severely learning disabled teens who had somehow fallen through the cracks and had almost no compensatory skills. As the Randy Newman song says, "you gotta dig a little deeper to find out who you are" (so that) "when you find out who you are, you find out what you need." It's very true, and once a good evaluator agrees to test your child, he or she should be willing to dig as deeply as necessary for the most accurate understanding, which will be the most help to you and your child.

Third, a skilled evaluator should have some knowledge of **all those other disciplines** whose testing contributes to the overall diagnostic picture. When they're testing, they should be considering the child's functioning in those areas, too, to look for things that aren't working well.

In my opinion, any competent psychologist should have been part of a team at some time in his or her professional life, and should know something about related disciplines—medicine, neurology, audiology, speech and language, occupational therapy, physical therapy and sensory integration. All those areas contribute to a child's functioning and success in school. I do not pretend to be an expert; I do some tests in many of these areas, and if I'm not happy with my results, I refer the child for additional testing. I probably do that for 1 in 4 of the children I see.

Fourth, any good evaluator needs to **write clearly**, and finish reports in a timely manner. They should be able to present their results (in a parent conference or other meeting) in a well-organized, calm, straightforward manner, to be sure of their numbers and confident of their conclusions. As I learned at the hospital, it's extremely hard to con a neurologist who's used to hard data such as an EEG or a blood test, and who's been seeing cases for 30 or 40 years. Effective presentation skills are an asset at Team meetings and other times when an evaluator is on the spot, including hearings.

When I was learning, my supervisor tore my written reports apart, week after week. His favorite phrase was, "What the heck does this mean?" He was so obsessed with customer satisfaction (i.e., having the parents understand the report and be able to use it) that he should have been a salesman. Or a judge—being precise and accurate in the testing and reporting were just as important to him. My words had to be carefully chosen to get my point across, and **the point was to get the team to recommend what I thought was best for this child**.

Finally, the most important parts of the report may well be the **summary and recommendations**. At case conferences, I'd watch the neurologist flip to those parts of the report, as though they were the only parts that mattered. I was actually a little insulted, until years later a number of school personnel told me they did the same thing—they basically read the summary and recommendations.

Well, I may be slow at times, but I'm trainable. Those sections of the report are the "fish or cut bait" parts—what do I think is going on for this child, and what do I want the Team (or other school personnel) to do about it?

Your evaluator should make sure that the summary tells the whole story, briefly, with all the important parts left in and a detailed synthesis of his or her diagnostic impression.

He or she should prioritize my recommendations, putting the most important ones first and limiting the total number. I've seen reports with ten pages of recommendations and thought, "Who's going to do all of that?" Not most schools, that's for sure.

I learned at case conferences that **the first few recommendations** had the best chance of being looked at and acted upon, if they were clear, explicit, and well-explained. You can always work out the smaller details later, once the big things have been agreed on. Frequently, **the most significant recommendations** are the ones we discuss, and sometimes argue about, at a Team meeting. They are the ones that a child **must have**. If they don't know you need a table on the main level because you have difficulty walking, and agree to put you there, who cares if you also want a pink napkin?

In terms of specifics, a worthwhile evaluation, especially one you as a parent have sought out and possibly paid for, should have all of the following elements, in my opinion.

# Overview

It should begin with an overview of the reason for referral. Why is this child being seen for an evaluation? One or two reasons are fine, but the evaluator should mention whether there are concerns about attention, reading, emotional functioning or some other significant cognitive function. This sets the tone for the report.

# List of Tests

The specific tests chosen will allow you to understand what areas have been evaluated, and the evaluator should be able to tell you whether these are "screening tests" or ones with more depth and greater accuracy.

# Background Information

A note to parents: One of the ways in which I am different from many evaluators is that I do not know anything about a child's history when I begin testing. All of this information is gathered after testing, when I read previous reports and school information, or during the parent conference when we discuss results. So, although this information appears at the beginning of a report, I hope your evaluator will have learned it after the testing is completed, so that he or she can form an independent diagnosis and understanding of your child.

Background information should include the child's family constellation—who they live with, who else they are related to that they don't live with (only parents and siblings), if they attend a boarding school and don't actually live at home, whether there is a positive family history of problems with learning, attention, or emotional functioning. It isn't necessary to provide a full tabloid listing of every problem in every family member, just those that are relevant to the child being tested. For example, if two siblings have been diagnosed with dyslexia or several people on father's side have attention deficit disorder, this should be noted. Grandma's poor sense of direction or a cousin who got pregnant and dropped out of school is much less important.

There should be information about pregnancy, birth, the early period of infancy (temperament, feeding problems, health problems), any later or ongoing health issues, and any medications the child is taking. Problems with pregnancy or birth are sometimes associated with later neurological or learning problems. If there have been head injuries, hospitalizations, allergies or significant illnesses, they should be listed. Sometimes the child's personal style has been distinctive since early childhood, and this needs to be discussed.

Developmental milestones for sitting, walking, talking, etc. can be glossed over unless they were delayed, but for many children referred for testing, this was an area of concern. Parents tend to notice these things, even with an only child. In general, if there was a problem, it needs to be described in some detail.

I also routinely ask, now, if a child was adopted, having reached the end of too many parent conferences and then found out this fact. There may be details about the pregnancy or early life experiences, sensory deprivation, learning or behavior problems for the parents, or family upheavals. These can also affect brain development.

There should be a section about educational history, beginning with day care or preschool. Again, an evaluator is looking for clues in a child's temperament or social skills, learning styles, and early success or failure. Often, there were early signs of what would become significant problems when a child entered grade school. I've had school-phobic children who were so inconsolable they had to be taken out of daycare, or children who did only parallel play until kindergarten, or those who didn't speak or make eye contact for several years even though they were with the same group of children.

One mother told me she had been using flash cards with letters of the alphabet for an entire year with her five year old, who still couldn't recognize them. She knew her daughter had a problem, and in fact she was severely dyslexic and needed a special school program. The good news was that by fifth grade, she was reading at grade level. An early evaluation, diagnosis, and placement allowed her to be taught the right way, and she slowly developed alternate neurological pathways for reading, since the "standard" ones that most of us rely on did not work for her.

Children sometimes arrive with folders containing reams of paper about their educational history. An evaluator should read it all, but then summarize it in the report. The most recent testing should be noted. The current educational plan may be reported in greater detail, especially if there is concern that a child is receiving too few services, or the wrong ones for his or her educational needs, based on the testing.

A good evaluator will also ask about a child's interests, habits, hobbies, friendships, and family relationships. They should be looking for what Dr. Robert Brooks calls the "islands of competence" that support positive self-esteem. Is a child a good athlete? Do they have successful friendships? Are they flexible or fussy, easy or difficult to live with? What are their moods like? Often, the answers support what has been found in testing, and influence the type of program that will be recommended to provide the best "fit" and support a child's learning.

# Behavior during Testing

This begins the "meat" of any report, the stuff an evaluator is being paid to figure out. It should include a description of how the child behaved and interacted, beginning from when they entered the waiting room. How they behaved with the parents, how they greeted the examiner, how easily they were able to begin testing. With a good clinician, it doesn't really matter what a child does—the testing gets done eventually—but it is diagnostic. Temperament, mood, behavior and attitude all have a strong influence on learning.

What about anxiety, you might wonder? Can that throw off the results? It could, but if a clinician is good at what he or she does, it won't. As the computer programming people say, it's a feature, not a bug. It's the neuropsychologist's job to measure the anxiety level and deal with it, as they will generally do within a few minutes. If a child stays anxious, that's a feature that needs to be considered in the summary and recommendations.

In more than 1600 evaluations, I've only had 2 or 3 children whose anxiety made it nearly impossible to complete testing. The one teen who took 8 sessions gets the prize, but we did finish with what I thought were valid results, I did get him placed in a good program, and he did attend and complete high school.

Some school personnel complain about my choice to do the testing in one session, generally from 9 until 1 or 1:30. They say the children get too tired and that lowers my results. I will explain my reasons.

First, children are in school for six or more hours each day, and they are expected to concentrate and complete work throughout the day. I want to duplicate that span of time and see how the child handles it. Anyone can concentrate for 30 minutes, but how do they do all day? We take breaks every 45 minutes to an hour, and more often if the child is very young or needs a break. They go to the restrooms whenever they need to, and bring their water or beverages in with them.

Many children come from a distance to my office, and say they prefer to do the testing in a single session. They are certainly tired when we finish, but are often surprised that it didn't "feel" like such a long time. This is because we are doing such a variety of tasks, at the child's own pace, with my full attention and support. Tasks change frequently, and I make sure they feel good about what they've done. I can and do schedule an additional session when necessary.

My scores, when compared with similar tests given by examiners with similar training (even those in a different discipline), are usually comparable. Parents generally nod their heads when I share the scores during the conference; most of the time, they know approximately where their children are performing. As long as your examiner is a skilled tester and is sensitive to your child's attention and energy level, the results will be valid.

The behavioral observations part of the report should also talk about what happens once the door to the testing room closes. How does the child relate over time—in an age appropriate manner, or not? What is their work style? Are they "slower than a glacier"? Do they have "the attention span of a fruit fly"? Are they fidgety, argumentative, or insecure? Do they need two or three tries before they're satisfied—or correct? Is it hard for them to say they don't know something, or do they give up too easily? Are they flexible when they hit a snag, or do they just sit there?

It's also very important to note how they handle the stress associated with testing—tests that are timed, or new and unfamiliar, or work that is too difficult for them. There's a certain "test style", a way in which things are often presented in standardized testing, such as being asked to reproduce things shown on a card, or provide answers in a certain format, or do a number of easier items first. Children being tested for the first time are often startled or puzzled by this. For these children, a little extra practice or explanation may allow them to relax enough to give their best performance.

Finally, what are their language and fine motor skills like? Both play an important role in testing, with many responses provided verbally, or with a pencil or actual manipulatives. The examiner should note how accurately the child analyzes what is said to him, how well-organized and complete his responses are, whether he is skilled with a pencil, how easily he remembers what he is asked to do.

## Test Results

This section should begin with the cognitive and neuropsychological testing, which is stuff most parents are unfamiliar with and may have difficulty understanding. Your evaluator should explain what is being asked of a child in each test or subtest, what specific skill or area is being evaluated, how a child did compared to norms, and what their performance means in terms of learning style or a learning problem. In general, when you've read this section, you should have a sense of your child's overall cognitive strengths and weaknesses.

My website (www.susanbrefach.com) includes 3 samples of partial reports, including cognitive and neuropsychological functioning, academic skills, emotional/personality development, summary and recommendations. I debated putting these in, since it is such a limited sample, but decided that parents would then have a sense of the style of these sections and a description of many of the tests that are given.

There should be an intelligence test. In 99% of cases, this will be one of the Wechsler scales or the Stanford-Binet Fifth Edition. The Wechsler Preschool and Primary Scale of Intelligence—III (WPPSI—III) is for ages 4 through 7; the Wechsler Intelligence Scale for Children—IV (WISC—IV) is for ages 6 through 17, and the Wechsler Adult Intelligence Scale—IV (WAIS—IV) is for ages 16 and up. The Binet is used from age 2 through adults.

The WISC—IV is the one most of your children will be given. It is the war horse of testing, sturdy and reliable. It covers a wide age range, so a child can be tested over time using the same instrument. It correlates well with school-related learning, and reasonably well with overall intelligence. By the time children get to school, intelligence testing measures what skills they've "learned" as much as it measures what they "showed up with" in the first place. It's thus not a perfect measure, but it's what we've got.

In addition, this test has been used for so long that hearing officers, teachers, doctors, school admissions people, therapists, and people in the field of education generally know how to interpret the results with a degree of accuracy. They know roughly what the scores mean. Many parents get good at this, too, over time.

I think the WISC-IV is a wonderful instrument, because it gives me such a wealth of information. I should caution you that not everyone makes such good use of it; some people report the scores and pretty much think they've done their job. However, since you will be selecting your examiner carefully, using the previous chapter, you can expect to gain a lot of information about your child's learning style, strengths and weaknesses, and certain aspects of their intelligence, just from the clinician's discussion of your child's performance on this test.

The test gives an overall, or Full Scale IQ, and composite or grouped scores in four areas-verbal reasoning and school-related knowledge; perceptual (visual and non-verbal) reasoning; short-term auditory memory; and fine motor speed and accuracy. These four are then combined for the Full Scale score. There are several subtests in each area.

The scores are fine for an overall picture, but a skilled evaluator will be more interested in the patterns, and the scatter between the subtests and within individual subtests. Here, they will find evidence of uneven learning or retrieval, inconsistent attention, linguistic confusions, limited memory, whether a child thinks better verbally or non-verbally, specific learning disabilities, and difficulty with simultaneous processing. This last one is important in school, since it makes it hard for a child to do two things at once (such as listen and take notes) or to prioritize tasks.

By the time the examiner is done with this test, he or she will know whether a child is a logical, sequential thinker or a more diffuse thinker, whether they're picking up rote information in school, and whether there is neurological interference with learning. They will know about persistence, flexibility, and whether a child likes novel or more familiar tasks.

Then, the report should move on to the neuropsychological tests. These cover a range of skills that contribute to a child's ability to learn effectively: receptive and expressive language, auditory memory span and auditory processing, visual motor integration, attention and concentration, executive functioning, and visual memory. Depending on the child's age and grade in school, certain tests are more important. For children younger than 9, examiners should do a developmental screening of gross motor skills, motor planning and sequencing, hand dominance, and left/right identification.

All of this information is then summarized briefly, telling the reader how the child's brain works and how well it works, where the areas of difficulty are, and whether their learning style makes it likely they will struggle with academic learning and performance.

# Academic Tests

Here is where most parents focus their attention. They are concerned, as they should be, with whether their child has the necessary academic skills to successfully handle grade level work. At any grade, there are a number of associated factors that influence learning and performance. These include the child's attention span, the ability to retrieve information smoothly from memory, the executive functioning skills, how automatic and smooth the academic skills are, the size of their memory span, emotional factors, and graphomotor (handwriting) skills.

Once a child has been diagnosed with a learning problem, parents know there is interference with the typical learning process. If this is the first evaluation, you want to know the **baseline**—what your child can do before specialized instruction or an adapted program is provided. Whether the problem is visual or spatial, language-based, behavioral, or due to attention issues, this evaluation should document performance levels and areas of weakness.

In a re-evaluation, there is a need to understand not only how much progress has been made, and in what specific areas, but also whether the **associated factors** have improved. A child can make gains in word reading or spelling or written arithmetic, but still fall farther behind peers if the pace has picked up in a higher grade, or they are still too inattentive to work accurately, or if nothing is automatic and they have to search and struggle to retrieve each piece of information. A good neuropsychologist will be watching these factors, to see whether the child's program is really making a difference and improving overall performance.

Sometimes schools point to one or two specific academic skills that may have improved, while ignoring the associated factors. I've tested children who are spelling better or solving more arithmetic problems, but who are confused much of the time in class because their language processing is so poor. They know things but can't retrieve them from memory, or they haven't learned to put them in writing accurately. Or, they just can't stay focused or organized or control their anxiety. These children are not making "effective progress", they are falling farther behind.

An independent evaluation should provide in-depth information about a child's skills in the following areas for **young children** (grades K-3):

- letter naming

- letter-sound associations for single letters or more complex patterns depending on grade

- the ability to read syllable types that have been taught

- phonemic awareness (the ability to hear, identify, and re-sequence sounds in a syllable)

- rapid naming

- phonemic memory

- word identification

- reading of connected text if appropriate

- single sound and single word spelling

- writing from dictation and independent written work

- number sense and number writing

- arithmetic skills and practical math

- simple problem solving.

For **upper elementary and middle school students** (grades 4-5 and 6-8), there will be more emphasis on:

- reading fluency (both rate and accuracy)

- reading for meaning

- silent reading comprehension

- less emphasis on phonics (though it may still be evaluated, especially for children with learning problems)

- Written language will be assessed in more depth, along with spelling

- arithmetic, conceptual understanding, and practical problem-solving skills (money, time, measurement, chart-reading) should all be included

At the **high school** level, the emphasis should be on:

- skill at synthesizing academic material from several sources

- analytic skills

- logical reasoning and problem solving. These are some of the higher-level executive functions that help a child be successful with a challenging and varied curriculum.

- the pace, accuracy, consistency and efficiency of the child's work should be noted and factored in to the summary.

- tests that measure a teen's ability to analyze abstract and inferential passages in reading (or spoken language), as well as longer reading passages.

- the ability to generate a multi-paragraph essay with appropriate vocabulary and thematic development

- the ability to solve a wide range of more complex, multi-step math problems.

At each age level, some of the same tests may be given, while others will be different. However, selecting age-appropriate tests is not the real issue.

# Not all tests are created equal.

Schools tend to favor certain tests, and some of these do not evaluate a child's skill in depth, or they give inflated scores. This seems to be more of a problem with reading, where schools routinely use tests that do not adequately measure real reading skill, either for oral fluency or comprehension. There are several tests favored by schools that, in my opinion, are not very good at providing usable information about a child's skills. There may be too few questions in a given area, suggesting that a child is good in "social studies", for example, when they only had to answer three questions. Some tests try to cover too broad an area, and don't examine key areas in the necessary depth. There are intelligence tests that are merely "screening instruments", which is not what you want if you're looking to really understand your child's cognitive strengths and weaknesses. Some don't compare well with the WISC—IV, which is important if your child will be tested more than once. The Stanford-Binet, for example, gives me very similar scores to the WISC—IV, in contrast to the Woodcock Tests, which generally do not.

Everyone seems to fall "within the average range" on some of these tests, even when that is absurd. This range includes everyone between the 25th and 75th percentiles, which is such a large number of people (almost 7 out of 10) that it isn't meaningful. It includes 67% of the population. You as parents want to know more precisely where your child performs, and you'd probably like a grade level, too.

Plus, it's easier to "guess" on certain tests because of the format of the questions, so kids score higher than their actual skills. I've testified in special education hearings in which the hearing officers actually agreed that these tests gave inflated scores.

Recently, I attended a Team meeting where the special education teacher presented her test results for a fifth grader whom everyone agreed was substantially learning disabled. On my testing, she performed at the mid-2nd grade level in reading. The teacher had given the Woodcock Reading Mastery Test—III, and the child fell "within the average range". When I asked how that was possible, since we all agreed the child had a significant reading disability, the teacher looked confused and said, "I don't know".

Some tests are not particularly helpful for parents. If a test provides only percentiles or a letter of the alphabet as a rating, it's hard for parents to know their child's effective grade level in reading. If a child went from an A to an E, but the class average began at D and is now at G, then has the child made progress or not? Well, they've gone up 4 levels, but they're only slightly ahead of where the other students started. It may mean they now are even less capable of handling grade level work, if the complexity of levels F and G went up at more than a linear rate. It's confusing, even for me.

A good neuropsychologist with a lot of experience in academic testing should be using instruments that are accurate, whether they are old, simple to give, and reliable, or new and trendy. Reading, after all, hasn't changed much in the past 30 years—or the past 200 years, for that matter.

Just because tests have standard scores and percentiles does not mean they are the best indicators of a child's skill level. They may be fine, or not. When I test a child, if I say they can read at a fourth grade level, the parents should be able to go into Barnes and Noble or the local library and pick out a chapter book that says RL4 (Reading Level 4) on the back, and the child should be able to read it with good understanding.

In fact, I think this is what parents are looking for, and expect, when they are told their child reads at a certain reading level—that the child can handle independent reading at this level of difficulty, and will be able to read readily available books, the same stuff their peers are reading. It seems reasonable to me.

I often give an older reading test that provides only grade levels. It drives schools nuts, and they get quite upset that they can't "compare" it with others that have percentiles. I give it as one of several reading and phonics tests for younger children. It has the advantage of asking the child to read **longer passages** (several paragraphs), even at a mid-first grade level, and asking them to answer **factual and inferential questions independently** (without looking at the questions and answers as the examiner reads them aloud, as another more "acceptable" test does).

Actually, I think these are two skills that are important for measuring reading: how are the child's "reading muscles" (can they read for more than 30 seconds) and can they tell you what they read, on their own? Plus, over more than twenty years of using it, I've found this test to be incredibly accurate. If I say a child can read at a mid-third grade level on this test, then it's supported by many other pieces of information. The parents agree, the teacher agrees, the other tests agree. As I said, reading hasn't changed much.

So, the testing should evaluate the different components that make up reading skill and competence, preferably using more than one instrument.

Written language is a complex task, and is often poorly developed when there is any type of a learning disability. Writing requires the ability to pay attention to several "parts" of a task at one time. A child needs to think about what he wants to say, how to structure the sentences, how to spell the words, what technical details (punctuation, capitalization) are needed, how the paragraph or story should be organized, etc. Writing the words themselves also requires sustained attention, and a degree of graphomotor (handwriting) skill. Most children who struggle with learning have a problem in one of more of these areas.

Writing is the last area of "language arts" skill to develop for most children, so a child may receive special education services and learn to read with good accuracy, and even improve her spelling, but still not be able to produce appropriate written work. Writing is a skill that needs to be taught in an organized sequence of steps, and practiced on a very regular basis. Academic testing should include a meaningful assessment of a child's independent skills for writing—not just the ability to fill in a single word to complete a sentence!

The math part of the evaluation may require several tests, since it's important to evaluate arithmetic skills, "number sense", pragmatic math skills and problem solving. Some children can do one type of problem, such as addition, but struggle with the reverse process of subtraction. Many children with learning difficulties struggle with time and money. For many, solving problems "in their head" is the issue.

In terms of tests, the Key Math—3 is good, and the Stanford Math tests are excellent at upper grade levels, though they take a long time to administer and may not be necessary unless there are specific concerns about a child's math skills.

# Emotional Functioning

A "screening" for basic emotional functioning is generally sufficient, unless the referral questions suggest a need to do more. For many of the children referred for an independent evaluation, the primary issues are learning, attention, or some aspect of neurological or cognitive development. As part of the evaluation, a good clinician will want to know how a child sees the world around him, and especially **how he sees himself in the world**. Does he see himself as generally being successful, capable in school, socially accepted, having talents and interests that are valued, as being supported by family members, "as good as the other kids"—or not?

Self-concept and self-esteem are important drivers of persistence and overall mood. A skilled clinician will generally have a good sense of these issues as he or she interacts with and watches the child in the testing session. A typical battery of tests should include things like a sentence completion test, several human figure drawings, and a semi-structured interview. I don't tend to give check-lists; I think it's easy for kids to rush through them and be less than truthful.

In some cases, there is such a strong **secondary emotional reaction** to the learning problem that it results in ravaged self-esteem, extreme discouragement, physical symptoms such as headaches and stomachaches, and withdrawal or outright avoidance. Children who are embarrassed by their learning problems, or who feel like failures, are at risk for giving up. The boy who hid his face from me while working was an extreme case, but he was far from being the only one. One young teen girl said **nothing** in school—I'm not sure the public middle school knew she could talk. To her mother's astonishment, she ran for student council once she was placed in a school for students with language-based learning disabilities, where her learning style, performance, and language skills were similar to those of her peers. For the first time, she felt comfortable, and was willing to "take risks" socially.

Sometimes being asked to do certain tasks results in tears, withdrawal, emotional outbursts or refusal. Most kids, however, will try to "tough it out" and give what is asked for. The emotional toll is very evident if one is looking, and **it is the evaluator's job to look**, so that changes can be made to a child's school program if necessary.

As children approach adolescence, it's especially important for the independent evaluation to monitor their emotional functioning. In my experience, the public school often does not pick up on these issues, or minimizes them, both in Team meetings and in testing.

For some children, **psychological functioning** is one of the primary issues in the referral. Here, more in-depth projective testing is required. "Projective testing" means that a child is asked to "project" his or her own thoughts and emotions onto stimuli that are deliberately vague, such as an inkblot or a picture where the people could be doing any number of things. They are asked to tell what the design might be, or to tell a story about the picture, including what the people are thinking and feeling.

This is a way to understand the thinking process at a very deep level—whether there is disorganized thinking or a clinical thinking disorder, whether a child "distorts" what is really there, whether they are logical or impulsive or out of touch with the world around them. This type of testing also looks at a child's major emotional states— whether they are seriously depressed or angry, how well controlled their emotions are, and how they handle emotional stress. Social perceptions and social functioning are evaluated as well.

It is important for parents to know that this kind of testing must be administered by a clinician with **a lot of skill and experience**. Many psychologists give these tests rarely or not at all. The tests must be given in a precise manner for them to be valid. The scoring is difficult and very time-consuming. The results must be integrated and then written in a way that is understandable to you as parents, and neither too bland nor too extreme. They are often intensely stressful tests for a child to take.

When done correctly, they provide almost an x-ray picture of a person's mind and personality, and this level of detail should be requested **only when needed**. They should not be given casually or routinely. Parents will generally know when they are necessary, and should try to ensure that the clinician has the appropriate experience.

When I need to do projective testing as part of a neuropsychological evaluation, I schedule a **second testing session**. The child and I are simply too tired to do them well after the other tests are done. They will probably take less than an hour to administer, but that will be an intense hour. I will sometimes also write up this part of the testing as a separate report, if there is information that the school system does not need to know. Parents should discuss this with the clinician ahead of time.

# Summary

Obviously, the psychologist needs to tie everything together. As I said earlier in this chapter, some professionals go straight to this section of the report, so it had better include the important scores, conclusions, and a detailed diagnostic picture of your child. It should present the referral concerns, and information about the child's current program, if that's relevant.

The **cognitive testing** should be summarized, with composite IQ scores. The areas of strength and weakness in cognitive functioning should be described, as well as the child's learning style and any signs of a learning disability. Remember, the WISC-IV is a **powerful instrument**, and the summary should emphasize the major findings from the different groups of scores.

The **neuropsychological testing** should then be summarized, highlighting strengths and/or weaknesses in the child's language skills (listening, analyzing, and speaking), fine motor and visual-motor integration, scanning and visual accuracy, attention and executive functioning, memory, processing skills, planning, and organization. A child who has difficulty with one or more of these areas will often struggle to **learn** or to **use his or her intelligence fully**. These skills are the "brakes and steering" that interfere with a child's basic "horsepower".

School personnel need to know about any problems in this area, since these are tests that they don't tend to administer. Often, a child will require one or more accommodations in the classroom to help compensate for neurological deficits. Schools may be reluctant to provide accommodations that are truly helpful, or they will agree but then not follow through. That is one advantage of having a psychologist who will continue to follow your child over time, and will attend Team meetings. The psychologist can help parents monitor what is actually being provided, and whether it is helping.

In addition, the neuropsychological testing may result in recommendations for additional testing in areas such as speech and language, occupational or physical therapy, sensory integration, or audiology. Some of the special services provided in schools are the result of recommendations based on this area of testing.

**Academic skills** should be summarized, including a breakdown of relevant skills for reading (such as skills for sounding out or "decoding" words, an awareness of the ways that sounds are combined into words—"phonemic awareness", oral reading fluency and comprehension, how automatic a child's skills are, etc.), spelling and written language, and both written and oral math. With a younger child, there will be more emphasis on basic "building block" skills such as decoding words and mastery of phonics. For an older child, it is important to know how well they handle more integrative tasks such as written language and reading comprehension. Strengths and weaknesses should be described. The more detail here, the better, particularly if a child has a learning disability.

**Emotional functioning** should be reviewed, and the most relevant aspects of a child's emotional state should appear in the summary. Especially if a child is experiencing some type of distress as a result of a learning problem, this should be noted so that appropriate recommendations can be made.

The child's emotional functioning should be discussed **to the extent it was part of the referral questions**. For many of the children I see, this is a paragraph about self-confidence, self-esteem, basic interactional style, and the impact of any learning difficulties.

For other children, the emotional issues are so overwhelming that a full projective assessment was done (I discussed this earlier in the chapter). In that case, I often write a separate report of 2-4 pages just to document a child's current emotional state and the major issues or themes that emerged during testing. Sometimes, this is a case of TMI—too much information for school personnel. The material is better suited for a child's therapist and the parents. Schools don't need to know all the details of what's going through the mind of a severely depressed child, or a teen with a thought disorder. They just need to know that a child's **emotional state** is having a **significant impact** on his or her functioning.

For example, the young man whom I mentioned in an earlier chapter, Peter, who was having hallucinations during the testing session, needed a short-term hospitalization so he could be stabilized and started on appropriate medication. The public school had completely missed the severity of his disordered thinking, and no one at the high school had the training to work with him, before or after his hospital stay. He needed a therapeutic day program for the rest of high school. The school needed to agree, and pay for it, but the details were private. I wrote a separate report that was used by his therapist at the new school.

At this point, there should be a **final, summarizing paragraph** or two—the Cliff's Notes version, that can be (and often is) put into an Individualized Education Program (IEP), to let everyone know the bottom line. This gives the most important findings, concerns, and diagnostic impressions. If the examiner has a point to make, he or she should definitely make it here.

## A Note about Diagnoses

When I was at the teaching hospital, early in my career, the head neurologist used to give nearly every child he saw the same diagnosis—"cerebral dysfunction". I asked my supervisor what this was all about, and he said it meant "something is wrong with the brain". He said the neurologist felt that was specific enough. Of course, that would describe **most of us**, including me! None of us have perfect brains, and I think that was the point. This neurologist was seeing many of these children for a third or fourth opinion; they all had some significant problems with learning, behavior or functioning or they wouldn't have been there. He wanted to **focus** on describing them and **getting them services**.

In general, I feel the same way. There are **very few** diagnostic labels that "have" to be given, in order to obtain the necessary services for your child. Some, in fact, are given **too**

**often** or **inappropriately**. A diagnosis that is more than a child needs can actually **interfere** with getting proper remedial services from a school.

The report can include a **medical diagnosis** in the summary, especially if the medical condition requires medication or treatment during the school day, or may have a significant impact on school performance—a seizure disorder, diabetes, Tourette's syndrome, and sometimes Attention Deficit Disorder. Some children who have seizures, for example, have disturbed sleep and interference with memory consolidation. As a result, they may be tired in school and have trouble recalling information, which the school will need to address.

To give another example, I tested Aaron, who had learning disabilities and also Crohn's disease, an autoimmune disorder that affects the lower intestine and nutrient absorption. This is a chronic disease that causes significant stomach pain and fatigue. Aaron, who was in middle school, had a history of going to the nurse several times per week. Not only did the school system offer inadequate services to address his dyslexia, they complained that he missed too much class time, implying that he had an "emotional problem". I asked whether they realized that he was in pain much of the time, and in fact should have permission to leave class **whenever he needed to do so**. In this case, I stated in the recommendations that due to his medical diagnosis, Aaron required specific accommodations and support, such as being provided with any material he missed when he was out of class.

In some cases, a clear **diagnosis** is what the school is looking for, to guide them in deciding if your child needs services. A skilled evaluator will diagnose a **specific learning disability**, particularly if he or she is recommending a certain remedial program or increased services to address it.

For example, the neuropsychologist should provide a diagnosis of **dyslexia** if this is clear from the testing. There will be signs that the child is significantly **unable to "break the code"**, and is not making sense of the abstract nature of the letter system (which is what we are really doing when we read). The Orton Dyslexia Society (www.interdys.org) provides a list of characteristic symptoms. Sometimes there is difficulty with a specific component of reading, or a language-based learning disability that affects classroom learning in additional ways. The examiner should say this in the report. Children can also have disorders of math (dyscalculia) or of written language (dysgraphia), and this should be documented and stated.

Over the years, I have become concerned about diagnoses that are over-used, or given to children at too young an age. In these cases, "less" is often "more than enough". The important thing is for behaviors and performance levels to be carefully documented, so that appropriate services can be put in place.

For example, **attention deficit disorder** is a diagnosis that is currently very "trendy". With the wide range of behaviors used to "diagnose" it, I could probably apply this label to nearly every child in the country. Some testers (both school and private) apply the criteria for ADD so loosely, the diagnosis could apply to me, to you, and to the clinicians themselves. The true incidence of attention deficit in the population is generally listed as 3-5%. A clinician should see **significant behaviors** that will need to be addressed throughout the child's day, and should **document what the child will need** to be successful—specific accommodations in school, check-ins at the beginning and end of the day, more structure and clear expectations at home and in school, the use of checklists, direct teaching of strategies to compensate, etc.

I certainly see children in my office who **definitely meet the criteria** for this disorder. Their neurological systems are unable to maintain the appropriate "level of arousal" to allow them to function in an age-appropriate way. With these children, I'm most concerned with school programming and accommodations, along with possible medication to help them focus until their neurological system matures. Other children show less significant signs. If I can describe and make recommendations without a label, I do so.

Many schools will suggest to parents (or state with conviction) that a child has Attention Deficit Disorder, when in fact there is an auditory processing disorder or an academic learning disability. This diagnosis can be an "easy out" for a school, since they will suggest medication instead of other services. It is your evaluator's job to make this **differential diagnosis** and list the appropriate recommendations.

I have a problem with elementary-age children being diagnosed with Executive Functioning disorder. This refers to a child's ability to plan, organize, initiate tasks and work independently, and use active problem-solving strategies. In high school, these are often areas of weakness that persist in children who were distractible and inattentive—it's sort of the "big brother" of Attention Deficit disorder. However, until children reach **middle school**, their **teachers** should be providing most of the executive functions in a classroom.

Bipolar disorder is another diagnosis that is currently popular. Psychiatrists have been encouraged by drug companies and their own peers to diagnose children as young as 2 with this serious disorder, and to prescribe medications that are not approved for use in children, or not approved for bipolar disorder even in adults. Dr. Stuart Kaplan, a clinical professor of psychiatry at Penn State College of Medicine, wrote a book in 2011 titled <u>Your Child Does Not Have Bipolar Disorder: How Bad Science and Good Public Relations Created the Diagnosis.</u> An article in Newsweek (June 27, 2011) highlighted the dangers to children of this mis-used diagnosis.

Based on my clinical experience, bipolar disorder is often applied to children who are far too young. The Diagnostic and Statistical Manual (DSM-IV R) lists diagnostic criteria for this illness, and describes the mid-teen years as the lower age limit for consideration of a Bipolar disorder. Professionally, I am reluctant to give this "label" to children until they are teens, although I often see children with unstable, highly variable, or depressed moods.

If I think a child has a mood disorder or some other emotional disorder severe enough to warrant medication, I'll say so. But many moody children either have difficult temperaments or have serious learning disabilities, which is enough to put anyone in a bad mood. Once they are labeled with a mood disorder, the focus is often on **medication alone**, when most of these children need a much more comprehensive program. They don't need a label to deal with as well.

A few years ago, I saw a boy in 5th grade, Harry, who displayed signs of clinical depression during the evaluation. There was a strong family history of depressed and anxious mood. Harry was often tired, withdrawn, and unproductive in school. He didn't act out, but he rarely chose to be with peers during free times. At home, he cried often and resisted doing homework. Clearly, these issues needed to be addressed, but Harry also had a language-based learning disability. The school had been trying to address both areas of need, but in both cases with much less service than Harry needed for effective progress.

One of my major goals at the Team meeting was to get the **school** to focus on Harry's **learning difficulties**, while helping the parents to be more aggressive in getting him help for his sadness and withdrawal. I needed to emphasize the diagnosis of **specific learning disability** with the school. Calling him "bipolar" or "mood disordered" was not helpful, since he was too young. Besides, I wanted the school to **focus,** to provide **a lot more** remedial instruction and speech/language therapy. I didn't want them to get "hung up" on his psychiatric diagnosis.

A skilled evaluator will discuss what he or she saw in the session, summarize the child's emotional functioning, and make detailed recommendations for services to help a child manage his/her emotions more successfully. Sometimes, a school will offer a service to address "emotional problems", but these will vary in usefulness based on the skills of the provider. It is often more important to focus on getting the **best remedial services the school can provide**, since these are needed for **academic progress**.

Often, children with emotional problems or social, pragmatic language weaknesses (both of which this 5th grader had) need to work in a small therapy group with a counselor or a speech/language pathologist, to improve both their language skills and their social functioning. It is often more an issue of "pragmatic language" than just social skills. The goals of the group, and the skill of the leader, both need to be geared to the needs of this type of child.

Since these groups are not always available in a school, I would rather have parents find the services through an outside agency or professional. This is also true for most children with any type of emotional or behavioral problem, unless their behavior is so disruptive they need behavioral interventions during the school day.

Besides diagnostic labels, the other part of a summary that I have feelings about is a "score sheet" or a chart of the scores from the tests that were given. Some clinicians put all of their raw data in charts at the end of their reports. The reports of school evaluators, in all diagnostic areas (education, psychology, speech and language, etc.) **often consist primarily of charts** of test scores. School systems would like me to do the same.

While you may think that this sounds like a helpful tool, I don't do it, as a matter of professional judgment.

It is very easy for a school or even a parent to **focus on the scores**, and lose sight of the child, who is a complex individual and deserves to be seen as such. For this reason, I consider it irresponsible and unprofessional, as well as unhelpful, to reduce my evaluation of a child to a list of numbers.

The numbers, in my opinion, are **much less important** than my ability to synthesize the huge amount of data I've gotten after four hours with the child. They are **much less important** than my ability to produce an integrated, clear, and useful diagnostic picture of the child's strengths and weaknesses and needs.

The **important part** is this detailed picture of an individual child, which I can pull together because of my skills, talents, and experience. The **final product** is as much art as science. I do not want people to think of this child as a list of numbers, a set of scores or percentiles. It really bugs me. It's an invitation to be superficial in the analysis—"Just the scores, ma'am."

# Your child is not the scores.

In fact, most school evaluators provide little by way of analysis or synthesis of their data. Whether this reflects school policy, lack of time, or lack of skill, I can't say. I do know that their reports are often of little use in understanding a child's learning style, strengths, and areas of need.

Sometimes attorneys with whom I work will make up a "score sheet" to compare several testing sessions, to see whether a child has made progress, and how much. Unless I was the person who saw this child over time, I don't feel comfortable comparing someone else's test data with my own. Unless I know the other professionals' work, I may be comparing apples to oranges.

Some clinicians, in schools and in private practice, use **computer programs** to analyze their data and produce part or all of a report. This is where some of these score sheets come from. Again, I feel as though this is the lazy or inexperienced clinician's choice.

I don't know about you, but I don't want a machine to be responsible for telling me anything more significant than my weight. When I consult a doctor, I'm looking for that professional's skills and expertise. Do some tests, get some results, but for heaven's sake, **pull it together** yourself. If you can't do that on your own, I'll consult someone else. So, these charts are not part of my reports, although sometimes parents or attorneys will make one to compare a child's progress (or lack thereof) over time.

The final part of an independent evaluation will be the actual **recommendations**. Here's where "the rubber meets the road", as they say. Does the clinician make recommendations that are specific, focused, appropriate, and still reasonable? This is often difficult for a parent to assess. You want the best of everything for your child, but may not know exactly what will be most helpful.

Specific recommendations should include a description of the **type of classroom** a child needs in order to learn. In many cases, this includes the type of student a child should be learning with, the teaching style that is needed, the type of language or visual aids that will support learning, and even possible programs that would best meet the child's learning needs.

**Many examiners shy away from recommending big changes in a child's program—even when these are essential for learning.** They may make vague recommendations but not come out and say a child needs a language-based class, or a program of direct instruction in phonics, or a certain number of sessions per week with a specialist to teach certain skills. The way these recommendations are incorporated into the IEP makes a big difference in how well, and how much, your child will learn.

Your examiner should make recommendations in all the major areas of an academic program:

- type of classroom and details of teaching style

- types of in-class support that are needed

- types of out-of-class remedial instruction, how often, by whom, and in what specific areas

- types of remedial programs that will best suit the child's needs (for example, specific programs for reading instruction, written language, math, phonics, etc)

- additional evaluations that the clinician believes are needed

- any professional consults, such as for medication or therapy, that the clinician thinks are needed

- possible summer services to prevent regression

- how soon the child should be seen for re-evaluation

I always recommend as much as I think is necessary, but I'm not out of touch with reality. If it's March, the schedule of the Speech/Language pathologist is already packed to the limit, and I know that. Asking for a child to be seen five times per week is simply not reasonable. Sometimes, I have to negotiate something less than ideal for a few months, with a promise of more in the summer or the next academic year.

Note that this is **not the same** as not recommending the services a child needs. I will put **in writing** what I want, and then negotiate with the school for the best possible plan at the time. If I want a certain type of classroom that is not available in public school in the child's town, I help the parents find it someplace else, and then discuss it with school personnel.

One final note about my recommendations: **medication**. When I think this is necessary (or would be very helpful) for a child's functioning in school or at home, I will recommend consultation with a pediatric psychopharmacologist—a neurologist, psychiatrist, or nurse practitioner who specializes in working with children and teens to prescribe and monitor medications. It is often a problem to find an **available**, affordable professional who also has the characteristics I'm looking for. I have a small list of people, but I'm always looking for more. This is because of the second criterion I look for when working with a medical professional—**monitoring**.

Selecting medication for most psychological issues is rather like throwing darts at a board from a long distance. Your dart will probably hit **somewhere,** but it's hard to tell if you've hit the **right place. Unlike** some medical problems such as diabetes, there is not one accepted medication that will almost always help. **Like** diabetes, biochemical imbalances that cause psychological problems need to be managed on a long-term basis.

Deciding on the best medication for childhood ADD or ADHD, anxiety, depression, moodiness, flexibility or behavior/thought control **is not an exact science**, and it is likely that your child's doctor will need to try more than one medication, at more than one dose. He or she may need to try several medications in combination. A doctor should agree to see your child as many times as necessary, and adjust doses or medications based on feedback from you, your child, and the school. He or she should be willing to do this **either** until your child shows significant improvement, or you all decide that medication is not providing enough "bang for the buck" to warrant continuing. There are alternatives to medication, and the Appendix lists several books that discuss these alternatives. I discuss this issue in detail in the chapter on working with other professionals.

**Recommendations** are a crucial part of an independent neuropsychological evaluation. We will discuss their use in greater detail in several later chapters.

## CHAPTER 6

# AFTER THE EVALUATION: NEXT STEPS, POTENTIAL PROBLEMS, AND KNOWING YOUR RIGHTS

*"I learned this, at least, in my experiment: that if one advances confidently in the direction of one's dreams, and endeavors to live the life that one has imagined, one will meet with a success unexpected in common hours."*
*Henry David Thoreau*

**Know Your Rights**
Trust Your Instincts

When I began evaluating children for a living, more than twenty-five years ago, I decided that I would present the truth as I saw it, regardless of who paid and what they were hoping to hear. I was idealistic; I saw myself as an advocate for children, who couldn't vote and didn't have much power in the educational system. This was my first and basically my only rule with regard to what I would say. Sometimes parents were unhappy with my results or recommendations; sometimes the school system was unhappy. Either way, I found I had to get used to often making people unhappy.

Once the evaluation is done and the report is written, I often find myself sitting in a meeting at the child's school and disagreeing with the current amount or type of help the child is getting. It's uncomfortable, a bit like telling the Emperor he isn't wearing enough clothes. I lay out what I want to see happen anyway, because based on my testing, I believe that different services are necessary for the child to make effective progress.

Often, the parents aren't surprised to hear my results, and are in agreement with my recommendations. They may even have been telling the school for years that what's being done isn't working. They've gone out on a limb and gotten an independent evaluation (possibly more than one, depending on the child's needs). They've set up this Team meeting, brought in the evaluator or an advocate to present the findings, and shared their own, often poignant, concerns.

There they sit, basically hanging out in the wind, hoping the school will agree with the results and provide the necessary help so their child can make **effective progress**. Most parents are pretty anxious as this scenario plays out.

The issue on the table is getting these recommendations **put into place and acted on.** Sometimes, it's not a problem; the school accepts the outside testing, agrees that the child has certain needs, has the right services and personnel available, and writes an appropriate Individualized Education Plan. Everyone smiles and tells one another how good this will be for the child. My work here is done (for the moment).

In fact, this happens with probably half the children I work with. Some meetings are like a Middle East rug bazaar, with a lot of negotiations and counter-offers, but in the end I am able to facilitate putting "the right stuff" in place.

The rest of the time, it's not as pretty. There's little happiness and few smiles. I know it's going to be like pushing water uphill. If you've been in this type of meeting, you know exactly what I mean.

I'd like to be encouraging, but the truth is, just because I'm an experienced professional doesn't guarantee I'm going to have any more success initially than the parents did. The difference is, the school system can't simply dismiss me. I have the right degree and training, and more than twenty-five years' experience. Going into the meeting, I know what the child needs, and how far below grade level his skills are. My reports are judged to be accurate by hearing officers. I know the next steps and the strength of my case. Most important, I will stay on this path as long as parents want me to work with them.

As you might imagine, this can make me unpopular at Team meetings, especially as school systems have come to know who I am. I'm not a person who enjoys confrontations, but the needs of children are more important than being "liked". My goal is to ensure that a particular child will get as much of the specialized instruction or accommodations he or she needs as possible.

If it sounds as though schools try to pretend things are **better than they really are**, I'd say you were hearing correctly. It's part of the "school culture" issue I mentioned in a previous chapter. It is generally frowned upon for teachers to admit that something "isn't working"—whether this is the class type or peer group, the currently available programs, an individual teacher's style or effectiveness, or the progress a child is making.

It's like asking a member of the Mob to "rat out" one of his colleagues. Not a great idea, if you want to remain a group member in good standing. This is why you need an **outside** evaluator, advocate, or other professional to work with you in getting appropriate help for your child.

As you might expect, the test results and recommendations that I present in a meeting are often not received well. Nobody enjoys being told that what they're doing is insufficient, especially if they've been able to hide that information from parents for years. I'm sympathetic, but I have to **keep my eyes on the prize.** It is my job to get your child what he or she needs to be successful. My goal is **to make school work for your child.**

Here, I'm going to offer you a graphic that shows what should be happening between you, the school, and your child. It's a **triangle**, and I will use it in another place in this book, to remind you of the essential **partnership** among the three parties involved. Triangles are inherently strong, stable, and self-correcting. Stools with three legs are the most stable, and thirds are used in music to describe intervals and harmonies that are pleasing to our ears. Your outside evaluator or other expert helper is not a direct part of this triangle, though ideally he or she is actively communicating with all three points.

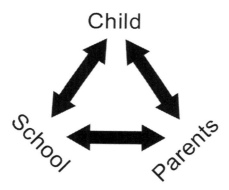

Child

School                    Parents

Flow of Communication
and Responsibility

Note: the triangle implies that **all three points** are of equal importance, and I believe this is true. Even young children need to feel as though their concerns and worries are heard and dealt with. After all, they are the ones expected to do the "heavy lifting" here; they have to learn to compensate for whatever learning or behavioral or emotional difficulty they were born with, and they have the smallest amount of actual power. **The least** we can do is listen carefully and make use of their feedback. As they approach the early teen years, this becomes essential.

School personnel may give lip service to the "all three points are equal" rule, but in my experience they have difficulty "walking the walk", especially when it means doing something different or thinking outside the box. You as parents may **often** have to remind them (and yourselves!) that this is a three-way partnership.

Let's look at some of the common objections schools offer. In many cases, parents are taken aback and don't know how to respond. After all, schools have been telling parents for years that **they** know what's best for your child.

Remember: **you are the expert on your child.** Don't let the school tell you that their cars can get 100 miles per gallon, or that your child really doesn't need more than one meal per day. It isn't true, and your independent professional should be prepared for these objections.

One of the current favorite arguments I hear from schools is that they must by law provide a "free and appropriate public education", also called FAPE. Of course, this is only true to the extent that the public school program allows the child **to make progress**. If a child isn't learning in the public program—or their emotional functioning is being destroyed—then **something else** is what they need, and that something becomes "appropriate".

The same is true with regard to a school's need to offer a child the "least restrictive environment" (this is defined in the state and federal statutes). As I've said in meetings and special education hearings for many years, **a substantially separate, fully language-based program** at a different school may in fact be the "least restrictive" place for a child with significant learning disabilities, if it allows him or her to learn and make progress. Some children simply will not be able to **overcome their learning problems** without a great deal of specialized, individual attention.

Another argument for the school's recommendation over mine is that "we can't be sure this is not just a developmental issue that will go away if we give it some more time". Federal law does not allow this to be used as an explanation beyond age eight. Still, that's how we end up with an 8 year old non-reader who's still in first grade, which just seems wrong to anyone who hears about it.

Another argument is that providing services as many times per week as I recommend is not necessary (read: too costly). Any professional who works with children, however, will tell you that you get more "bang for the buck" when you provide remedial services to children at the **youngest possible age**.

Perhaps you've heard that a young child can learn many different foreign languages if they start as infants or toddlers and are immersed in the language. The brain simply picks up the new language and files it on its own track, one language next to or overlapping the other. There is a period of receptivity for language, when many things are possible. Starting in 4th or 6th or even 8th grade, as many schools do, is often much less effective, if the goal is to actually be able to speak and read this language, since the children are past the point of greatest receptivity, and have many more subjects and activities to pay attention to. They will learn some, but less than if they started younger.

The older a child is, the more intensive the instruction in learning a new language (or correcting for a learning disability) needs to be. Unfortunately, the type of multi-sensory immersion provided by the Rosetta Stone language videos, for example, are rarely used by school systems. These programs use a computer, are fully individualized, provide immediate feedback and correction, allow more practice per session, and help focus attention and memory. This enhances learning, even for adults.

The same is true for improving a child's expressive language and vocabulary, articulation, language processing skills, memory span, pencil control, fine motor skill, gross motor planning and coordination, and the baseline fundamentals for understanding reading and math. The sooner you start, and the more often you practice and review, the better.

It makes sense, doesn't it? If you work out at the gym, is once a week or four times a week better? Much **brain power** is like a **muscle**—use it and improve it, or don't and it won't. Kids who are not picking up these skills on their own need direct instruction in Kindergarten through 3rd or 4th grades, so they make the **maximum growth** before the nervous system is mature and the neurons fully grown, at around age 9. More bang for the buck, but I still get an awful lot of arguments.

One of the hardest arguments for a parent to counter is that the school's offerings are "research based" or "research driven", as though that makes them somehow sacred and sure to be correct. It's here, I'm afraid, that I encounter the Emperors with the fewest clothes.

There have been numerous teaching methods and even styles of classroom management that I have observed in my years as a psychologist, and even some that I remember from my childhood, that were out-and-out disasters for significant numbers of students. I am sure these were considered "well researched" or even the current buzz-word, "research driven". **It didn't matter**.

Whoever these researchers were, they weren't testing this stuff in the **real world**, where I observe and where your kids try to learn. It's a darn good thing the quality of research in other areas is monumentally better, or we'd still be relying on blood-letting to cure disease, and our space rockets would all have blown up on the launching pads. One article I read compared the criteria used in designing current education policy to "using astrology to design a space program".

The fact that something has been "researched" does not mean it has been **researched well**. In fact, the standards for research in education appear absurd to anyone trained in hard science research. If you subject this "research" to a hard scientific analysis, with only rare exceptions you can readily determine that it did not prove what it claimed to prove. If we built bridges the way we design academic programs, they would mostly fall down.

Whatever the state of "research in education", the products or programs it recommends often seem to need revision or outright disposal. I attended a school of education for my doctorate, but before that I studied biology and human genetics. I don't believe most of the research I read in education would have been published by scientific journals with more rigorous standards. The fact that they use human subjects is not an excuse. No, they can't manipulate students or heat them up or keep them in a dark room; it's not like testing chemicals to see if they work, or doing stress tests on metals. However, medical research manages to produce reliable results in many cases, and evaluate different protocols using human subjects, so I know it can be done. I just don't think the researchers spend enough time in the "real world" of schools.

If you think about it, reading and math have been taught in a way that clearly "works" for at least the past 150 years in this country. In the Little House on the Prairie books, Laura Ingalls Wilder began teaching school at age 16, and described her methods for teaching the basic subjects in some detail.

She would present the material—letters, letter-sounds, words, spelling lists, methods of doing arithmetic—and have the students say it aloud and copy it in writing. She reviewed the material a number of times, and drilled the students in the facts she wanted them to know, and then tested the students to be sure they knew this stuff automatically. Only then did they get to move up to a higher level. Introduce, copy, drill, repeat, test, then continue.

If it sounds simple, it's because it really isn't rocket science. It's a method that worked then and still works for teaching the basics, at least for children who do not have severe learning disabilities.

One of my own children was in a semi-professional theatre performance for a number of years. There were about 40 adults and 10-15 children. The children's group would consist of ages 5-11; they would be part of a 2 ½ or 3 hour production in which they needed to sing (often in parts and in foreign languages), dance, move about on stage, and be part of the larger scenes, for several weeks of shows. A friend asked him how the kids managed to learn all that stuff.

My son replied that the music director would teach the songs in small parts and go over them, as many times as it took, during weeks of practice, until everyone knew every word and note. They simply kept at it until everyone had mastered it. Then the stage director would watch them perform, to be sure they really had it down cold. The same methods were used for the dances and stage movements. Introduce, copy, practice, review, test.

For years, I've said that I think some teachers get bored. They would like to be doing something different or new, that would be more exciting for them. What they forget, I think, is that **each class of children** that comes in, each and every year, needs to learn the same things as the year before. This means the methods used will be generally be **the same** from year to year. They did it on the prairie in the 1880s, for heaven's sake.

But it works. And many of the shiny new things that your children and mine have been asked to use simply don't work as well.

As I said before, schools often don't make good use of **the resources they have**. Boredom could be alleviated in several ways. By making use of technology, children who needed more practice could get it, and those who were ready to move on could be exposed to more challenging material. Alternatively, they could use the model of Waldorf Schools. These are schools that teach according to the educational principles of Rudolf Steiner, a German educator and researcher. In these schools, one teacher stays with the same class of students from first through eighth grades. This would require teachers to be competent to teach a wider range of subject matter than many currently are able to do, but it would mean they didn't have to teach beginning reading every year.

I recently read an article about management and the late Peter Drucker, considered by many to be the world's greatest management thinker. Some of what he wrote is startlingly relevant to the field of education. He wrote "**management is not a progressive science**: the same dilemmas and difficult trade-offs crop up time and again." The problems of management, he felt, were always basically the same, decade after decade—and I believe **the same is true for educating children**. Children simply don't change that much, and they need to learn the **same things** to be well educated—how to read for meaning, write accurately and honestly, deal with numbers, manage their time, and understand how the world works.

Drucker also believed that "all human organizations need clear objectives and hard measurements to keep them efficient." (Economist, Nov 21, 2009). The education establishment needs these desperately. Management consultants and business-school professors have struggled to be taken seriously, he thought, because **they were prey to fads and fashions**—great ideas that didn't turn out to work, and great companies that went belly up and took lots of people with them (such as Enron). If that doesn't describe much of **education**, I don't know what does.

When I began observing classrooms several decades ago, there were still schools with "open classrooms"—a cluster of rooms with partial walls, with different classes taking place in these rooms at the same time. I was appalled at the level of auditory distraction; no matter where I sat in some rooms, I had trouble hearing the teacher because there was so much noise filtering in from the other classrooms—and I didn't have a problem with auditory processing or attention! Children with a variety of learning disabilities often failed to learn in these classes. They were "in vogue" for some years, and I'm sure someone somewhere "researched" them. I thought they deserved to be scrapped, and they have been.

Then there was "whole language"—the idea that lots of reading out loud together as a class, with a teacher pointing to the words in a big book on an easel, would somehow "switch on" the ability to read, without all that boring phonics. Again, I was appalled, but I figured it had been developed through research and maybe they knew what they were doing. To me, it was like asking children to bake a cake without a recipe or even a list of ingredients, just by showing them lots of finished cakes. Some children managed to produce cakes, but many did not.

For the roughly 85% of children who are "wired for reading", the method almost doesn't matter. Expose them to print, any time between ages 5 and 8, and most of them will figure it out, even without good instruction. All of them, of course, will benefit from a well-taught phonics program.

For the other 15%, however, the "reading switch" does not turn on automatically. There is some interference, some part of learning to make sense of the abstract nature of print that they don't understand. It can be due to a range of problems—visual, auditory, memory, attention, developmental delays, or other things. For these children, **direct instruction in the letter-sound system**, known as phonics, is required. The only exception to using phonics instruction, in my experience, would be the few children with significant cognitive or developmental limitations who will acquire a limited "whole word" reading vocabulary.

For years, I tested kids with no phonemic awareness, no inner sense of the letter-sound relationships, and thus poor reading skills. I complained that they needed to be taught phonics, the building blocks of learning to read. In several cases, I was actually told that phonics was "boring", and that neither teachers nor children wanted to do it.

Well, yeah, it might be boring, but I don't care. I care that these children needed what had been done in 1880, but was not being done in 2002. Finally, some of the more astute teachers began **doing what worked**. They taught their classes the letter sounds, how to sound out words, the rules to use and the exceptions to those rules. At this point, phonics is again "in style"—but for how long?

Where I live, there is a math program in use in many towns called "Everyday Math" that showed up about 20 years ago. My oldest child was in a "field test" class—the teacher would get a box each month or so with the next set of lessons to use. It was developed by the University of Chicago, so you could be forgiven for thinking it was based on good, solid research. I honestly don't know who they used for research, but it has more holes than a screen door. It is very language-dense, meaning that you have to be very good at analyzing language in order to understand the lessons and assignments. There is hardly any drill of math facts. Five different "strands" or math topics (including algebra, measurements and graphs, and word problems) are presented all through the year—even to first graders, with the teacher moving back and forth between these strands on a lesson-by-lesson basis. The homework typically includes 4 or 5 different kinds of problems on one page, including tricky word problems. There is nothing to challenge the child who is advanced or even adept in math.

Do you see any problems here? To pick just one, the program is a nightmare for a child with any type of language-based learning disability. They sit and stare at the word problems and cry. Kids with weak rote memories don't know their math facts, and inattentive kids can't keep track of the different strands of instruction, since the teacher seems to be doing something different all the time.

Again, I complained, and again I was told how "exciting" and nifty this new program was. I was clearly an old fossil who didn't appreciate updated teaching styles—until desperate parents and teachers finally started plugging the holes by drilling math facts and going back to simpler, more numeric and less "wordy" math texts.

For years, "invented" spelling was encouraged, and we were told that children would simply "pick up" and "prefer" the correct spelling over time. This was presumably another "research-based" idea. Written language skills were supposed to be absorbed through the air or something, since they weren't taught in an organized, systematic way, and kids were not asked to write very often. Both ideas turned out to be wrong, as they realized when many children in upper elementary school couldn't spell or write a sensible paragraph.

I even have an article, about 10 years old, from a journal of education, titled "Writing: It can improve, but it has to be taught". Honestly, how could they have thought otherwise? Don't these people talk to one another? In many classrooms now, teachers give spelling lists that teach basic rules, though I don't believe there's enough follow-up to ensure mastery. Writing is getting more attention, but often the skills I see are still so poor that I know many children need much more practice, proofreading by a teacher, and models to follow (called "templates").

There's plenty of blame to go around—the "developers" who aren't designing educational methods that produce **real-world learning** and mastery, researchers who don't design appropriate studies, teachers looking for something "new", administrators who don't fully evaluate whether a new program will **produce better results** for students. All of them are supposedly "well educated" **already**, and all of them, in my opinion, should be doing better.

**You know what works?** I'll bet you do, even if you don't know the "technical" names for this stuff. So much of early learning involves common sense—introduction of material in small segments or steps, repetition, practice, review, and being able to see, hear, and touch the teaching materials while learning.

Teaching letter sounds, and how to blend sounds together, and how to "sound out" (decode) words or syllables **works**—whether it's Phonics workbooks available at your local bookstore, or Primary Phonics, or Lindamood's auditory sequencing programs, or SRA's phonics (these last 3 are listed in the appendix so you can learn about them, though they need to be taught by professionals). Teaching reading with controlled, repeating vocabulary **works** (think Cat in the Hat and Hop on Pop). Drilling spelling rules **works**. Clapping out math facts **works**. Writing every single day and correcting what you write **works**. Cursive handwriting reinforces reading skills for weak readers—just ask the Orton-Gillingham folks who use it daily to help teach dyslexics.

The next time the school tells you that the newest, most research-driven teaching methods are being used with your child—and that people like me who want simpler, more old-fashioned methods that have worked for 150 years don't know what we're talking about—I hope you can control yourself.

I usually can't, which is why school personnel often cringe when they see my name on a report. They act as though I want to drag them back to the Dark Ages, instead of merely wanting them to do what works for the children who actually need skilled teaching in order to learn.

That's the nub of the problem, really, if you have a child with any kind of learning difficulty. You can throw just about anything at half the children in a class, and they'll pick up enough to make sense of the curriculum and acquire a decent set of skills.

It's the **other half** of the class, the ones with an area of weakness or confusion, whose brains don't always make sense of input or who can't find the information in their memories reliably, who need a teaching style that does not allow them to fall between the cracks. In essence, this is mastery-based education. It is what you want for your children—to help them achieve mastery. You want them to be able to **use** what they have already learned to **master** the curriculum being taught. You want them to become independent learners.

To get them there, you may have to fight some battles, which is why I'm writing this and you are reading it. So, what are your rights? Equally important, what are your **child's rights**?

The federal special education law is formally called **20 United States Code 1400 (USC 1400),** which is known as the Individuals with Disabilities Education Act (IDEA). The federal regulations that describe how this law is put into effect are called **34 Code of Federal Regulations 300 (CFR 300).** This law and its regulations have several purposes, but one of the most important purposes is "to ensure that all children with disabilities have available to them a free appropriate public education (FAPE) that emphasizes special education and related services designed to meet their unique needs and prepare them for further education, employment, and independent living."

All of the information related to this law and its regulations is available on-line from the federal government at http://idea.ed.gov. You can look them up and read them for yourself, but I am hoping that you will be working with a skilled psychologist who is aware of the basic rights you and your child are entitled to. Eventually, if problems persist or get worse, you may need to consult and hire an educational advocate or an attorney who specializes in special education law. He or she will certainly be aware of your rights, and will help you decide how best to proceed in getting the help your child needs.

Each state also has laws and regulations that govern special education services. In Massachusetts, the statute is **Massachusetts General Law, chapter 71B.** The state regulations implementing this law are called **603 Code of Massachusetts Regulations 28.00.** These are available on-line at www.doe.mass.edu/sped. For each state, there is a website with the state regulations and rights, found through the department of education (doe) for that state. There will be a category for special education, with links to the relevant laws and regulations.

The Federation for Children with Special Needs (http://fcsn.org/index.php) publishes a wonderful summary of your rights, and those of your child, under special education law. While this is a Massachusetts organization and thus addresses requirements that are in effect in that state, there are many rights and services that are mandated by the Federal laws and will be the same across states. The Federation's booklet will not answer every specific question that a parent might ask in a particular situation, but it will give you an overview and a place to begin. The appendix of this book also has a list of books that deal with special education and the law.

There is also an additional body of information pertaining to these laws and your rights. Since the laws were passed, parents have brought cases to federal and state courts, as well as to the Bureau of Special Education Appeals in their states. The decisions resulting from these cases are part of the legal record, and are used in deciding future cases. As a result, there have been many additional interpretations of what services school systems must provide, where the limits are in providing these services, and what rights you and your child have. In some cases, these decisions have made it easier to get services, and in some cases more difficult.

For example, the Massachusetts special education regulations state that their purpose is "to ensure that eligible Massachusetts students receive special education services designed to develop the student's educational potential in the least restrictive environment."

**Special education services** are defined in both state and federal statutes, as "specially designed instruction (that is, adapted in terms of content, methodology, and delivery)...to meet the unique needs of the eligible student, or related services necessary to enable a student to access the general curriculum."

The law in Massachusetts **used** to require that students be educated so they could achieve "maximum feasible benefit"; this has been watered-down to merely ensuring that they make "effective progress" and achieve their "full potential". As you can imagine, all of these phrases are subject to interpretation, and have been argued over in meetings and court cases for many years. What constitutes "effective progress"? Who decides what a child's "full potential" is? When is the "least restrictive environment" a small, substantially separate class, or even an out-of-district placement, rather than a regular classroom?

As I write this, I am preparing to testify in a Bureau of Special Education Appeals hearing for a 14 year old boy whose cognitive abilities scatter over a wide range, but generally fall mildly below the average. He also has severe learning disabilities, but the school system decided he was essentially incapable of learning due to his "low intelligence", and did not provide even minimal remedial services to teach him to read, write, and do math. He has spent most of the past four years "putting in his time" but learning very, very little in the way of actual academics. My testing emphasized his learning disabilities, which meant that he would be capable of learning with specialized instruction, but the school placed him in a 9th grade program designed to teach life skills—cooking, buying things in a store, filling out a job application, being polite—all very helpful, I'm sure, but not as important as being able to read at a functional level (which is 6th grade, approximately) or do basic math with good understanding. With what they offered for high school, he would not be able to live independently or get most minimum-wage jobs, even though he is cognitively capable of those things.

So, here we have the issue of "educational potential". Could this boy read at a functional level with the right instruction? I believe he could, and so do his parents, which is why they rejected the education plan and are spending money they don't have to try to get their child appropriate services.

To take another example, think about "effective progress". What does it mean to you? You might think making a year's progress in one school year is pretty reasonable, maybe somewhat less if a child is struggling with a significant learning disability.

How about no progress? For two years in a row? Plus having an instructional aide yell at your child for working too slowly and not being able to remember material, when these are listed as areas of deficit in his Individualized Education Program? It didn't seem right to the parents, or to me—which is why this particular child is now attending a private school for children with language-based learning disabilities. However, he's also more than three years below grade level in his skills, and it will be a real challenge to help him access a grade level curriculum **as well as** improving his independent academic skills.

A child in public school, from preschool (age 3) through high school (or age 22) is expected to make "effective progress" in the "general education program". This is their right, and **when a child can't do this**, special education services must be offered to correct the situation. In Massachusetts, a child must make "documented growth in the acquisition of knowledge and skills, including social/emotional development…with or without accommodations, according to age and developmental expectations, the individual educational potential of the student, and the learning standards set forth in the Massachusetts curriculum frameworks and the curriculum of the district."

Well, there are plenty of words in that sentence that are open to debate. Who decides **how much growth** is enough? In what ways will this growth be **documented**? By the school's standardized testing or by more independent tests given by specialists? If the child could succeed in **general education** with the right accommodations, how do we ensure they are being provided? What if a school insists that a child is merely "**developmentally slower** to learn to read", when my more in-depth testing clearly demonstrates a reading disability? And once again, who gets to decide a child's **individual educational potential**?

Obviously, the sooner parents realize that their child is having problems with learning or behavior in school, the sooner they can get an accurate evaluation and use the laws to get more appropriate services. Knowing your rights is one part of that process.

## Remember- you know your child best. If you think there is a problem, listen to your instincts.

When considering what rights you and your child have under state and federal laws, it helps to know how certain words are defined by these laws. Many cases hinge on whether a child meets certain criteria, or whether the school district has followed the law in terms of time deadlines, determining eligibility, or preventing a child from being successful in the regular education system by not providing necessary accommodations. This is not meant to be an exhaustive list of definitions, just the ones I find most helpful. I am not an attorney, and there are many smaller details that they are qualified to deal with, while I am not.

For example, **eligibility** is an issue that arises when a child is evaluated for the first time. The Team considers whether the child is eligible for an IEP or 504 Accommodation Plan based on certain disability categories (described below). Eligibility is also readdressed every time the child is re-evaluated, to ensure that he or she still qualifies as having a disability.

**Eligibility** becomes a critical issue when a child is close to graduation from high school. An "eligible" student is one between the ages of 3 and 21 (up to 22nd birthday) who has not attained a regular high school diploma, and who has one or more disabilities that prevents him/her from making effective progress in general education without specially designed instruction or some other related service.

This means that an eligible student can receive special education services until he or she turns 22, including transition services to enable them to live independently and hold down a job. Services available to children are almost always better than those available to adults (due to decades of cutbacks, and services that are mostly provided less intensively in the community rather than in specialized settings). So, most parents would like their children to receive specialized services for as long as possible, if they are needed. Not surprisingly, school systems would prefer to give a diploma as soon as possible.

Now, I'm afraid most parents assume that getting a high school diploma means a child has something close to 12th grade level academic skills, but of course this is often not the case. Standardized testing and grades in courses do not give parents accurate information about their child's skills, in my opinion. As I mentioned, the assessment tests given to Massachusetts students in 10th grade are at approximately an 8th grade level in terms of difficulty. Children on IEPs are allowed to take the test multiple times, with increasing assistance or accommodations. For students with learning disabilities, these tests may not tell a parent where a child is performing, or whether they are prepared to graduate from high school.

There have been numerous cases dealing with the issue of a high school diploma, and the need for school systems to provide extra, compensatory services so a child will have the necessary skills for higher education or work. The decisions are part of the public record; parents can look them up on-line on a state by state basis, and advocates and special education attorneys know about them.

Schools can award a diploma if a child has the necessary credits and passing scores on the state mandated assessments, unless a child is protected through an IEP or 504 Plan. In that case, a child is entitled to a Transition Plan starting at age 16, that details what goals the student will need to master in order to be successful in post-secondary educational pursuits, in adult daily living skills, in the job market, and in pursuing outside social activities. A student is not obliged to take a diploma until these transitional goals are met or the student turns 22.

A few years ago, I tested a 19 year old who had been placed in a residential setting at age 17, due to a combination of emotional and learning issues. After 2 years, the public school was planning to give him a diploma. However, the placement had, in my opinion, not provided adequate help for his emotional problems (neither in therapy nor through medication), his language weaknesses, or his learning disabilities. This young man was completely unprepared and unable to live and work independently, based on my testing and observations. The parents agreed. They wanted another placement for the next 2 years. The school claimed the student had "done his time" and was entitled to a diploma (his math skills were at approximately a 3rd grade level, and his independent reading at a 6th grade level).

In many cases, it's hard to convince a student **not** to take a diploma and graduate with his peers, even when he isn't adequately prepared. It often comes as a shock that they aren't academically at grade level, or even close. They've "muddled through", or been passed because they are quiet and well behaved, or they've been in special education classes with modified expectations. I've seen all of those scenarios, more than once. Being older than your classmates can become a social problem, and many students get discouraged. But they **are** eligible, and parents should do everything they can to encourage them to stay and continue improving their skills for as long as possible.

What constitutes a **disability**? Both federal and state laws say one or more of the following impairments:

- Autism or autism spectrum disorders such as Asperger's syndrome
- Developmental delay, for children up to 9 years
- Cognitive impairments, including mental retardation
- Sensory deficits, including vision and hearing impairments
- Emotional impairment
- Communication disorders or difficulties
- Neurological, including a traumatic brain injury
- Health issues, including ADD/ADHD, diabetes, epilepsy, Tourette's syndrome, severe allergies, or another syndrome that affects academic learning and performance
- Physical issues, such as cerebral palsy or a birth defect, if it affects academic performance
- Specific learning disability

This last is the one most parents are dealing with. The law states that a **specific learning disability** is "a disorder in one or more of the basic psychological processes involved in understanding or using language, spoken or written, that may manifest itself in an imperfect ability to listen, think, speak, read, write, spell, or to do mathematical calculations."

So, this is a disability that affects a child's language skills and language-based learning. It includes diagnoses such as dyslexia, developmental aphasia (problems with speech production and word retrieval), perceptual problems, and brain injuries. It doesn't include disabilities that are the result of motor, hearing or vision problems, mental retardation or emotional problems, or environmental or economic disadvantage (e.g., poverty).

In practice, the evaluation Team at your child's school will determine which disability they believe your child has, with input from you and any outside professionals who attend the Team meeting (more about this in the next chapter). The diagnosis may change over time. Sometimes, a child will no longer display a developmental delay or an emotional disability. As academic expectations increase, a child may display a more specific learning disability. If a child is seen for additional evaluations, such as a neuropsychological or a speech/language assessment, there may be documentation of Attention Deficit Disorder or a Communication Disorder.

With a **Specific Learning Disability**, the Team decides that in spite of age- and/or grade-appropriate instruction (as determined by state standards), a child is not making age- or grade-appropriate progress in one or more areas: oral expression; listening comprehension; written expression; reading skills, fluency, or comprehension; math calculation or math problem-solving.

The Team can also base the diagnosis of a specific learning disability on a child's uneven performance or achievement, compared to age-level norms or expected levels based on intelligence. In other words, if you have a child whose intelligence falls at the 90th percentile, but they read, write, or do math at the 10th percentile, the discrepancy is considered a sign of a specific learning disability.

A statistically-significant discrepancy between composite IQ scores on the Wechsler Intelligence Scale for Children- Fourth Edition is also an indicator. I have tested children with discrepancies of up to 50 points (one standard deviation is 16 points)—Verbal Comprehension may be in the low average range (composite IQ score of 80-90) while Perceptual Reasoning is in the superior range (composite IQ score above 120). These are not accidents or random events, assuming the testing was reasonably competent. They are signs of a specific learning disability.

One of the problems with evaluations conducted by the school, in my opinion, is a tendency to add up scores such as these and come up with a Full Scale IQ that is in the "average" range. There are 4 Composite scores on the WISC-IV, but if you take my example and add just the 2 I mentioned (80 plus 120), and divide by 2, you get 100, which is dead average. However, with discrepancies that are more than one standard deviation, this is not only inaccurate, but tends to prevent the recognition of a learning disability. Most parents realize that if their child is low average in Verbal Comprehension and superior in Perceptual Reasoning skills, then they are not "average" in either area!

Another problem, in my opinion, is that schools do not tend to notice significant discrepancies between subtest scaled scores on the WISC-IV, or within the subtests themselves. All of these instances of scatter are important diagnostic indicators, yet many of the personnel who administer the WISC-IV do not analyze the data in enough detail, and are thus less likely to pick up on a child's inability to learn or perform consistently or smoothly.

In my experience, the children most likely to be "missed" by this tendency to compute the average are those with a non-verbal or a visual-spatial learning disability. These children may have average to above-average language skills. They can read and often write fairly well until the material begins getting too abstract in middle school. They tend to be quiet, because they often have no idea what is going on socially. For these reasons, they may seem to be "doing fine", with the exception of math.

Teachers are often more aware of language-based learning disabilities, in which children will struggle to read and spell. Yet I have tested children with Perceptual Reasoning IQs in the 55-70 range, while their verbal performance is above average (110 and above). These children struggle with as many aspects of learning as their peers with dyslexia, and often get diagnosed much later. Again, I see this as an argument for an independent evaluation by a psychologist with more extensive experience than most school psychologists.

The final step in diagnosing a specific learning disability is deciding that the child's inability to learn and achieve at an age-appropriate level is not the result of low cognitive ability, emotional disturbance, problems with vision, hearing, or motor skills, or outside factors such as poverty. In practice, a child is entitled to services if they have those problems, too, so this is just a matter of being specific in diagnosis. In terms of a child's rights, he or she does not have to have the "correct" diagnosis to receive appropriate services. Remedial instruction or classroom accommodations should be provided to **address specific deficits or weaknesses in learning**, that prevent a child from being successful when he or she is presented with a grade-level curriculum.

# Other Programs

What about children who attend **private school programs** or are **home-schooled**? They are also entitled to special education services from the towns in which they live. Parents of these children can request evaluations if the child is struggling with academic performance or has other areas of difficulty (such as speech or visual-motor problems). Public school systems must offer services to these children if they are found eligible.

In practice, that may mean taking your child to the public school first thing in the morning or at the end of the school day to receive special education services. Sometimes, a teacher or therapist will come to the private school to provide services. Your child has a right to services, but he or she may not be able to receive as much service, due to scheduling issues. You can't, for example, insist that a reading specialist come to the private school every day during the child's language arts time. Ideally, your child may need speech therapy 3 times per week, but you may only be able to get him to the public school on two mornings, because of your work schedule.

Often, this situation becomes a scheduling nightmare, especially if the child needs daily services to address a significant learning disability, or if there are multiple areas of need. If a school system has made a "good faith" effort, it is reasonable for them to say that the appropriate services can only be provided if the child is placed in a public school program. This may cause a dilemma for a family, if they are very committed to a certain school or program (such as a dual-language curriculum or a Montessori method).

Over the years, I've tested children who were too distractible and disorganized to handle the expectations for independent work at a Montessori school, or who had language-processing and memory weaknesses and were flunking the Hebrew or French half of the day, or who lacked the motor planning and fine motor skills that were emphasized in early elementary classes at a Waldorf school, or who needed more individual attention or a slower pace than their private school could provide. Children with some degree of dyslexia often need more specialized reading and phonics instruction, on a daily basis, than any private school offers, unless the school is designed for this type of learning disability (these are few and far between).

So, your child in a private program definitely has rights under special education law, but how this gets put into practice will depend on the schools involved, the specifics of scheduling, and the severity of a child's needs. Sometimes, parents hire outside tutors to "top up" what a public school is able to offer, but this can be a slippery slope as task expectations increase with age.

# Service Options

There are many different **services** that a school system can provide to a child who is determined to have special needs. Many children with learning disabilities will receive specialized remedial instruction in the areas of reading, written language, and math, provided outside the general classroom in a learning center or tutorial. They may be placed in separate special education classes (often designated as language-based classes, though they vary in the amount and quality of language-based instruction that is provided). There is also academic support that is given in the regular education program, by a specialist or paraprofessional.

Other **related services** are designed to help a child benefit from special education instruction, or be more successful in general education. These include (but are not limited to) speech and language therapy, psychological counseling and social work services, sensory integration and behavioral services, physical and occupational therapies, early intervention services, diagnostic medical services, audiology evaluations, school health and nursing services, and parent counseling. Some of these will be more available in a school district, depending on the town's resources and the specialists they are able to hire. In other cases, a town will use outside agencies for certain diagnostic or therapeutic services. If a child attends an out-of-district school placement, transportation to and from the program will usually be provided.

If you believe your child needs a specific therapy, or support for a documented area of deficit, then you should bring this up at a Team meeting. This includes services provided over the summer.

Often, parents will request that a particular remedial method or type of instruction (a specific reading program or an individual tutorial, for example) be continued over the summer. The limiting factor in this situation may be proving that this service is needed to "prevent regression". The school will look for evidence that a child has shown noticeable regression, usually over the summer. Since this can disrupt a child's learning quite substantially (summer represents 20% of the year, after all), many parents choose to provide this instruction privately. However, regression can also be documented over holidays, weekends, and school vacation weeks, helping a parent to get summer services approved more easily.

The laws pertaining to related services are likely to differ slightly from state to state, so the Department of Education website for your state is a good place to start if you have questions about whether a given service is covered under special education law.

Now that you understand your child's rights, and why there may be a problem in getting the best services to meet your child's needs, the next step is negotiating with the players at a Team meeting.

CHAPTER 7

# TEAM MEETINGS AND THE INDIVIDUALIZED EDUCATION PROGRAM

*"If you only have a hammer, you see every problem as a nail."*
*Abraham Maslow, psychologist and author*

Team Meetings

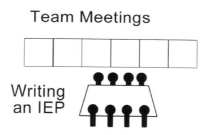

## Your Goal for the Team Meeting

Once any testing done by the school system or by outside professionals is completed, and the reports written, there will generally be one or more meetings to discuss the results and decide if your child is eligible for any accommodations or direct specialized services. This is the point you, as a parent, have been waiting for. Your goal, simply stated, is to obtain the **highest level of service** for meeting your child's needs, from **the most qualified persons,** and to set **clear, measurable, ambitious benchmarks and goals** to insure that your child makes the best progress and moves closer to a grade-appropriate performance.

The testing may be done, but you are still only a short way down the road to your goal. At this point, the "heavy lifting" is about to begin—getting school personnel to provide the amount and type of service that your child actually **needs,** rather than what they happen to **have.** If you are like most parents, this is where you need the support of a professional who will advocate for **your child.** Even for parents with some training or experience in special education, it can be overwhelming to face a full team of school personnel on your own.

# Bring Someone With You

Given the complexities of both special education law and the forms that are used to determine need and describe services, I strongly advise parents to take a professional with them. I will be describing the process of a Team meeting, the writing of an Individualized Education Program (IEP) or a 504 accommodation plan, and how to set goals and expectations for growth. However, the laws and procedures are likely to vary from state to state. It's a good idea to have someone with you who is familiar with the laws in your state.

If you have followed the advice in an earlier chapter and used an outside neuropsychologist who will attend Team meetings with you, this is your best bet. This person can explain the testing that was done and can describe your child's performance and needs. He or she can also help you interpret the school's testing and recommendations. Most important, the evaluator can articulate and discuss what they see as the appropriate services to meet your child's needs. Expertise, experience, and a willingness to advocate for sufficient services are important reasons to bring the right person with you.

There's another reason I want parents to bring someone with them: it's really hard to play **more than one role** in your child's life. It's the reason pediatricians take their own children to another pediatrician. Surgeons don't operate on members of their family. You are going to find it nearly impossible to be the parent **and** the attorney, advocate, psychologist, speech pathologist, therapist, or whatever. It confuses school personnel and greatly reduces your effectiveness. Trust me, you will not be taken as seriously, **regardless** of your credentials. To give just one example, many parents I've worked with try hard not to "make waves" with school systems. When **I'm** at a meeting for your child, it's my **job** to make waves if necessary. Getting outside help just increases the likelihood that you and your case will be taken seriously.

If you can't bring the person who did the testing, then hiring a special-education advocate is another good option. Sometimes a child needs an assessment only in a certain area, such as speech/language skills or sensory integration. These professionals are less likely to have time in their schedules to attend meetings than an independent psychologist. Hopefully, they have been recommended to you by someone you know and trust, and the evaluations are comprehensive and written with clear results, recommendations and goals. It then makes sense to bring an educational advocate with you to make sure those recommendations are considered.

Special education advocates come from a variety of disciplines and have different backgrounds. I have worked with many in the Boston area who are experienced, organized, good at negotiating, and well-informed with regard to special education law and regulations. Some were special education teachers or even administrators, some have backgrounds in social work or school psychology. In Massachusetts, there is an advocacy training course offered by The Federation for Children with Special Needs (their website and a publication, A Parent's Guide to Special Education, are listed in the appendix). The advocates I work with are all highly skilled and have been very effective in helping parents. They attend meetings, help write IEPs, advocate for services, and help parents determine if their children are making effective progress.

Have you seen the print ad pointing out that people lose half their memory capacity once they are wearing a paper exam gown in a doctor's examination room? It sounds silly, but patient advocates advise people to bring someone with them to the doctor's office, if test results or a serious diagnosis are going to be discussed.

It's the same with a Team meeting. I've had lots of parents tell me they were overwhelmed by all the data being presented. There are often 4 or 5 separate reports with results, just from the school personnel. The different tests may have produced different or contradictory results. Teams typically include administrators, such as the Team chairperson and the principal; each of the people who did testing; teachers; service delivery professionals; school counselors—everyone but the janitor, it seems! With so many people and so much data, it's easy to become confused.

I would even suggest bringing a relative or close friend, if that is your only option. It's another pair of eyes and ears, someone who can take notes for you, or ask questions you may hesitate to ask (or forget to ask!). By law, you are entitled to bring a person of your choice with you. You don't have to explain why. The person doesn't have to have any professional credentials. Your plumber or the Fed-Ex delivery person will do, though they might not be my first choice. Just give yourself some support.

## Scheduling the Team Meeting

The law states that schools need to schedule a meeting to discuss an outside evaluation within ten school days of receiving the report (not including holidays or school vacations). Ideally, this means that you bring the evaluation to the special education office or the Team chairperson at your child's school, and within two weeks you are sitting down with the full Team to discuss the services your child needs.

In practice, it often takes longer, especially if the school decides they want to do their own, additional testing. You are still entitled to an initial meeting, but a school is not "obligated" to accept outside test results. They can meet, but refuse to write an IEP until they have their own testing to compare with the outside testing. This can push things out another two months, since they have 30 school days to complete testing. It's also a huge hassle for your child, since testing may be done in sessions as short as 20 minutes. If 3 to 5 people do testing, each with a total time of 2-3 hours, that adds up to a lot of interruptions of class time. Fortunately, many schools will do abbreviated testing when a comprehensive neuropsychological has been done.

Sometimes, a school system will agree that no further testing is needed. A child may not have learning difficulties in other areas, such as fine or gross motor skills, and thus testing by the occupational or physical therapist is not needed. The school may have evaluated the child fairly recently, and may decide that those test results are still valid. Many school systems won't have a neuropsychologist on staff, and will accept the outside testing and agree to discuss it as part of a Team meeting.

Even with a cooperative school system, the process may take two meetings—one to discuss the outside testing, and one to write the actual IEP itself. I recommend asking for a two-hour block of time, and specifically asking whether it will be possible to write the IEP during this time, if your child is found eligible for services. Sometimes raising the issue ahead of time can allow school personnel to be mentally "prepared" for the task, and it can all get done in one meeting. Since you will be paying for your specialist's time, plus travel, this saves you time and money.

# The Individualized Education Program

An Individualized Education Program (IEP) is a document that serves as a legal framework for the services your child will receive. It describes your child's special needs and the types of accommodations that are necessary for learning in the regular classroom and in other school settings. It lists the types of services that will be provided: consultation by various professionals, services provided in the classroom, and services provided in a specialized setting, such as the speech pathologist's office or a language-based class.

The IEP format is determined by state and federal laws. The federal Department of Education website (www.ed.gov) will have information pertaining to an IEP under the Code of Federal Regulations (CFR) 300.32- 300.328. Each state designs its own IEP form, which must include space for administrative data and all the information that is required by federal and state law. In the appendix, there is a blank IEP form used by the state of Massachusetts, which I will use as a general guide in discussing the different parts of an IEP and what a parent will want to see in one.

These forms are long, complicated, and sometimes hard to interpret. I still get confused when we are discussing accommodations needed for the student to be successful in **academic classes** (Present Levels of Educational Performance A: General Curriculum, page 2) vs. the accommodations needed in **other areas,** or due to **other disabilities,** such as communication or behavior (Present Levels of Educational Performance B: Other Educational

Needs, page 3). It always seems as though they are making this more difficult than it needs to be. Yet another reason to have the psychologist, an advocate, or an alert friend with you.

# A Team Meeting – Introductions and Testing Reports

The meeting will generally begin with everyone signing in on an administrative sheet, to show who was there and their role in the Team process, and then introducing themselves and stating their role. You can ask for a copy of this sheet, but it is better to take the time to get these names and roles in your own notes. You can ask for repetition and take your time. If your "support person" is the one taking notes, make sure they are done before allowing the meeting to proceed. Any expert you bring will also be taking notes.

Try not to be intimidated by the size and "formality" of this group. You need to **set the expectations of the group**, as well as the pace, right from the start. Remind yourself of why you are here, and what you hope to accomplish. The worst that can happen is not that the meeting takes longer, but that you don't understand something important and don't achieve your goal.

**Remember – You are the expert on your child, and thus the most important person at this meeting. Your primary goal is to understand your child's needs and get the necessary services to help him or her succeed in learning.**

If, like many parents, you find these meetings overwhelming, let your expert or advocate do the "framing" and control the pace. The team leader may want to rush through some parts, but it is important that you know who these people are, especially if they tested your child. Your expert should "check in" with you to be sure you are ready to proceed.

Some parents ask to tape record the meetings, so they can be sure they haven't missed anything. In my experience, this causes anxiety in school personnel, who worry that something may be said that cannot be delivered on later (such as a specific person to deliver services) or that a school evaluator may say something more definitive about a child's needs than the Team leader is expecting. Often, the Team leader will say that prior permission to tape was required. Sometimes, they will ask for a copy (which may be a pain for a parent to produce). They may interpret the request as being confrontational. While I have no problem being direct or even disagreeing with school personnel when necessary, I'm not sure this particular request is worth the hassle, as long as someone is there taking complete and accurate notes.

The Team leader for one of these meetings may hold a variety of positions in the school system. In some schools, it will be the assistant principal, the school psychologist, or the special education teacher. In other schools, there is a specific job of Evaluation Team Leader (ETL) or Team Chairperson; there may be one who has this role in several elementary schools, or there may be one per team or grade in a large high school.

Who it is doesn't really matter. It is this person's job to chair the meeting, write up the document that results from the meeting, keep track of the paperwork and dates for annual reviews and re-evaluations, and send the proper information to parents—whether this is a request for the school to do testing or the IEP itself. This person's job most likely includes other duties, but for now these are the ones we care about.

Generally, the Team chair will ask the classroom teacher(s) to summarize how your child is doing in their class. This can take awhile, since many teachers do care about showing that they know your child and his/her needs. However, given the time limitations in a general classroom, with a range of 18-30 students, any teacher will have a very brief amount of focused, uninterrupted interaction with your child each day, sometimes only a few minutes at the elementary level.

I once sat in a 2$^{nd}$ grade regular education classroom with 27 children for an entire morning, approximately 3 hours. The teacher was competent and hard-working, but I timed it, and she spent 5 minutes paying mostly-undivided attention to the child I was observing—a bright, sober little girl who'd been a premature baby, and who worked and processed information more slowly than her peers. The girl was often confused and overwhelmed, and needed far more attention than she was able to receive.

At the high school level, a teacher may teach 4 or 5 classes, with between 15 and 30 students each. In practice, this means that the teacher may not interact with a very quiet student at all during a typical class. Teachers also vary greatly in their observational skills and their ability to pick up on difficulties. So, this teacher "check-in" is likely to be a mixed bag, at times providing useful information and at times clearly showing a lack of knowledge of your child's needs.

It's not as though they are spending an hour each day working just with your child. There may well be other children in a class who are more needy or more demanding than yours, further reducing the attention he or she receives. Of course, if your child is the one demanding attention, for whatever reason, you may get an earful!

I have sat in **hundreds** of Team meetings and listened to teachers taking 10 minutes each telling parents what a great kid they have (completely unrelated to the purpose of the meeting) or being so vague that it's clear they have no idea of your child's level of academic performance. Sometimes, they review a child's current grades, but in my experience these can be unrelated to the actual level of academic skill. Some children with significant learning disabilities are so persistent or so well-behaved that their grades reflect effort rather than reading level. Some get huge amounts of help with homework, which thus will not show what they can do independently. The bottom line is, grades **can** be arbitrary, or they can be accurate. I certainly can't tell by listening to the teachers. The only information I trust is my own test scores.

I will generally ask questions of some teachers, to get some sense of whether a child volunteers, participates, works well in a group, can do the work independently, seems distracted, etc. However, this is often just "for form", since **few teachers are going to tell me anything other than positive information in a group meeting.**

After this, if the school has done testing since the last time you met with them, the Team leader will ask these professionals to summarize their findings. Sometimes, the particular evaluator won't be able to attend the meeting, and the Team leader will read the summary. There should be copies of all reports for you to have for your records, if they have not been sent to you ahead of time.

Don't be surprised if the school's test results do not agree with those of your outside evaluator(s). There are a lot of reasons why this may be so, and you will have time later to discuss this. Don't worry about taking notes on these summaries, as long as you get a paper copy of the report. Your expert (or companion) will be taking notes.

The only important thing to note would be if an evaluator seems to agree with **your own belief** about your child's areas of weakness. If the reading specialist or the speech/language pathologist report low scores or say there was a problem in some area, this is significant. Many times, in my experience, they will be under pressure to **not** find signs of a problem, report it, or say it out loud.

That may sound cynical, and I can hear the howls of protest from school evaluators across the country. I am merely stating what I have personally found to be true, over the past 32 years and more than 1600 evaluations. If school personnel could be relied upon to **accurately** evaluate your child, **honestly** report the results, and **consistently offer appropriate services,** I would be out of a job and you would not be reading this book. It is not in their best interests to call attention to the huge needs within **any** school system, since, as I mentioned before, they simply do not have adequate resources to meet all those needs.

Sometimes it takes a long time for these reports to be presented. I have found that the less useful information there is in a report, the longer the evaluator will take to present it. Again, it sounds cynical, but it happens so often, in so many school systems, that I can't explain it as merely an anxious or very slow evaluator. I believe it is a subtle attempt to "run out the clock" and make everything leading up to **deciding on services** (the part you care about) take longer.

By comparison, I will have done as much testing as most of them put together, and I'll summarize it in 5 or 6 minutes. Nobody remembers more than the high points, anyway. I make sure that I don't waste anyone's time with anything other than the most important aspects of your child's performance, the relevant scores, and the key diagnostic categories.

Once the school's reports have been given, the Team leader will generally ask me, or your other outside evaluators, to present their findings. Every once in awhile, they will try to get the school psychologist to summarize my report, as a way to diminish my findings and my relevance to the meeting. Needless to say, your expert should not allow this to happen.

The school personnel will usually, but not always, have had time to read my report before the meeting. Occasionally, if the child is in crisis or they really want my input, we will meet as soon as my report is typed, or even before then (I will speak from my notes). It's all fine with me. My goal is to get the best services for your child, and I don't care if they've read my report ahead of time. Some people will have highlighted the report, or have questions, concerns, or disagreements about some parts. Sometimes, my diagnoses or conclusions are a surprise to the school (this often happens with visual-spatial or non-verbal learning problems). Often, they will want to "haggle" over my tests or results vs. theirs.

I'm prepared for this. It's what I expect at a Team meeting, though it can be upsetting or confusing to parents. Remember that **you know your child best.** I am there to be objective and thorough. I also know your child by now, very well. It is my job to negotiate with school personnel **on your child's behalf.**

I will present my test results, in cognitive, neuropsychological, and academic areas, and my conclusions, but I wait to give recommendations. There are many steps remaining before we get to talk about "service delivery", and that's where school personnel the rest of the Team will discuss my recommendations.

If things go the way you would like them to, the Team will now begin to decide on your child's eligibility for services, and actually write the Individualized Education Program that will document the particular services and accommodations your child needs, why he needs them, and how they will be provided.

One other point: I have seen a number of books that present a very positive relationship between parents and school personnel, with everyone "getting along" and agreeing on services for children. I have experienced this level of rapport on many occasions, and I have seen many successful, effective, and even brilliant classes and learning environments in public schools.

However, if that were the norm, here in my area of the country, I believe I would not see so many children year after year who are struggling or failing, or so many frustrated, despairing parents. I also don't believe these problems are unique to New England. Because of my experiences, I feel it is important to tell parents why there might not be perfect harmony at these meetings, and what to do about it.

## The Decision Tree

In Appendix 1, I have included a blank form of the type used to determine eligibility for services. Basically, the Team needs to decide—as a group—whether there is evidence of a disability and what type it is, whether your child is making appropriate progress in the regular curriculum, whether he or she needs specially-designed instruction to be successful in learning, and how best to provide the specific instruction.

The first form is a "flow chart" to determine eligibility in general. The team decides:

- if your child has one or more of the listed disabilities (these were also listed in the chapter about your rights. If the answer is "yes",

- then the next question is whether, because of this disability, your child is unable to progress effectively in the general education program without specially designed instruction, or unable to access the general curriculum without one or more related services. If the answer is "yes",

- then the Team will find your child eligible for special education services, and an IEP.

This sounds straightforward, but there are a number of possible snags at each point. You and your expert(s) will need to be actively involved in this decision-making process.

If the school personnel decide that there is no disability, in spite of the information your expert has presented, the entire process stops here. Yes, you hope to reach consensus, but that doesn't always happen. If they find your child "ineligible", they are required to write you a letter, within 10 days, telling you what they decided, why, and what your rights are.

At that point, to be honest, your "rights" are fairly limited. You can obtain more outside testing, if what you have is not comprehensive enough to prove your point. Sometimes, parents go to these meetings without any outside testing, or with only one type of independent evaluation, such as a speech/language or occupational therapy evaluation. If your child was not seen for a complete neuropsychological evaluation, you may need to get one and have the psychologist come to the next meeting.

If you do have a full set of relevant, well-done testing and the school system still declines to find your child eligible, then your only recourse is to request a mediation or a special education hearing. These are both described in the chapter on "Further Options". In both cases, you get to present your case to an impartial party, and request the services your child needs. In mediation, the mediator tries to get both sides to agree, but he/she has no authority to force a school or parent to do anything. In a hearing, which is definitely the "nuclear option" in terms of time and expense, the hearing officer decides, and the decision is binding.

However, in most cases a school will agree that the child has some type of disability. But which one? While this is not the most important decision, it is one that should be considered carefully, since it will determine which services are offered.

I recently attended a Team meeting for a 12 year old boy whose language-based learning disabilities were "covered over", to some degree, by his task anxiety and his excellent intelligence. That meant that the school personnel often saw a bright but anxious child who struggled. He had an IEP, but the disability was listed as "emotional", not "specific learning". As a result, he was offered a counseling session and one period per day in the Learning Center, but not phonetic training or an individual reading tutorial.

When I saw this boy for testing, his skills for reading fluency, decoding, spelling and written language were several years below grade level. He struggled to analyze more complex language, in class and in print. He worked slowly and lacked confidence, and he didn't have solid skills for isolating the sounds in words so he could decode unfamiliar ones.

Clearly, he met the criteria for a specific learning disability, but as long as the school focused on his emotional state, they weren't going to give him the remedial reading instruction he needed. At the Team meeting, this was my main goal—to get the disability listing changed, so I could advocate for the services he needed to compensate for his learning problems.

School personnel will often pick a single disability, or a minor one, when the child struggles in several areas. I will argue for checking several boxes, especially the one for "specific learning disability", so I can get the most specialized services.

If the Team is considering a "specific learning disability", remember that the discrepancies between Composite IQ scores, or between/within specific subtests, or between IQ and achievement as measured by the school or your independent evaluator, can also be used to justify checking this box. Your expert will be prepared to present this data and argue this point if necessary.

So, let's assume we get past the first question. School personnel agree there is a disability. The second question is often tricky to prove, if the child is bright, hard working, or has a lot of outside support. The "bar" for meeting academic expectations at a given grade level is fairly low, in my opinion (school systems across the country have standards for "appropriate performance" that do not specify or require true grade-level mastery, as you and I would hope to see). It is possible for a child to have a substantial learning disability and still manage to "get by" in terms of grades or tests.

I have tested children and adolescents who miss a lot of what is being said in class, or whose reading fluency or writing skill is years below grade level, but who "pass" with a "C" or "D" grade in many classes. These children are often above average in intelligence (sometimes significantly above). They have parents who sit with them every night for homework, often for hours. They are willing to work for as long as it takes each night, until they reach the point where they are just **too frustrated and confused** to keep it up—which may happen in 3rd grade or as late as 9th.

They work with outside tutors, during the school year as well as in summers. I've talked with parents who drove their children 45 minutes to an hour **each way**, several times per week, to attend individual remedial reading tutorial sessions offered at Massachusetts General Hospital in Boston, or the Masonic Lodges in Lexington, Worcester, and other cities (the Masons offer free, high quality Orton-Gillingham tutoring to children, though this is only part of the solution for a child with dyslexia). They take the child to a therapist to help with self-esteem and depression resulting from chronic school failure. Sometimes this goes on for years.

Most of the parents I see are willing to do anything to help their children. I am often awed by their dedication and sacrifice. However, many of these outside services will enable a child to barely "make it" in school. This can cause a serious dilemma for parents who believe their children need more services during the actual school day.

School personnel will say, "she's a hard worker", or "she's doing fine", or "he's passing", which does not address whether the child has anything approaching grade-level mastery of skills. **Parents think** a "B" or better shows a child understands the material, while **school systems** will accept a "D-" as a passing grade, in every year and every subject.

All of these factors influence whether a child will be seen as making "effective progress". It's where a lot of the arguments happen, at a Team meeting. I'm looking for mastery, automaticity, fluency—not merely the ability to hang on by one's fingernails.

It's not that I feel kids shouldn't need any support outside of school. I've done my share of helping with library research, making poster boards, and studying math facts, vocabulary words, or types of rocks. I've helped my children review material they understood, as well as material that needed more practice or explanation. I don't think we can expect any school to "do it all"- that is, after all, why children have parents and don't spend 12 hours per day in school.

However, I **do** think it is the school's responsibility to ensure that students master the basic skills in literacy and math, and gain an appropriate knowledge base in science and world affairs, as well as thinking and problem-solving skills, to enable them to reach something close to their potential. They need to be able to live independently, work at something worthy of their intelligence and gifts, and continue their schooling if they want. I do not think that is too much to ask.

I often need to argue that a child "should" be making better progress, given their intelligence. I also point out the things they can't do "on their own", without help, based on my testing. For some children, there will be one or more classes where they are clearly having difficulty meeting expectations, as even the school will admit.

A parent's description of the anger, exhaustion, tantrums, or other "meltdowns" at home will sometimes make the point that effective progress is not being made. Most schools don't see these behaviors, since a child will usually do anything to "hold it together" during the day. It's only when a child is "past the point of no return" that it shows in school. I also discuss the emotional effects that I saw during the testing, which are sometimes dramatic in spite of the child's desire to hide how he or she is feeling.

One "administrative" point—the school personnel may say they need more information, or the parents may realize they need to get one or more additional evaluations. The school can ask for additional time, an "extended evaluation" period of up to 8 weeks, to do extra assessments or observations. Parents must consent to this. In this case, a partial IEP should be written, so a child can begin receiving some services while the Team (including parents) gathers more information. This can be used as a stalling technique, but in some cases it is legitimate. Your expert can help you structure things so your child begins getting support, if he has been found eligible. At the second meeting, a complete IEP can be written.

By now, with the Decision Tree completed, it probably feels as though you've been in this meeting for a week! Don't fade just yet—it's time to write the actual IEP.

# CHAPTER 8

# THE INDIVIDUALIZED EDUCATION PROGRAM—WHAT IT SHOULD AND MUST INCLUDE

*"If you think education is expensive, try ignorance."*
*Benjamin Franklin*

The Individualized Education Program (IEP) is one of the most important documents in your child's file. It is the roadmap that states where your child is performing at the present time, where you and the school would like him or her to perform in the future (essentially, over the next year), and how the school will help your child reach that level of performance. Appendix 2 includes a blank IEP form, used in Massachusetts. Each state designs its own form, but these should be very similar since the federal laws must be followed in each case.

An IEP is designed to meet the educational, emotional, and social needs of children from ages 3 to 22, so this is a broad document with a number of specialized sections dealing with areas such as transition planning for children older than 15, transportation to an out-of-district placement, justification for a longer/shorter day or provision of summer services, and the transfer of rights when your child reaches age 18. These sections will apply to a relatively small number of students, and I won't address them in detail. If these issues apply to your child, you will most likely be consulting an attorney as well as your independent expert, to be sure your child receives the necessary services.

An IEP must include the following key elements:

- a statement of parent or student **concerns**

- a description of student strengths and **key evaluation results**, including results of independent testing

- a **vision statement,** usually written by parents but sometimes compiled by the Team, of where the parents would like to see their child performing over the next 1-5 years, in terms of academic skills, mastery, social and emotional development, self-esteem, and any other area of importance

- a description of the **specially designed instruction** that will enable your child to make effective progress in content areas (reading, math, language arts, science and social studies) and make effective progress in reaching the annual goals

- a description of the **related services** that are needed to allow your child to make use of the specially designed instruction, as well as access the general education curriculum and non-academic subjects

- a description of your child's **present levels of academic achievement** and performance

- a statement of how the child's disability affects her progress in the general education setting

- a statement of **measurable annual goals** in the areas of difficulty

- a statement of **benchmarks**, which are shorter-term goals

- a statement of how the child's **progress** towards these goals will be measured, so a parent can clearly tell whether gains are being made

- a statement telling how often parents will receive progress reports (which is as often as children receive report cards, usually 3-4 times per year)

- a list of **accommodations** provided in the regular education and special education settings, that are designed to help your child access the curriculum and provide his/her best performance

- a list of accommodations that will be provided during testing situations, including standardized testing

- an explanation of the issue of **non-participation** (that is, when and for what reason your child will not participate in regular education activities, as well as non-academic or extracurricular activities)

- a description of transition services, transfer of rights at age 18, extended year services, and other more specialized situations

- a statement of **which specific services** will be provided to your child, how often, where, by whom, and for how long at each session (this is the Service Delivery page, page 5)

If this seems like a lot of information for one document, you're right. It is a legal document, and has much more detail than many parents can absorb without a lot of effort. I'll go through the sections in some detail, but it will also be important to review your child's IEP with your professional partner (psychologist, independent evaluator, or advocate).

The front page of the IEP (not pictured) is an Administrative Data Sheet, which includes the name and address of the student and each parent, information about the meeting (date of this meeting and the annual review, when the next 3 year re-evaluation is due), and the assigned school information.

Often, a Team leader will anticipate that a child will qualify for an IEP. In other cases, this is an annual review or a 3-year re-evaluation, and the child has a current IEP. In these cases, the Team leader may prepare a "draft IEP" for parents and team members to discuss and add to during the meeting. Some information can already be written in, which saves time. These drafts are collected at the end of the meeting, and the "actual" IEP is then prepared. Some Team leaders use computer software and enter the information as the team agrees on it, then print a draft for parents to review at the end of the meeting. The method doesn't matter, only the services that will be offered.

# Parent Concerns

This is the first numbered page of the IEP. Here, you want to list any and all of your concerns about your child, in all significant areas. These areas include specific academic subjects, emotional functioning and self-esteem, peer relationships, attitude towards school—anything you see that worries you. If you don't feel the current services are adequate, **say so.** If you don't think your child is making progress, **say so.** If you are worried about an upcoming transition to middle or high school, **tell them why.**

**Be as specific as you can in stating what you are concerned about, and why.** If possible, write this paragraph out at home and bring it with you, so you don't waste meeting time trying to pull it together. However, you should not feel pressured to write this "on the spot" in the meeting, if you didn't write it ahead. It is perfectly acceptable to say that you will bring it to the Special Education Office or the Team leader at your child's school the next day.

It is important that you list all relevant areas of concern, since the school may later say that you "weren't concerned" about written language, for example, if you didn't mention it.

Give supporting details of your child's weaknesses or examples of your child's functioning, if you can.

Here are two good examples: Anthony, age 8 in 3rd grade, and Cynthia, age 14 in 8th grade.

"Anthony has been receiving services for 2 years, and he still can't read independently. He often can't read his homework on his own, and when he reads a first grade book out loud, he stumbles over most of the words. He avoids reading and writing, and he usually can't spell the words he tries to write. In math, he does not know his addition or subtraction facts. He can't add money or tell time. We are concerned that he is falling farther behind his peers. He is starting to cry when it is time to do homework, and says he "hates school". He has been teased, and we worry about his friendships and his self-esteem. We are concerned about the amount of help he gets, and feel that he needs a lot more one-to-one instruction to learn reading and math. He is going into 4th grade and does not have the skills he needs for independent work."

"Cynthia is often confused and overwhelmed when she gets home from school. Her binder is a mess, and often she doesn't have the necessary books or papers. Her notes from her classes are not complete. She says she understands most of the material in her classes, but then she can't remember it at home. She is still reading very slowly, and when we question her she doesn't seem to understand what she has read in a grade-level textbook or a novel. We are concerned about her organization and her reading comprehension. She also seems confused about her math class, and can't do the homework independently. We are very worried about the transition to high school next year. We feel she needs more help with basic skills and organizing her work."

Do you see the level of detail here? These paragraphs say that the parents know **what** their child is struggling with, and they want **more direct service** to address the areas of weakness. It helps to focus the minds of Team members if the parents have a clear picture of their specific concerns and an idea of what needs to happen to fix the problems. Your independent evaluator can help you cover the bases here, and may even have a few suggestions.

## Student Strengths and Key Evaluation Results

Sometimes the Team leader will have collected this information and filled in this part of the IEP, with the school's latest testing, standardized test results, independent testing results, and the child's strengths. Often, there is a narrative paragraph describing the child's performance style, strengths and weaknesses. This information can run to more than one page for a child with significant learning disabilities, and you want all of it in this one place for reference. Other than the first paragraph, it should consist mostly of facts—the IQ scores, achievement levels, and test scores.

Be careful here, and insist on honesty. I certainly want to recognize a child's strengths, such as athletic ability and friendliness, since these are often the only things that "keep them going" while they struggle with academic achievement. However, there is a tendency for the "she's so polite, sweet, hard-working and well-liked by peers" part to be followed by the "she'll be fine" part, and we can't let that happen. Being a "nice kid" is irrelevant when considering academic skill levels, and the more "capable" a child sounds, the easier it is for a school to argue that she doesn't need much in the way of services.

Some school systems will resist putting in the test results from an independent evaluation, either because they differ substantially from the school's results, or because they disagree with them for some other reason. Usually, when I point out the absence, they will agree to add the scores. It is your right to have them in the IEP, even if the school puts in a note that they don't agree with the scores.

If a neuropsychological evaluation has been done, you will want the scores from cognitive testing, neuropsychological testing, and academic testing included. If there are other outside evaluations (occupational therapy, speech and language) these need to be listed as well. It is also appropriate to include a brief summary of the key findings from the evaluation. For example, from the summary of one of my reports:

"John struggles with all aspects of language functioning: with processing what he hears, storing information in short and longer-term memory, retrieving information, and organizing what he wants to say. He displays reduced verbal fluency and limited skills for written language. Reading comprehension, decoding and spelling are significantly below grade level expectations, consistent with a diagnosis of dyslexia in the context of good intelligence."

The child's type of disability should be listed here for reference. This section of the IEP forms the **baseline**, and in the future you will be able to note progress (or its lack) by comparing new scores to these. If you don't understand the way a score is presented, ask to have it clarified in this section. For example, the school may list the child's raw score on the English Language Arts section of the Massachusetts Comprehensive Assessment Scale (MCAS) but not whether this is a "proficient", "needs improvement", or "warning" score.

# The Vision Statement

Here, the parents are asked for their vision of what they hope their child will be capable of, and will be doing, in the next 1 to 5 years. This isn't part of the federal or Massachusetts statutes, but is required by the state Department of Education, so your state's IEP may or may not have this section.

If it is included, this is your chance to put the school system "on notice" that you want your child to achieve a certain level of performance. For most parents, this would be reaching age or grade level skills, though other goals may be most appropriate. Some parents want their child to make a years' growth in reading, math or writing skills in the next year. Some want better social skills, self control, or organization. If you think your middle-school or high school age child should be able to attend a college program, or live independently, or have a successful social life, this is where you say it.

Again, it may be helpful to prepare this statement ahead of time, so it can be inserted at the meeting. Other Team members may have additional ideas to include, but you are the parents and your goals are the ones that matter.

# Present Levels of Educational Performance

This is page 2 of the IEP, subtitled Part A: General Curriculum, and is often referred to as "PLEP A".

Here is where the Team will document the **academic areas** that are **affected** by your child's disability. They will list specific details of **how** the disability affects progress, what **accommodations** are needed in order for your child to make effective progress, and the **types of specially designed instruction** that is necessary to support this **effective progress**. As a result, this is an important page in the IEP. You and your expert will want to carefully consider each of these four areas.

In many cases, your child's learning disability will have an impact on learning in most or all subjects. At the very least, the major subjects should be checked. A reading disability will interfere with his learning in math class, because he won't be able to read the textbook or teacher handouts. A visual-spatial disability will make it difficult to read maps in social studies, or to do geometry problems in math. Emotional problems will show up in different classes throughout the day. A sensory integration disorder or attention deficit disorder will affect performance in every class, since there will always be sensory information to process (competing sounds, too much language presented too quickly, a need to stay seated at a desk or to line up close to one's peers) and a need to maintain attention and concentration.

The Team leader will probably have no difficulty checking all the areas you think are relevant, as well as noting other curriculum subjects such as Health or foreign language, music or physical education.

In describing how the **disability** affects **progress**, you want the Team to be as specific as possible. Your child's disability should be named. The types of tasks that are affected by the disability should be listed. Anyone reading this part should clearly see **how** this particular learning problem or limitation would make it difficult for your child to be successful in the academic tasks that are presented each day. A few examples:

- slow processing speed and weak memory skills will affect the ability to take notes in classes, or to listen and work at the same time

- a language-based learning disability will affect the ability to understand what is said in a regular education classroom

- a reading disability such as dyslexia will mean that a child can't read the texts, hand-outs, homework, tests, or additional reading materials that are at grade level

- a visual-spatial disability will interfere with accurate visual analysis in reading and spelling words, proofreading, analyzing graphs or maps, and understanding math concepts or doing sequential tasks, such as solving more complex arithmetic problems

Some of the sections of the IEP may feel repetitious as you sit there listening. Didn't the Team already discuss how your child can't do certain grade-level tasks because of his or her learning problems? Didn't the independent evaluator provide a list of test scores, showing that your child is not performing at grade level in some important cognitive and academic areas? Haven't you all agreed that he or she has a learning disability? Isn't some of this stuff obvious? Haven't you done this movie already?

Well, yes, but remember: an IEP is a legal document, with actual legal requirements. Up until now you've all just been talking, discussing your child and his or her needs. An IEP **protects your child's rights**, and most important, it sets up **accountability** on the part of the school system. Once this document is written and signed, certain things have to happen. Services must be provided, accommodations must be made—and **effective progress** must be demonstrated by your child. If this does not happen, there are **consequences.**

So, in the next section, the Team will list the types of **accommodations** that are necessary for your child to make this effective progress we keep talking about. Remember, "effective progress" is defined as "to make documented growth in the acquisition of knowledge and skills, including social/emotional development...with or without accommodations, according to...the educational potential of the student."

The list can include anything and everything, from the essential to the impossible. It includes accommodations such as preferential seating; homework that is modified in difficulty and/or quantity; extended time on tests; use of a calculator; having a teacher check the child's assignment notebook; pre-teaching new concepts or vocabulary; re-phrasing instructions or lecture material; providing a complete set of class notes; and putting less information on a page (such as fewer math problems).

In the next chapter, I will discuss accommodations and how to monitor their effectiveness in greater detail. To be honest, this is one of the parts of an IEP that I have a problem with.

Let's look at the situation realistically. This list will include the things that a **regular education teacher** (and in some cases, an aide or paraprofessional, or the special educator if she is in the class) is **expected to do** to ensure that your child can understand and access the curriculum that is being taught. Depending on your child's particular learning problems, this could be a **very long** list.

In fact, just to show you the scope, I am listing the accommodations that were in the IEP of an 8th grade girl with a significant language-based learning disability and above average intelligence, placed in a public middle school and receiving a number of special education services:

- present material in small steps using simplified language and slow pace of delivery (remember, this was supposed to happen in **regular education classes)**

- preview or pre-teach new vocabulary and concepts to connect to prior learning

- provide opportunities for frequent repetition and review

- use multi-sensory approach to supplement and reinforce concepts

- provide copies of class lecture notes

- frequent check-ins and breaks for comprehension

- clarify all directions and instructions when needed

- preferential seating

- provide positive feedback and reinforcement

- limit or modify reading assignments when needed

- provide reading guides to accompany textbook assignments (should be consistent between classes)

- break down long-term assignments into smaller steps

- provide timelines and templates for longer assignments

- provide study guides for tests and quizzes (one week ahead)

- allow her to take tests in small group/separate setting

- word bank and modify format of tests

- additional time on tests

- limit number of new concepts presented at one time

- modified homework as needed

- use of rubrics for all writing assignments

- portfolio assignments as necessary

- prompting or cueing when needed to help formulate a response or complete a sentence; encourage student to "talk about" a word to help with retrieval

- pre-alert prior to calling on student

- provide additional "wait time" or visual cues

- define idioms and figurative language

My first thought when I saw this list was, "wow, can these teachers also walk on water?". My second thought was, "and what are the other children in the class doing, while this teacher is spending the entire class period providing these accommodations for this one child?" The expectations were unreasonable, in my opinion.

I brought up my concerns at the Team meeting, after I'd done an independent evaluation and realized how substantial her needs were. The Team leader looked more than a little insulted and informed me that if the accommodation was in the IEP, then the school was obligated, by law, to provide it. The teachers were perfectly capable of doing everything listed in this section, and would do so, because that is what the IEP required.

Well, excuse me for being suspicious, but these teachers are only human, like the rest of us. I consider myself a reasonably competent person, and I know many people as competent as I am, or even more so—and I tell you, none of us could have implemented this entire list while teaching a class of 22 eighth graders. Not happening.

In fact, I observed this child's regular education classes, and they were a disaster for her. There was **so little attention** being paid to this enormous list of accommodations that were supposedly being "provided by law" that she might just as well have been attending school in a foreign country. The girl had no idea what was going on in several of her classes. She was anxious, withdrawn and discouraged. My detailed observation notes showed that she was not being provided with any effective accommodations, and was unable to learn **or remember** what was being taught.

In social studies, for example, there was a constant flow of conversation from the 22 students. The teacher lectured, gave instructions, presented factual material and asked questions in a loud monotone, but rarely paused or emphasized important information. He never asked this girl if she understood. The text was at grade level, dense with dates, names, locations, and sequences of events pertaining to European history between the middle ages and the present time. The class was discussing a list of kings and their various wars and alliances, with no outline or visual organization on the board or in front of them. It was a noisy group. Homework was shouted by the teacher as the class scrambled to gather their belongings when the bell rang. The girl never opened her mouth for the entire period. So much for helping her "access the curriculum".

Bottom line- this is a section where "quality", not "quantity", is required. As a parent, you want your child to make as close to a year's progress in a year's time as possible—maybe even a bit more, if your child is significantly behind her classmates and the special education services are skilled and frequent enough. You may think that the more accommodations your child receives, the more progress he or she will make.

I'm afraid it isn't so. You do the math. A class is usually 18-25 children, give or take a few, with one teacher. Other children in the class will have needs, too. On a good day, a competent teacher may be able to consistently provide 3-5 accommodations for a single child in a given class. We need to be sure the first few listed in the IEP are the essential ones.

Sometimes, there will be an instructional aide or a paraprofessional in the class, to assist the children with IEPs. I have found it difficult but not impossible to persuade a school that a given child should be provided with an aide. If I am successful, or when there is already an aide in the child's class, this may or may not allow more accommodations to be provided.

Paraprofessionals vary tremendously in terms of ability, training, and effectiveness. I tested an 8-year old boy with sensory integration, attention deficit, mood regulation, and learning difficulties. He was struggling with every aspect of being in a classroom and trying to learn the material. The aide working with him was the only reason he was able to perform at all. She was tuned in to his moods, could help him regulate his behavior, noticed when he was struggling and getting frustrated, adapted his work, took him out to a quiet room or out for a walk when he needed one, and helped him focus. She was patient, flexible, and consistent. She was amazing, but until I can figure out how to clone her, I can't assume that any other children I evaluate will get the same level of help.

In each case, it depends on the "fit" between child and aide. Most of the time, what I see is far less individualized or appropriate, and thus much less helpful.

In most classrooms, there will be 3-8 children with special needs who need the help of an aide. Schools will often place a group of children who have IEPs in the same classroom, so that one aide can help them all. These children may or may not have similar needs, and there may be other children in the class who ask for, and receive, the aide's assistance. You can see the potential for overload here, I am sure.

In my opinion, more than 3 children who need help is too many for **your child** to reliably receive the help he or she needs to get real benefit. Some aides can remember to monitor a dozen aspects of performance, while others struggle to keep up with taking notes. The same is true for special education teachers or their assistants. Some are extremely helpful, and some are pretty much useless in terms of helping the children in the class who need it. This is based on **years of observations of actual classrooms,** not just baseless criticism.

Sometimes, an older student can self-advocate for the accommodations he or she needs, but this isn't likely in elementary or middle school, and even many high school students would rather fail than draw attention to themselves by speaking up to request a calculator or an agenda book check. They **rarely** will ask, "Could you repeat that? I didn't get it." So we can't rely on your child to ask for what he needs, even when the school says he knows he needs it.

If we assume, on average, that there will be one adult in your child's class who will be charged with putting the accommodations in place, it is essential that the most important ones—**the ones that raise the likelihood of helping your child make effective progress in understanding the curriculum**—be the first ones listed in this section of the IEP.

Regardless of what the Team leader says, when I observe classrooms, as I do for hundreds of hours in each school year, I often do not find that the most important accommodations are being implemented.

As they say in diplomatic circles, "Trust, but verify." Once the IEP is put in place and your child is receiving services, it may be helpful to have your independent evaluator observe several classes, to see what is actually happening (more about this in a later chapter).

The last section of page 2 on the IEP deals with the types of specially designed instruction (special education services) that are necessary for your child to make effective progress. For most students, this will involve adaptations in **content** and **methodology,** and specifics about how your child's performance will be measured and monitored.

Children with learning disabilities frequently need modified **content** in several or all major subjects, which should be specified.

**Methodology** means the type of setting and the specific type of instruction. For example, a small group setting or one-to-one instruction, using a structured, rule-based, phonetic reading program or a particular program to enhance phonemic awareness and decoding skills, or a process writing approach.

In terms of **performance**, you should expect to see several different types of assessments, including teacher or specialist input, quarterly progress reports, the annual review, and any standardized group testing done by the public school. Individual testing will not be listed here, since the school is only required to re-evaluate every 3 years.

**A note about testing**: when a child is quite young or has a complex diagnostic picture, or is several years below grade level in academic performance, or if you as parents have concerns about whether the services being provided are enough to support "effective progress", then it makes sense to evaluate your child more often than every 3 years. While the school system will not do this as a rule, many parents will have an independent evaluation done more frequently, to monitor a child's progress or growth in skills. By way of comparison, most out-of-district placements, such as a school for children with dyslexia and language-based learning disabilities, will do **annual individual testing** to measure academic growth.

A child's performance and overall profile can change substantially in one year, in both positive and negative ways. I base my recommendations for re-evaluation on my level of concern for an individual child. There are children whom I ask to see again in 1 or 2 years, because I need to be sure they are making sufficient growth. In some cases, I know that the services offered are not adequate, and I need to document the child's lack of progress so I can help the family get more appropriate services, or even an alternative placement.

As a parent, you are free to have your child re-evaluated at your expense as often as needed. The school's performance criteria will often not be adequate to tell you if your child is moving closer to grade level, or is making only limited progress. **Independent, objective, precise testing** is the best way to monitor how much your child is learning. This applies to other outside testing, such as speech and language evaluations, as well.

# Present Levels of Educational Performance

This is page 3 of the IEP, labeled Part B: Other Educational Needs, often referred to as "PLEP B". In this section, the Team will note services **other than** special education services that your child may need, or times **other than academic class time** in which his or her special needs will affect performance. The format and purpose are similar to PLEP A.

At the top of the page are boxes to check for all appropriate needs and considerations. In many cases, social/emotional functioning or communication skills will be the major areas of difficulty across the school day, but parents should carefully consider all possible areas of need. Noting "age-specific considerations" is also important, since a child's needs will be very different in preschool compared to mid-high school, when issues of transition planning should be addressed.

Again, there should be a statement about the child's specific disability and areas of difficulty, a list of how the disability affects performance in non-academic areas (including unstructured social times such as recess and lunch), the types of accommodations the child needs to be successful in these situations, how instruction or expectations will be modified (for content and methodology) and how progress will be evaluated.

It is here that the Team will list the best ways to support your child in communicating with staff and peers outside of academic classes, or how he or she will receive help if their emotional difficulties interfere with behavior when they are with support staff and teachers of "specials". Services such as adaptive physical education, Braille materials, or extra support for field trips will be listed in this section.

# Goals, Objectives and Benchmarks

Here is where the Team will document and commit to working on each of the goals of the IEP—the specific areas in which the Team agrees that your child needs help, so he or she can make "effective progress". In the appendix, I have included only one page for goals in the blank IEP, although in practice this part of the IEP will usually run to several pages, if a child needs specific help in a number of areas.

Federal and state law require the IEP to include "measurable annual goals, including academic and functional goals designed to meet the child's needs resulting from his disability, and enable him to be involved in and make progress in the general education curriculum."

A school system may attempt to limit the number of goals in an IEP, though there is no rule about how many goals a child can have. I have seen IEPs with one goal, and others with 5, 6 or 7. How many does the child need? You want this part of the IEP to be as specific as possible, with fairly narrow goals, so it is possible to measure progress objectively. In general, all major areas in which a child's performance is below age or grade level expectations should be addressed by goals in the IEP.

It is especially important that parents understand **exactly what skills** will be worked on (**goals**) and **how they can tell** if the child meets those goals (**benchmarks/objectives**). How else will you be able to tell if your child is making progress during the course of the IEP?

These are some of the major areas of difficulty usually addressed by the goals of an IEP:

- reading fluency
- decoding skills (the ability to sound out words)
- reading comprehension
- written language
- math calculations and/or problem solving
- peer relationships/social skills
- organizational/study skills
- self-advocacy
- articulation
- communication skills (a speech/language goal, often)
- fine motor and visual-motor skills (an occupational therapy goal)
- gross motor skills (a physical therapy goal)
- behavior/self-control
- transition planning
- extended year services (summer services)
- sensory integration

This list is not exhaustive, but you get the idea. If it is an area of deficit for your child, it can and should be addressed by a goal in the IEP. Often, an independent evaluator will have a list of goals, and can help ensure that major concerns are written into the IEP.

After agreeing on a particular goal, the Team needs to describe your child's **current level of performance** in this particular area. For academic skills, this means listing the most recent, relevant test scores. One possible problem is that there may be school testing and independent testing for a given skill **that do not agree**. As I mentioned in a previous chapter, some tests used by schools do not provide **fully accurate levels** of performance. They may over-estimate skills or provide wide percentile ranges ("between the 25th and 75th percentiles) that aren't very useful to you as a parent. When you read this part, you should see some **objective measure of performance** that **makes sense** to you. You may need to insist that the independent test results be included in the paragraph.

This is important because, again, it serves as a record of your child's **baseline** performance—what he or she can do right now, independently. It is one piece of data that you will use to determine if your child is **making progress** over time. Believe it or not, I have seen many children who have made limited or **no** progress for several years, in one or more areas. The school may be reluctant to point this out, since it may mean that the child requires services the school **does not have** or **has not provided** with appropriate frequency.

It is your job (along with an independent evaluator) to monitor, notice, and demand that your child's progress be meaningful and **effective.** Remember: **you know your child best. If it seems that he or she is making hardly any progress, you may well be correct. Your child is entitled to better, under the law.**

Once the Team has agreed (with any luck) on what your child can currently do, in this area, then you need to decide on some **measurable** annual goals. These are the skills you want your child to attain over the next year.

Note that this is "one year" in terms of the IEP, which probably won't be the same time frame as the school year. It depends on when your Team meeting is held—if it's in January, then the IEP runs from January to January of the next year. This makes it a bit more tricky to determine how well your child is "keeping up" with the class. You will be comparing your child with his own previous performance, when you meet to write next year's IEP. If you don't have a good sense of whether your child is making progress in catching up to grade level, you may need to do some outside testing.

**Measurable annual goals** can cause serious heartburn for many parents. You know your child is performing below grade level, or you wouldn't be writing an IEP. **How far below** has just been agreed on, but how far does the Team think your child will **progress** in the next 12 months? Parents assume a child will make a year's growth, but school systems often resist such an unambiguous, measurable goal. They want to write goals such as:

- With teacher support and assistance, Carl will solve arithmetic problems with 70% accuracy

- Amy will complete modified homework assignments for 4 out of 5 assignments

- With teacher support and assistance, Kevin will produce written responses in class with 80% accuracy

- Given 3-4 verbal cues, Samantha will maintain task focus to initiate and complete a task, 75% of the time

- Mark will improve his understanding of core content curriculum by developing individual learning skills

There are a lot of words with unclear meanings in those examples. How do you "quantify" teacher assistance and support? To what grade level of difficulty will the homework be modified? What grade level of arithmetic problem are we talking about here? What are "individual learning skills" and how do we measure them to see if they are improving? You see the problem.

## Make the goals clear, and make them measurable.

Teams like to use percentiles such as "75% of the time", or specify "3-4 verbal cues". It sounds precise, but it's awfully difficult to measure. If your child grows 2 inches, we can measure that. Unless you are in the class every day, how the heck do you know how often your child is helped, prompted, or begins working on a task independently? You don't.

What you are looking for are goals that are both challenging and able to be measured in some way other than by a psychic. Believe me, the school will tend to tell you these percentiles are being "achieved", and will even increase them the next year—but based on my experience, it doesn't mean that your child will have made any progress towards being an **independent learner,** or is working any **closer to grade level**.

If the **goal** is to improve math skills, for example, and the Team has documented current skill levels in a comprehensive way that makes sense to you, then it is reasonable to take **the areas of greatest need** and set measurable goals to improve skills in those areas. That's basically all we're asking for.

I reviewed the IEP of a 14 year old girl with severe dyslexia, language and memory weaknesses, and poor executive functions (skills for organizing, planning, and monitoring her work). In math, her current performance was at a mid-elementary level. She needed a multiplication chart, a number line, and a template to solve word problems. She struggled to remember how to do certain problems without a lot of spiraling back to review. She had difficulty following complex instructions due to her language problems.

The **math goal** was "to demonstrate an increased understanding of a 4<sup>th</sup>/5<sup>th</sup> grade basic math curriculum. The student will be assessed using daily assignments, weekly quizzes, and tests, with an 80% accuracy rate expected."

Now, the first sentence may not be as precise as I'd like, but all those assignments and quizzes are going to let the parents and the school know whether she understands and can use the material. More important, the **benchmarks and objectives** were very specific and targeted her areas of greatest need. They were:

- To identify a number's place value up to millions, with 80% accuracy

- To show an ability to solve math word problems at the 4/5 grade level with 80% accuracy

- To solve arithmetic problems using four operations (addition, subtraction, multiplication and division) and whole numbers, with 80% accuracy

- To demonstrate an understanding, at the 4/5 grade level, of fractions and their functions, decimals and percents, with 80% accuracy

- To solve problems involving adding and subtracting fractions and decimals at the 4/5 grade level with 80% accuracy

- To understand and solve problems involving multiplying and dividing fractions and decimals at the 4/5 grade level, with 80% accuracy

- To solve problems using money, time, and measurement at a 4/5 grade level with 80% accuracy

These are specific, challenging, and most important, **measurable** benchmarks. They emphasize pragmatic math skills that this child will need in her life, and they recognize (honestly) that she is not ready for more "abstract" math such as pre-algebra. I can re-evaluate this child in a year and see whether she can do what they've been teaching her to do, whether she understands the processes and can solve the problems at a 4/5 grade level with reasonable accuracy. Did she learn the skills and can she use them independently? I can tell the parents yes or no.

You might be thinking that a 4th or 5th grade level is pretty low for a child in 8th grade, and you'd be right, but this is a child with significant learning disabilities, who only learned to read in her first out-of-district placement—in 5th grade. Given that, she has made close to a year's growth each year since then, in her specialized school placement. I can't ask much more of her—or the school—than that.

If she's as strong as she appears to be, and continues to work **very hard** in her special education school, I have hopes that she can get to an 8th grade level in reading and math by the time she finishes high school. She may surprise me and do better. Remember, 8th grade is approximately the level of difficulty in the Massachusetts assessment tests given in 10th grade to determine eligibility for a diploma, so she would have managed to pull herself up to an acceptable public school minimum.

The take-away point here, which you may not be expecting, is that if she'd been placed in an appropriate special education program in **first grade,** when her parents suspected she was dyslexic, she might well have been able to master basic reading and math skills at a **much younger age** (when her neurology was still quite plastic and developing). She might have acquired improved memory and language skills, and been able to access more of each grade's curriculum. This would have **increased her options** for a fully independent and contributing life. **Sooner is better. Always.**

For each major goal area such as "fluency" or "math" (the numbered ones at the top of each section) there will be 1-5 specific goals that your child will be working on, with help, during the IEP period. **The number of specific goals should depend on your child's needs**.

Fluency may be addressed using one specific program designed to improve the smoothness and accuracy of a child's reading, such as Great Leaps or Read Naturally. This may be the goal for that area, to use the program and make "x" amount of progress (higher grade levels of difficulty, speed of reading, reduced number of errors, etc., all of which can be measured).

In math, children are generally learning to do a number of different processes, and are being taught a number of concepts to support those processes. If a child struggles with math, he or she will need specifically designed instruction in a number of areas, including problem-solving, learning math facts, accurately completing arithmetic problems (addition, etc), using practical math skills, and so on. In this case, there should be a goal for each area of difficulty, and a way (or ways) to measure progress and mastery.

So, you and the rest of the Team will decide on major areas of need (goals), list current skill levels in these areas, identify specific tasks that need specialized intervention in order for your child to improve, and agree on how progress will be measured, so you will know whether your child is making "effective progress".

Finally, we get to page 5, the **Service Delivery Page**. This is the last major step in terms of writing the IEP. Here, the school lists the **exact services** to be provided, **who** will provide them, and **when, where, and how often** they will be provided. As the IEP itself states, "services should assist the student in reaching IEP goals…to (allow the student to) progress in the general curriculum, and to participate in extracurricular/nonacademic activities."

However, there is a potential problem with this ideal. Since **services, specially-trained teachers, and programs all cost money**, there is often disagreement between school personnel and your independent evaluator or advocate over **exactly what** will be provided.

Things may have been going along quite smoothly and pleasantly, but now we're talking **money**. We've already talked about the fact that the budget for special education services is limited in a given school district. There is tension between the need to provide for the educational needs of all students, especially those with learning disabilities, and a fixed budget for the school year. Special education directors are administrators, and are responsible for the bottom line. They are certainly aware, as are Team leaders, that resources are limited. This results in a tendency to offer less help than a child may need to be successful.

This is not the way you want your child's services to be decided. You want the program, services, and supports that will give your child the best chance of making "effective progress". Remember, this phrase may mean something different to you than it does to the Team leader. Effective progress is a term that is still argued about in meetings and Special Education hearings. To you, it probably means "a year's growth, at least, in a year's time". For the school, it means the amount of growth they can probably achieve with the resources they have available. In actual situations, it may come down to as few services as a school system can get away with offering.

As parents, you and the school have somewhat different goals. I am always very aware of this fact when I advocate for a child. I am able to work successfully with a school system and get the help I think is appropriate in the majority of cases, but not all.

There are some services that are negotiable, and some that are not. I try to "keep it real" and not ask for more than I think the child truly needs. This means that I tend to have less "wiggle room" when discussing possible services, and am often considered stubborn as a result.

Sometimes, I am asking for services the school does not have. In that case, they will try to justify what they **do** have. This results in arguments about the relative merits of different remedial programs, group vs. individual help, or in-class vs. out of class services. There may be disagreement about an offer of a pull-out group to teach certain skills vs. a separate language-based class for an entire subject, such as Language Arts or Math. And the biggest problems come when I know the child needs a more substantially-separate program, possibly for all academic subjects—and that such a program does not exist at the school.

This is why most parents benefit from having an independent advocate who can discuss these issues from a position of experience, and keep the conversation focused on your child's needs. Often, my test results will show a significant gap between the child's skills and grade level expectations. I can argue for more services based on this gap, often successfully.

With other children, I may **know,** based on my professional experience, that they are vulnerable learners, that their skills are not automatic or solid, that they need something a lot more comprehensive, that they're going to "hit the wall" in the next grade because the expectations will increase. However, if the test scores are not significantly below grade level, and the child still has some self-esteem left, I **may not be able** to get what I think the child needs. We may have to watch, wait, re-test, and put together a stronger case (thus wasting valuable learning time for the child). The need to wait is particularly painful with some children, and can seem very unfair.

This part of the IEP process is often uncomfortable for parents. If you haven't done this before, you are probably expecting a rational discussion. You may believe that the school wants the very best for your child, as you do. However, a school's assessment of what is "best" may not agree with yours. If they've got what your child needs and it's not more than they can afford to give, then we're golden. Otherwise, it's going to be a struggle.

A few years ago, I evaluated a 7 ½ year old boy with severe dyslexia and a moderate attention deficit. He was completing 1st grade in a private (non special-education) school but was not yet reading, writing or doing math, and he was pretty reactive to all of these tasks. The parents had gotten some tutoring services through the public school, but it was not enough. Since the public school did not have an appropriate, comprehensive program, the parents placed him in a school for children with dyslexia and language-based learning disabilities, where he made slow, steady progress with a **lot** of individual instruction and **very** structured classes.

At the beginning of 3rd grade, the case finally came up for a pre-hearing. I was distressed when we were told that the parents did not have a "good enough" case, because the child had been "too young" at time of placement. He wasn't "3 years behind" in academic skills. They hadn't placed him in the public program and "let him fail". The fact that the public school's program (which I had observed) was completely inappropriate didn't matter. Such is the state of special education law.

I'm still furious about that case. How was a 1st grader supposed to be 3 years behind? He was being penalized for being "too young", and the parents were being punished for getting an accurate diagnosis of dyslexia when their child was only 7. They'd done the right thing, but eventually they would have to place their son in the public program, hope he "failed" quickly and decisively, and then deal with the emotional fallout—before they would be eligible for public funding of his placement.

Sometimes, children just won't "fail" badly enough. They have easygoing temperaments and enjoy school for the friendships. Parents get tutors several hours per week, and the children "muddle through". I'm currently following a 3rd grade girl with significant auditory processing problems and a reading disability. When I observed, it was clear that she missed a lot of what was being taught in the regular class. The school did not have the type of reading tutorial I wanted for her, so they gave her what they **did** have. Parents also hired an outside tutor. She's made modest progress, but is not at grade level in reading, phonics, or math. The "special education class" that was offered for part of each morning was not a good fit for her—too much going on, too many kids at different skill levels coming and going, a teacher who was not fully certified to provide remedial instruction, and **still** the wrong reading program—but the attorney has told the parents they have to put her there (where she will almost certainly "fail"), before we can get the placement she needs.

I've worked on many cases like these, but fortunately there are others where I've been successful in getting an appropriate placement to enable children with significant learning disabilities to develop better skills. Remember—**You know your child best. You know what he or she needs.** Working with an independent psychologist, you will keep trying until you get what your child needs, or something close enough to allow "effective progress".

The only time I feel there is a legitimate argument for limiting services is if the child's schedule is going to be destroyed by all the pull-out services. I have seen schedules for children in elementary school that were more complex than those for CEOs. Each day, the child had a different schedule, with pull-out services, small-group instruction, individual tutorials, and services provided in the classroom—and this happened several times per week. Since elementary schedules often vary from day to day, due to specials such as gym or music, this resulted in a fragmented and confusing day.

In these situations, careful coordination is essential. The child should not be **expected** to complete class work that was missed while he received services. Either the regular education teacher or the special education teacher should be responsible for coordinating all of one subject, such as language arts (including homework, spelling lists, and reading expectations). One would like remedial reading instruction or pull-out math services to be given at the same time each day, but classroom teachers don't always teach one subject at the same time each day. There are times when I simply have to agree to less service than the child needs, or look for an alternate such as a language-based class for part of each day, which may actually be **more** than she needs.

The right services may be available at a different school in the district. All of the language-based classes may be placed at one elementary school, for example. Changing schools may be difficult for your child, but if the program is appropriate (observation by you or your expert is recommended) it may be the best option.

There are 3 options for **service delivery**—consultation, services provided in the regular classroom, and services provided in an out-of-class setting (also called "pull-out" services).

**Consultation** (on Grid A) means that a specialist, such as the speech and language pathologist, occupational therapist, or school psychologist, consults with the classroom teacher (or the team of teachers, if your child has several) to monitor the child's progress, answer questions the teachers may have, and ensure that the necessary accommodations are being provided in the regular classes. Often, this is listed as 10 or 15 minutes per week, or per cycle if that is longer than 5 days. This is a low-cost service, but given the busy schedules of specialists, they may be consulting about several children during that time. They may not focus on your child each week, or come in and observe on a regular basis, and as a result it may not make much difference to your child's experience in the regular classroom.

**General Education Services** (Grid B) lists the services your child will receive while in the regular education setting. This includes:

- having a specialist come in to a class during a period of academic instruction to provide direct service to your child. This could mean the occupational therapist working with your child on fine motor or handwriting tasks during a writing lesson, or the speech/language pathologist working on vocabulary, or a special education teacher helping a child organize material in science or social studies, or working with a small reading group during reading time.

- Having a special education teacher or paraprofessional sit in on a certain class on a regular basis. Depending on grade level and the learning needs of the children on an IEP, they could be taking notes, answering questions during a lecture or test, or helping students complete classroom assignments (also called a "supported class").

- Co-taught classes in which a special education teacher (it may also be a paraprofessional) is present in an academic class, for the purpose of providing **adapted instruction** or **clarification** for those students with special needs. Note that this is what is **supposed** to happen. When I observe **co-taught classes,** I rarely see **any** co-teaching. The whole point of these classes is to offer a child with language-based learning disabilities an adapted language experience that will presumably be easier for them to understand. In my book, that means the special education teacher **should be doing a lot of the talking.** Makes sense, right? Unfortunately, it doesn't happen very often. There should be adapted handouts and readings for the kids with reading disabilities, pre-organized or "skeleton" notes for kids with auditory processing problems, and clear, simpler language when information is being presented. I rarely see these things, either. I can count on the fingers of one hand the number of times I have seen a truly co-taught class, and they were great. However, this is one service that schools will offer to avoid pull-out services or fully-adapted, smaller classes. As a parent, you need to know that what it is **called** and what it actually **is** are two different things. Children will often be just as confused or overwhelmed in these classes as in regular ones, because the special educator is not doing his or her job.

**Direct Service** (Grid C) is where services delivered outside the general classroom are listed. For the most part, these services will be the **most helpful** to your child. They are also the most costly. To illustrate both points, when a child is placed in a special school setting (an out-of-district placement) designed to meet significant learning or emotional disabilities, the services provided in that setting are all listed as Grid C services. Work on your child's special education **goals** will generally occur during these Grid C services.

Each type of service will be listed on a separate line, along with the relevant goal numbers, the type of personnel delivering the service, the number of times per cycle and the amount of time per session, and the starting and ending dates. The Team will specify which **goals** will be addressed by which **service.**

Sometimes one goal will be worked on in several settings, such as a speech/language goal in which the specialist will both consult with the child's team and see the child for direct service. Sometimes one type of service, such as a reading tutorial, will address more than one goal, such as fluency, decoding and comprehension. This is typical and acceptable.

Grid C services include:

- Individual or small-group sessions with a special education teacher or other specialist (speech/language pathologist, occupational or physical therapist, psychologist, etc)

- Specific tutorial sessions, often for phonetic programs, specific reading instruction, or math (certified reading instructor, special education teacher)

- A class period spent in a learning center or resource room setting, in which a number of students will work in various groupings with one or more special education teachers/ paraprofessionals

- Special education classes, which are self-contained for a given subject. The students are generally similar in terms of their skills and their needs. These classes substitute for a regular education class in that subject. One example would be a language-based English class or Social Studies class.

I am often in the position of trying to get a child increased Grid C services, whether it be more frequent reading tutorials or sessions with the speech pathologist, or substantially separate classes for one or more subjects. My recommendations will be based on my test results. Often, parents have been asking for increased services for years, without success. Other times, they won't have realized the extent of their child's needs, but they will know that he or she has not been learning and achieving appropriately.

I have a simple rule: **the younger the child and/or the farther below grade level he or she is, the more special education services they need per week per area of difficulty.**

Thus, for a child in 1ˢᵗ or 2ⁿᵈ grade who has not effectively "broken the code" and shows signs of a reading disability, I often want a daily reading tutorial by a reading specialist, with work on phonics, sight words, decoding skills, and fluency. For a middle school child who has struggled for years with auditory analysis, organizational skills, and grade-level reading and writing, I want small, adapted, language-based classes for some (if not all) of the major subjects.

The term "language-based class" is often used loosely by school personnel. They may act as though it applies to **any class** in which audible **language is used** (I guess American Sign Language class would be excluded), but in fact, it is something far more specific. Since decisions about placement often depend on the availability and adequacy of this type of class, I will describe it in more detail in the chapter on accommodations.

The type of personnel who work with your child can have a significant impact on the amount of learning that takes place. In general, Grid C services should be provided by specialists with training and experience in the area they are trying to remediate. It is not essential that they be "certified" by the state—this is not sufficient to ensure a skilled provider. I have watched "certified" speech pathologists or special education teachers who did not provide quality services, and I have observed teachers without full certification who were brilliant at helping children learn.

The one area where I do think **full certification** is necessary is in **reading.** There is an enormous difference between a reading specialist who has had **several years of training** in one or more specific remedial reading methods (such as Orton-Gillingham, Wilson Reading, or one of the Lindamood programs) and one who has merely read the materials or taken a weekend "introductory" course. School systems will not volunteer this information unless a specialist **is** fully qualified, so it is up to a parent or advocate to **ask.** Since I spend a lot of time in schools, I have sometimes had experience with a certain teacher, and know his or her skills. I can ask for this person to provide the service for a child. Educational advocates tend to work locally, and may also know the skills of many teachers.

When I observe, I find the **effectiveness** of a specialist is strongly dependent on the **level of training** and **amount of experience** he or she has. I only wish I could videotape the two ends of the spectrum, because the differences are stunning. With an ineffective or inadequately-trained teacher, children are confused and not as focused. The session will be slow and halting, as the teacher fumbles with materials. I've seen lessons conducted incorrectly, and children learning very little. For a child who is already behind grade level, this is unacceptable.

That said, there are fully trained specialists who are not very good at what they do, because they are only human and not everyone is cut out to be an effective remedial reading tutor. Schools will never admit this, but in the "real world", not everyone who wants to be a neurosurgeon or an F-16 fighter pilot is successful, either. Teaching children with learning disabilities requires **training, skill and talent.** Not everyone can do it.

A fully-certified reading teacher is a **minimum**, but it guarantees nothing. Often, other parents will be of help, if their children have worked with a particular teacher. Nearly everyone in a school "knows" who the best and most effective teachers are, just as every first grader "knows" who the best reader is in his or her class. Just don't expect school personnel to offer this information.

The "type of personnel" listed in the grid determines the **minimum qualifications** for providing the service. This is **all that a school system needs to provide to be in compliance with the law.**

Thus, if "sped staff" is listed, this can include fully qualified special education teachers as well as special education aides. The same is true if they only list "staff" for any other skilled remedial service. However, I do not believe that paraprofessionals or aides should be providing Grid C services. Aides are not required to have a college degree (at least in Massachusetts) and (more important, frankly) may have **very little specific training or experience in remedial instruction.** This is true of both classroom and "special education" aides.

Some school systems hire aides with some college credit, and at times a certified teacher (even a special education teacher) may work as an aide if there is no suitable job available. This would be a bonus for a school system, but you can't **specify** only a certain "level" or "type" of aide on this grid. You would have to trust in luck, or at least the willingness of the school system to hire people who **happen** to be more skilled than the minimum requirements, assuming they are available.

In my opinion, that is just too large a risk, given your child's needs. If he or she could have made "effective progress" without **skilled, specialized instruction**, they would have been making it in the regular classroom. Since this has not been the case, or you wouldn't be reading this book, it is essential to know who will be providing the out-of-class services you are trying so hard to obtain for your child.

This means **you want Grid C to specify the most qualified person, for the most amount of time that you or your expert think is needed, in the smallest possible group.**

When discussing the **amount of service** (frequency and duration), remember my rule about needs: **younger child/farther behind = more often/smaller group.**

The specific times for each service should be listed objectively—3 X 30 (three times per cycle for 30 minutes each time) or 5 X 45 (five times per cycle for 45 minutes each time), for example. Note the number of days in a "cycle" in your child's school, so you can figure out how many times per week the service will be offered.

Bear in mind that this includes transit time to and from the classroom, "settling in" time, switching between tasks and cleaning up. If your child is seen in a group, there will be additional time spent getting everyone focused and productive. I've seen 30 minute small group therapies in which there was 5 minutes of direct service! This is obviously one step away from a waste of time. It's why I ask for more time, in as small a group as I can get.

Ideally, a remedial service your child needs will be offered on an individual basis, every day, for the amount of time that allows maximum progress. In most cases, I would be laughed at if I asked for this. I know, it makes sense to you, but remember that services and personnel **cost money**, and the Team leader needs to keep the bottom line in mind.

Some guidelines:

- A child with a reading disability should be seen daily if at all possible. Many remedial programs, such as the Lindamood Phonemic Sequencing Program (LiPS), Wilson Reading, and Orton-Gillingham are meant to be offered **daily**, so the skills and strategies will be able to "stick".

- With speech, occupational therapy and physical or sensory-integration therapy, young elementary children (K-3rd) should be seen 3 times per week for best results while the nervous system is still maturing

- Services in the classroom are almost always less effective than out of class services, due to distractions and interference. If your child is going to receive both in-class and out-of-class services by the same professional, make sure the out-of-class services **are frequent enough to address the areas of weakness**, and consider the in-class services a bonus. For example, **remediation** for written language or math should be provided in separate sessions with the specialist. Additional in-class support, that can be provided as often as every day, will **reinforce** what is being taught in private sessions, but **is not a substitute**

- If an adolescent is placed in a resource room or learning center to support classroom learning, this should be offered several times per cycle **for each course to be supported.** This means that a child who needs help with 3 academic classes (fairly typical) will most likely need to be seen daily if the services are to be effective in monitoring, reteaching, organizing, and helping with longer-term assignments

- A substantially-separate class for a given subject should be offered as many times per cycle as the regular education class meets

- Don't let school personnel tell you that a young child "can't pay attention" to a 45 or 60 minute tutorial. It isn't so. I've observed **hundreds** of tutorials. If the instruction is right for a child, and the service provider is skilled, nearly all children are focused and learning the entire time. I've found that children are particularly good at telling when a service is something they need to help them learn. When it is, they participate eagerly and fully. Children **want** to learn, and **want** to improve. School personnel will almost always err on the side of **too little remediation**, rather than too much.

- If you are meeting in the middle of an academic year, the specialist's schedule may already be packed, and the time they have available may be less, and at a less convenient time, than you would like. There may need to be compromises in one of these two areas. Go for **more service**, even if it messes up your child's schedule for a few months. Plan to meet at the end of the school year, or right at the beginning of the next one, to schedule the remedial services at a better time for your child. For example, remedial reading services should be provided when the regular class is doing reading. It is better to miss a "special" such as art or music than to miss science or social studies, if your child isn't confused by the language or reading in these two academic classes. Classroom teachers will often have a block of time set aside for reading, math, and writing. Try to get the matching services offered at those times. Be sure the child won't be expected to "make up" what he or she "misses" while getting remedial help.

Note when the services will begin. It should be no sooner than the date of the Team meeting, and even that is a fudge, since it will take days or weeks before the IEP is fully written and then signed by you. Until it is signed, services do not need to be provided. Lawyers are often concerned with accuracy in this area, but I just want the services provided as soon as possible. At times, a specialist will start working with a child immediately, if you give consent at the meeting. Sooner is better, in my opinion.

The last 3 pages of the IEP deal with matters that may or may not be significant for your child, depending on his or her age and type of disability. These include:

- Nonparticipation Justification- why is your child being removed from class to receive certain services? This is probably not a big deal for most parents, who **want** their child to receive specialized services. However, here the Team will list whatever learning difficulties make it "critical to the student's program" that he or she be treated outside the classroom. It's a further acknowledgement of need.

- Schedule Modification- a longer or shorter school day or year. The important part here is most often the need for summer services. These are especially important for children with substantial learning disabilities. Many children show notable regression in skills during vacations, when they are not receiving specialized instruction. They may even regress over a three-day weekend, or during school vacation weeks. If this is the case for your child, he or she is **entitled** to an **extended year program.** It doesn't matter if your child's needs are different from those of other children in the summer program, or if they are more or less severe. Summer services must be designed to meet **your child's** needs and **prevent substantial regression.** In practice, a parent might have to consider a legal challenge in this area, since schools rarely have the types of services in the summer that are available during the school year. It may be worth fighting for a 12-month program if your child has severe needs, but many parents choose to pick their battles and hire a tutor for the summer. Unfair, but true.

- Transportation services- if a child is placed in an out-of-district placement that the school pays for, or even another class at a different elementary school, then he or she is entitled to transportation to and from the program. If a child needs specialized transportation due to his or her disability, the details of what is needed should be listed here.

- State or District-Wide assessment- if standardized tests will be administered during the time the IEP is in effect, the Team should note whether your child will take these tests without or with accommodations, and should list the accommodations. This can run to quite a list, to the point where it seems the child doesn't need to do **anything** independently. I will discuss accommodations in the next chapter. Be aware that the **more** help your child is given, the **less** you can rely on the test results to give you reliable data about your child's functioning. There's a difference between being able to ask a clarifying question or have extra time, and having the test read to your child, with possible vocal "hints" as to the correct answers. My professional opinion, stated several times in this book, is that these tests are **a poor measure of grade-level mastery** even for children with no special needs. For children with learning disabilities, they often do nothing but cause anxiety and distress.

- Transitional planning information, transfer of rights at age 18, and a box to check if the parents do not attend the meeting. There's also a space for "additional information", such as medications the child is taking or outside services provided by the parents.

- Response Section- STOP HERE. At this point, you need time to digest this document, discuss the details with your expert or advocate, think about how well the services offered match your child's needs, and consider your options. You have 30 days to respond. Unless the IEP includes everything you think your child needs, take the time to think about how best to respond. I will discuss your options in the chapter "How to know if your child is making progress".

Congratulations. Wasn't that easy? With any luck, you now hold in your hands a completed IEP that provides **some** of the services that will allow your child to develop improved skills, understand the general education curriculum, and make "effective progress". Depending on your child's disability and the particular school system, there are unresolved issues that we'll deal with in a later chapter.

You may have a fabulous memory for details, such as the services a given program needs to provide, or your legal rights. Or, you may have found this book before you get to the "team meeting" stage, and be able to read this chapter a couple of times before you really need it.

If you are like most parents, however, you've probably already sat through plenty of meetings with school personnel, feeling overwhelmed by details and unsure of how to get the services your child needs. That's what most parents tell me.

It's why I'm writing this, and why I believe in working with the best independent psychologist or advocate you can find.

# CHAPTER 9

# PLACEMENT AND ACCOMMODATIONS – TWO AREAS OF POSSIBLE CONCERN IN AN IEP OR 504 PLAN

*"In these days, it is doubtful that any child may reasonably be expected to succeed in life if he is denied the opportunity of an education."*
*Brown vs. the Board of Education (1954)*

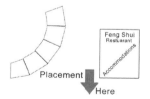

Dealing with placement issues is a little like rolling a large boulder up a steep hill. The higher you go, the more effort it takes. The higher you go, the more special education services your child will receive, and it may not be possible to deliver these services within a regular class setting. As part of writing an IEP, the Team will need to decide issues relating to placement.

There will be times when a separate meeting will be scheduled to determine placement. If the Team has already met for two hours to discuss the outside testing and needed services, they may be out of time. If your child's needs are complex, or the Team is considering a significant change in setting (possibly an out of district placement, or an increase from Title I services to several language-based classes), this is a reasonable plan.

By law (both state and federal), the school system must place your child in the "least restrictive environment" that meets his or her needs. This bar is set fairly high, which favors a school district.

In my dealings with schools, including my testimony at hearings, this is a phrase that is hotly debated. Many times, my success depends on convincing a hearing officer that the placement sought by parents **is the least restrictive environment** in which this child can make "effective progress".

The laws describe Least Restrictive Environment as "the educational placement that ensures that, to the maximum extent possible, students with disabilities are educated with non-disabled students, and that special classes, (or) separate schooling…occurs only when the nature or severity of the student's disability is such that education in regular classes, with the use of supplementary aids and services, **can't be achieved satisfactorily**".

This means that the Team must consider the child's right to be educated with non-disabled peers if that is possible. It is almost **always** possible, though in many of the cases I see, it is not the **best choice** for a given student.

**As parents, you know your child best.** I assume you will know when the current situation is no longer appropriate for your child. Rarely do I see parents who want something **more restrictive** than what their child **needs.** Parents appreciate the benefits of a neighborhood school or the "home school" advantage, being in a regular class, being placed with non-disabled peers, playing school sports with friends and neighbors. However, these are only **true advantages** if your child is able to make "effective progress" towards his or her potential in such a setting.

Parents tell me they often feel intimidated when school administrators or other personnel talk about their child's needs as though **they** know best what the child needs. **You know your child best.** You, along with your outside experts, are an important part of the Team. The goal should be to reach **agreement** about a child's needs.

At meetings, it has been implied, or stated outright, that I am somehow "shortchanging" your child by asking for more services. That I want to rip a child out of his "friendly community" where he "has friends" and is "successful". That I'm recommending a "watered-down curriculum". That small classes or individual services are "isolating" or "unfair to your child". That anything more than the services offered by the school will be "damaging" to your child and will "ruin his future". I do not believe that any of this is true.

The **real issue**, as I've said before, is one of **money.** If a private school cost the same as a public one, if specialist services cost the same for five sessions a week or for one session, if a class of 8 children and an individual tutorial cost the same as an inclusion class—there would be no debate about "principles".

Let's look at the school's objections.

- For a child with significant expressive language (communication) or receptive language-processing problems, a **small class size and special education teacher** allows them to receive **adapted instruction** for the entire class period. It allows them to process information at their slower pace of understanding; to listen to information and instructions presented in clear, simple language; to get clarification as soon as they need it; to experience consistent repetition, review, and spiraling; and to receive multi-sensory support from visual aids and organizers. Things move at the **right pace** and with the **appropriate language,** so students can "access the curriculum" to the limits of their intelligence.

• For a child with dyslexia, **language-based classes** also ensure that the reading material will be presented at their current level of independent reading skill, again so that they can effectively "access the curriculum" and read the material on their own.

• The brighter your learning disabled child is, the **greater the benefit** he or she will get from more **specialized instruction.** In my experience, they may "survive" with fewer services, but they won't make the same academic gains.

• In my opinion, the more significant your child's learning disabilities are, the more important it is that he or she be taught in a **homogeneous grouping,** meaning a group of children **like himself** in terms of needs, intelligence, and learning style. Public schools are designed to teach heterogeneous groups (everybody mixed in together), and thus they will defend this approach. My rule: **the greater the learning disability, the greater the need to be taught exactly the way you learn, so there is the least amount of wasted time.**

• In a small, structured, language based program of the type offered in some public schools or a private special education school, the curriculum presented is likely to emphasize **what your child actually needs to learn,** which is very different from things being "watered down". When I observe, I see fewer distractions, interruptions, and confusions. There is much less "wait time", less "filler", and fewer assemblies or special events to interfere with actual learning. A much higher percentage of class time is devoted to actually teaching and learning skills, vocabulary, and information. There is more review. Teachers emphasize how new information relates to what children already know.

• Many times, I have been told by parents that their child with significant learning disabilities has few, if any, friends. Their learning disabilities interfere with communication, "keeping up" with peer conversations, initiating or maintaining friendships, playing games at recess, being part of a group project, or participating in outside activities. They may not be invited to parties or play dates. This is not true for all children, of course, but in my experience it describes the social situation for about 75% of my cases.

• When I test and observe **teens** with substantial learning disabilities who've been placed in either regular education programs with some specialized services added on, or in programs designed specifically for their needs, I see **distinct differences.** In fact, I can often tell where a teen has been placed, **just from their approach to the**

**testing, their mood and their attitudes about learning.** For example, the teens with language-based learning disabilities who have spent several years in programs that provide small, language-based classes (either private school programs or public ones that are fully adapted) almost always display higher self-esteem and self-confidence. They have been taught **strategies** for problem-solving and compensating, and they are willing to **use** them. They often assume they will be able to solve a given task with the skills they've been taught, and they don't give up as readily. They take their time and **persevere**, because they are less frustrated or discouraged. **In addition,** I find they maintain their **IQ scores** over time—especially scores for Information and Vocabulary. This contradicts the public school system assertion that they receive a "watered down" education. They are being taught the important stuff, and more important, they seem to **retain** it better.

So, with regard to deciding on the "least restrictive environment", the right answer **depends** on **the needs of your child.** It's not a matter of principle, research, or caring about your child's welfare, regardless of what the school says. It is only a matter of how much different programs cost.

My attitude is—I **know** these services are expensive, and giving them to this child will stress the rest of the system. I know, and I'm sorry. However, as I say to administrators and teachers, **you already have your education. You already know how to read. My job is to make sure this child gets an education and learns how to read.** In order to do my job, I focus on one child at a time, until their needs are met.

# Placement Determination

In the previous chapter, I discussed the service delivery page, which shows where (either in or outside the classroom) your child will receive the services designed to help him or her make "effective progress". This page also lists the type of personnel providing a given service, how often the service will be provided per cycle, and for how long a time.

The specific details of what is written in the Grid B (in class) and Grid C (out of class) portions of this page will determine the **placement.** For example, if a child is placed in language-based classes for all academic subjects, and receives specialist services in one or more areas, this is likely to take place in an out-of-district placement, since few public schools have such a comprehensive program in-house. A child who needs a structured, behavioral program across the day and direct therapy services will probably require a consortium program (several school systems sharing the cost of a more specialized program) or a private school placement for continuity and quality of service.

The issue of placement can be discussed separately from the issue of services, though the two are related. It is better to nail down the **services** a child needs **first**, specifying the maximum amount of time, smallest group size, and most qualified personnel that a school can be persuaded to offer. They will be "watching the meter" as these services are requested and agreed to, because at a certain point the total "amount" will trigger the need for a more restrictive placement.

In other words, each time the boulder is pushed farther up the hill, it costs more money. **More services=more specialized setting=higher cost to the system**.

A school system will obviously make an effort to supply services **in the classroom** whenever possible. This includes the direct services of a special education teacher, another specialist such as a speech/language pathologist, or a paraprofessional, provided on an individual or a small-group basis.

We've already discussed the qualifications these people will bring to your child's program, and the fact that even two professionals with the same credentials may differ greatly in their skill and effectiveness. The only way to tell is by observing the class or program yourself, and if you still have concerns, by having your independent evaluator do an observation.

Services provided in the classroom have both strengths and weaknesses. If a child is **mildly** below grade level, **sometimes** confused by the language being used, or **often** works more slowly, it can be helpful to have another adult to clarify and provide interpretation. Please note the qualifying words I used, because they were chosen deliberately. Children with **more significant or widespread difficulties** will generally need out of class services to make "effective progress", in my opinion.

If a child or teen is easily distracted but **understands the concepts** in the curriculum, and **reads well enough** to access the material, then having another adult provide occasional structure or re-direction may be what is needed to keep them "on task". However, without solid academic and processing skills, too much information will be "lost", even **with** support. The material will need to be re-taught in the learning center (if we are lucky) and the child will end up **wasting** his or her time in class.

Services provided in the classroom will be affected by the **number and frequency** of distractions in that setting. Depending on the age of your child, the regular classroom can be a tough place to work. For a young child with poor attention, concentration, or filtering skills, a regular-education first grade class can be a really tough place to be. There are **so many visual and auditory distractions** in that setting—bright colors, stuff on the walls and on every flat surface and even hanging from the ceiling at times, chairs scraping, children and adults entering and leaving the room, peer conversations, instructions being given and repeated, multiple work stations, things to remember, papers to do—that the level of stimulation is frequently overwhelming. When I observe, even I sometimes have a hard time focusing appropriately.

If there are other children with learning needs or behavioral issues (including ADD/ADHD) in the classroom, they will also be using the services of whatever specialists are there to work with **your** child. This will, of course, reduce the amount of help your child can receive.

Please don't let the school convince you that **one** aide or speech pathologist or learning specialist can meet the needs of half a dozen or more children during a certain class. **In most**

**cases,** this will not happen, based on my observations. Unless you are sure that no other child will need help from the in-class specialist or paraprofessional, you should divide the amount of time they are in class by the number of children, to determine **how much help** your child is likely to receive.

It's the same arithmetic, whether your child is scheduled to be seen in a small group, or whether the specialist will be going around the room "checking in" with individual children. One person can answer the questions, clarify the material, or reinforce the skills of one child at a time, in most cases. If there are people working in schools who can address the individual needs of several children **at the same time,** I haven't met them. What I observe is that children have to wait, or they don't get their needs met, which affects their ability to make "effective progress".

If in-class services are offered **and you think they may meet your child's needs,** it is still important that someone have a few minutes at the beginning and end of each day to monitor his or her performance. In particular, do they have the necessary materials and written assignments to complete homework, do they have unanswered questions about what was taught or about assigned work, are they working on longer-term assignments and preparing for tests, is there a teacher they need to consult? Make sure this support service is written into the IEP, as a **separate line item** in Grid B. Be sure that you understand exactly **what type** of monitoring will be provided and **how** you will receive feedback about it.

Co-taught classes are also offered on Grid B. School administrators will tell you that this is the "perfect solution" for many children: curriculum provided at the **same rate and complexity** as for a child with no learning difficulties (so your child won't "miss out" on anything), but with a special education teacher there at the same time to adapt the instruction to meet your child's special needs. Again, this is only an appropriate option if it actually meets your child's needs.

There are children who can "follow" the instruction when it is given, but who can't write it down or remember it well. Being given notes, outlines, and clarification during class can be a big help. Some inattentive or poorly organized children may also benefit from this model.

However, once there are language processing problems; reading, math, or writing skills that are substantially below grade level; or significant neurological issues that interfere with learning, your child may need much more adaptation than this type of class can provide.

This type of class **still** leaves the students with learning disabilities to interpret complex, abstract or figurative language. They **still** are expected to handle a grade level pace and quantity of information, and will need to read grade level materials. They **do not** get language-based instruction, and may be left with many questions or "holes" in their understanding. These are all issues that school administrators claim **will be addressed** in a co-taught class, but during my observations I often find this is not the case.

My biggest problem with co-taught classes is that **most of them are not co-taught.** To me, "co-taught" means that **both teachers should be teaching.** Makes sense, doesn't it? Unfortunately, in more than 8 out of 10 co-taught classes that I have observed, this is not taking place. In about 25% of classes, the special education teacher does nothing observable during class. In another 25%, he or she walks around for part of class, looking over the shoulders of students and answering an occasional question. Some take notes, or pull a small group aside to work with them (often **while** the regular teacher is teaching, so there is a lot of auditory interference). Some will try to monitor the entire class, so those with special needs do not feel "singled out". This means, of course, that the neediest students get even less help.

In about 10% of classes, I see actual co-teaching, and it is often very good teaching, too. The specialist re-phrases and simplifies what the teacher has said, defines additional vocabulary words or concepts, explains figurative language, draws attention to visual aids that enhance understanding, and has pre-organized notes or handouts that list concepts, facts, dates, or other important information. The specialist does this in front of the entire class, and the two teachers often alternate the bulk of the teaching, which provides the students with **two styles** and multiple opportunities for clarification.

Since this is **rarely** what a school means by a "co-taught" class, it is best to observe before agreeing to this placement for your child. In some cases, it will be available (in whatever form) for only 1 or 2 subjects, leaving your child confused in other classes.

The placements listed on Grid C (instruction provided outside the regular classroom) include specialist services and tutorials to address specific learning issues (provided on an individual or small-group basis), time in a resource room or academic learning center (the names vary), or a special education class that replaces an academic subject or area (a language-based English or Social Studies class, or a special education math class).

Specialist and tutorial services have been described in the chapter on the IEP. It will be clear from what is written in Grid C **how often** your child will be seen, for **how long**, and in **what size group.** The quality of that instruction will need to be verified.

Resource room services are as varied as the school systems providing them. I have honestly seen everything, from quiet, well organized, effective classes to chaotic ones that were a waste of time. There have been classes where students were learning exactly what they needed, and even receiving remedial reading or math programs. Others functioned mainly as places to do homework, without any focused assistance. In the worst cases, there has been no effective teaching or learning taking place.

The number of students, the ratio of students to teachers (and aides), and the range of grades permitted, are regulated by special education law. In most classes, there are too many students, in my opinion, for the help available. And even when the class happens to be small, and the remedial help is appropriate, I know that more students can be added at any time.

Depending on the size of the school, resource classes will be more or less specialized. In some high schools, there may be one resource period designed to specifically support one or more academic classes for one grade level of students. These tend to be more focused, and thus more useful. Other high schools or middle schools will have one academic support class to teach study skills **and** provide help with any academic subject, for one or two grades. Unless the room is divided so that these instructional areas can be addressed in **much smaller**

**groupings** and with **adequate sound barriers,** it will be very difficult to address students' needs appropriately. In a small elementary school, there may be **one** resource class for **all the children** in grades 1-3 or 3-5 who need pull-out academic support. This is likely to be a group with a **wide range** of needs, and the layout of the room and number of staff available will have a huge impact on the quality of learning.

Classes that try to do "too much" are often less helpful. In general, the rule is: **the more specialized and narrow the grouping, the more your child will be able to learn.** This, of course, assumes competent teaching from the learning specialist or the paraprofessional.

Academic support of this type may be offered as little as once per 10-day cycle (which is likely to be useless to a child with **any** special needs) or as often as twice per day. Here, as always, you as parents want **enough service** to enable your child to make "effective progress" in mastering the curriculum. But once your child needs daily or twice-daily support to keep afloat, it has been my experience that they are often too confused and overwhelmed to be able to learn effectively in their regular education classes.

Remember, it's called **support**—this means that your child should be understanding **most** of what is taught in his or her classes, and using this time to answer a few questions or boost specific skills (such as previewing vocabulary or learning how to study for tests). They should not be trying to play "catch up" or re-learning the entire curriculum.

As I said in an earlier chapter, the **amount of academic support** provided in the C Grid should be related to the number of classes for which support is needed. Your child should have 2-3 periods of support per cycle for each major subject in which their performance is affected by their learning problems. That means if they struggle with **every subject,** then academic support will not be enough to enable "effective progress".

The last option for a C Grid **placement** is a **special education class.** This class should provide specially-designed instruction to meet your child's needs, and should be taught by a certified special education teacher. The other children would be **expected** to have similar needs, though often we find this is not the case. The class size is limited by law to 8 children with one teacher, and more if there is a paraprofessional or assistant. This means class sizes can reach 12-16 children, which is not always appropriate for a child with significant learning difficulties.

There are many advantages to this type of class when it is done well: the smaller size, specialized instruction, and group of similar peers. Direct remedial instruction is often available during the class, and the material presented is adapted to meet the needs of the students. Public school systems that provide these classes are attempting to meet the academic, emotional, or behavioral needs of children with significant learning issues.

These classes can include language-based classes, special education classes (such as for math), and classes for children with behavioral or developmental problems. Since a majority of learning problems involve reading and language (because they are essential skills for getting an education), most of the classes offered will be described as "language-based classes".

Here's the thing—I have a **very specific set of criteria** for a good language-based class, and many of the so-called ones in public schools don't make the grade. Plus, there's the additional problem that a school will offer these classes for 1, or at most 2, subjects and think they're done. Do they think that the child, through some miracle, does not have a language learning disability in the rest of his classes?

Years ago, I dealt with a special education director whose main goal in life seemed to be **preventing** children from getting the services they needed. She constantly told parents that what she offered was "research-based", as though this made it better than what I wanted (I've already discussed the severe limitations of research in education. In my opinion, you can't tell **anything** about the value of a program based on any so-called "research").

I sat in many meetings with this woman, arguing for much-needed and more appropriate services for the children I had tested, some of whom had significant learning disabilities. *"What exactly do you want?"* she demanded at one point. *"All our classes are language-based classes."*

Well, yes, I guess so, if what she meant is that the classes "use language", as opposed to just drawing pictures. This is like the waitress in Switzerland who informed me (a bit sarcastically), "**All** our cheese is Swiss cheese," meaning that I had not been **specific enough** in my request, so she couldn't fill my order. Just **calling** something a "language-based class" doesn't mean it **is** one, or that it has the **necessary components** to help a child with a significant learning disability to access the curriculum. A regular education class does not meet my criteria for a "language-based class", and neither do some special education ones.

This woman was trying to trip me up, figuring I didn't really know what I wanted, and couldn't describe it in sufficient detail to convince the parents that what she offered wasn't good enough. She was mistaken on both counts.

Here are the major components of what I expect from a language-based class, whether offered by a public school or a private school:

- A class consists of no more than 8 children; teachers are generally special education certified, or at least are experienced and skilled in working with learning disabled children (**based on my observations**); and language-based instruction is used throughout the class

- Language-based instruction means that teachers use short, linguistically-simple sentences, they provide repetition and review of what they've said, they consistently spiral back to reinforce what has been taught, and they "check in" with students to ensure comprehension. They ask clarifying questions and re-phrase information or questions if necessary, to be sure students understand. They provide "wait time" or cues to help children retrieve information. They consistently use multi-sensory techniques such as visuals (maps, charts, time lines, photos) and hands-on materials to reinforce concepts. They define and explain unfamiliar vocabulary (and they **recognize** when vocabulary is "unfamiliar"!). They discuss figures of speech and explain what is "inferred" in the reading, they make abstract concepts more concrete, they give (and ask for) lots of examples, they summarize, they tell students "what this means" or "why it is important". They **do not** simply speak in a louder voice (I've actually seen this, I'm afraid).

- Students are placed in homogeneous groupings (students in a given class are all very similar in terms of skill levels, severity of their learning problems, and cognitive ability)

- All reading material in the class is adapted to the current reading level of the students. This includes textbooks, handouts, homework, books that are read together in class or at home, tests, and study guides

- Material is pre-organized for clarity, and includes the most important information without much "filler" or non-essential information. New material is related in a meaningful way to what has already been taught

- Homework is adapted so it can be completed independently by students, regardless of their current level of skill. Homework is designed to reinforce and practice what has been taught in class

- Test formats include cues, to help with retrieval for children with poor memory skills. This can include a matching or multiple-choice format, or fill in the blank with a "word bank". Major formulas or vocabulary are provided for students, so they can focus on demonstrating their understanding of material.

- There are **two other services** that will be part of an out-of-district language-based special education program, but which **may or may not be offered** by a public school program. In my opinion, they are **essential** for any child with a language-based learning disability, including dyslexia and communication disorders. These are a **daily reading tutorial** and a **daily written language tutorial.**

This is not an exhaustive list, but you get the idea. If this is what your child truly needs, than something **less** adapted and **less** specialized is not going to do the trick. As parents, you will have to address **three problems**: getting the school to acknowledge your child's need for this type of class, finding the appropriate class or classes in-district, and determining whether what is offered will be enough to allow your child to make "effective progress".

Sometimes, the "language-based class" will be part of a "special education program" that may last for more than one class period (often 90 minutes to an entire morning). These are sometimes designed to replace the entire "literacy" block, or all of English Language Arts time, including spelling, reading, written language, and phonics. This is done more often in elementary school. The same criteria and standards apply for this "program" as for an individual class.

Obviously, if you are discussing Grid C services at a placement meeting, then there is some recognition of your child's substantial learning needs. The school is at least willing to discuss the fact that your child is **sufficiently far behind grade level** that he or she can't make "effective progress" in a regular classroom.

The next issue is whether a school district has the appropriate classes. If they **say** they do, you or your independent evaluator (or both) will need to verify this with an observation (by now, you've probably figured out that I don't take **anything** I'm told on faith; I should have "Show Me" tattooed on my forehead).

Often, the proposed class will not meet your child's needs, for one or more reasons. If you end up rejecting the proposed IEP in whole or in part, you will list these reasons in detail (your independent expert should provide this information). Even if the class (or classes, if you are lucky) is appropriate, you still must consider your child's entire day. If English and Social Studies are going to be provided in small, language-based classes, how will your child handle the expectations of Math and Science? What about foreign language and specials such as music and technology?

A child with a significant learning, behavioral, developmental or emotional problem, who does not have the necessary skills for success in school, does not "pick up" these skills like a pencil, at the classroom door. In many cases, if there is concern about lack of skills and failure in one academic subject, that concern applies to other subjects as well. Not always—many children have more intact skills in one area (math or reading, depending on the area of disability), and science is very concrete and hands-on into middle school, so even children with language or reading deficits are often able to get the concepts and facts.

However, this is an issue to be addressed in the placement meeting. It is often an issue where you and the school will disagree. As I said earlier, schools try to save money by providing specialized instruction in as few areas as possible. But—**you know your child best.** If **you and your expert** believe your child will not be able to make "effective progress" without language-based instruction, or some other type of a separate, specialized class, for **all or most academic subjects,** then what is offered in Grid C **must include** that level of service.

The Team may offer a **combination** of separate special education classes and less-specialized but still supported classes, such as a co-taught class or one with a paraprofessional to assist your child. They may offer increased remedial services or tutorials outside the class, to improve skills. There are many potential combinations that can "work" for your child—but only if you and your expert believe that **the whole "package" will provide sufficient services** to allow "effective progress" in accessing the curriculum. This can be a complicated equation, and most parents will benefit from the help of an independent expert, who has **only** your child's growth and success in mind.

If it becomes clear that what is offered will **not** ensure this progress, then parents will need to consider their options. These are discussed in detail in the chapter on dealing with problems. Essentially, as moms everywhere have said, you have two choices—"take it, or leave it".

"Taking it" means you accept the school's services, and either wait or supplement with outside ones (or both). "Leaving it" means deciding to try for a program that is a better "fit" for your child's needs. Sometimes, this is an outside placement in a private school or consortium that has the services and type of class your child needs in order to learn. This option is not for the faint of heart, but I will discuss in detail the steps to take and the support you will need.

These private programs not only provide language-based classes **across the curriculum**, but a number of other remedial services designed to help your child develop improved skills, particularly in **reading** and **written language**. Because these two areas are so important throughout school (they are the major performance skills that teachers use to tell if a child understands what is being taught) they need to be taught in ways that allow a child to compensate for his or her learning difficulties and develop increased mastery.

- A **reading tutorial** will usually be offered on an individual basis to a child with a reading disability. Depending on a child's needs, the reading specialist will use one or more programs designed to develop or solidify skills for understanding sound/symbol relationships, and for hearing the difference between sounds. Most remedial reading programs are highly structured, rule-based, and generally phonetic. They teach the types of syllables that make up words, the rules and exceptions for decoding (sounding out) and encoding (spelling) words, reading fluency (both scanning and accuracy), sight words and more complex vocabulary, and comprehension. This is a big list, but all of these skills need to be learned and become automatic if your child is to reach a level of independent reading skill. Skimping on services **does not work.**

- There will be daily a **written language tutorial** using a "writing process" approach. This structured, sequential method begins by teaching a child to write simple sentences that are complete and accurate, then more complex sentences, and then paragraphs. It uses visual templates and graphic organizers to teach brainstorming and "webbing" skills, how to produce an outline and add details, and the editing skills necessary for accuracy. Learning to write is a complicated, demanding task that requires **daily practice and active collaboration with a well-trained teacher** if any level of skill is to be achieved. Short-cuts **do not work**.

- Most private language-based programs will also include **direct instruction** in expressive language and communication skills, literature (including listening to more grade-appropriate literature that children could not yet read on their own), strategies to improve skills for memory and retrieval, and thinking/problem solving skills. These will generally be woven into an integrated daily program that supports learning across all curriculum areas. It is one reason these programs are more appropriate and more successful with children who have significant learning disabilities.

The **severity** of your child's needs is only one factor to consider. There are financial, social, and emotional issues as well. The **timing** of your decision is also important, and may influence whether there is a "place" for your child in the school of your choice.

If you believe your child needs placement in a special education program outside your school district, you will submit applications to one or more schools (if you and your school district had reached agreement that an outside placement was needed, the school would be sending out packets of information to these schools). Decisions about admission are made in late winter/early spring. It can take several months for a school to receive materials and review them, interview parents and their child, and make a decision. The availability of a peer group whose needs are similar to your child's will also be a factor. Sometimes the timing is right, but not always.

Schools designed to meet the needs of children with specific learning disabilities are often few and far between. There are several in the Boston area, where I live, but they focus primarily on children with language-based learning disabilities. It is much more of a challenge to find a program for a child with nonverbal learning problems, or a child with a combination of language and emotional, or cognitive and learning, difficulties. Depending on where you live, it may be very important to work with an independent evaluator or advocate who knows the programs in your area. In some cases, the best school is many miles away (or halfway across the country) and will require boarding, which is not an option for a young child.

The best outcome would be for you and the Team to reach a decision on placement that provides your child with the necessary services and classes to meet his or her needs, **no matter where that happens to be**. Now that you know more about the different choices available for service delivery, you can advocate for those with the best chance of bringing your child closer to grade level, and the point where an IEP is no longer needed.

# Consent for Placement

Parents may accept the IEP as written, if it accurately and completely describes their child's needs and the types of services needed to meet those needs. They may accept part of the IEP and reject another part (for example, if parents like what is offered but feel their child needs additional services to make "effective progress"). They may choose to reject the entire IEP. Regardless of what parents decide, they **also** need to agree to the proposed **placement**. This page follows the Response page of the IEP (page 8) and is designated **PL1**. There is one form for 3-5 year olds, and one for children ages 6-21.

Just because the Team has agreed that your child needs services doesn't mean they will agree to the **type of placement** you feel is necessary. This is another potential roadblock, but by this point in your discussions it shouldn't come as any big surprise. You and your expert will discuss your options, hopefully using the information in the next few chapters.

During the placement meeting, the Team fills out the top portion of the form, indicating the recommended type of placement based on the child's needs. Note that it may not represent **your** choice for placement. Parents then either consent to or refuse the placement. A rejection of placement will "trigger" the same response from the Department of Education as your rejection of the body of the IEP itself.

# A 504 Accommodation Plan

Some children will not qualify for an IEP under state and federal rules. You may disagree, in which case you will seek an independent evaluation and re-convene the Team to discuss the new findings. However, you and the school district **may agree** that your child **has** some type of disability but **does not need** specially designed instruction in order to access the curriculum. Instead, the Team decides that your child needs **accommodations** that will facilitate "effective progress" and learning.

Section 504 of the Rehabilitation Act of 1973 states that a school district must provide every eligible student with a "free appropriate public education" (FAPE). If a child does not qualify for an IEP, but **does** have a disability, then FAPE is provided through the use of **services or accommodations** during the school day. An **eligible student** has some type of "physical or mental impairment", which includes any physical disability, a learning disability, or ADD/ADHD. In my experience, this plan is often provided to children with Attention Deficit Disorder or reduced processing speed, as a way of helping them achieve success in their classes.

Basically, this law allows your child to receive accommodations during the day even when he or she doesn't meet the criteria for an IEP. That's the good news. The bad news is, the 504 Plan **can be** a way for schools to "satisfy" parents by promising services that they won't "deliver". Every year, numerous parents tell me their child has a 504, but **nothing** about his school day has actually changed. This clearly does not satisfy even the spirit of the law.

Prioritizing and selecting the right accommodations is like reading the menu at a Chinese restaurant—a bewildering array of possibilities, many of which sound good. You can't possibly sample them all, but you want to pick the "best" ones—the ones that give your child the most benefit. Your server (the public school) may not be much help, since her suggestion will be to choose as many as you want. But when there are too many choices, you (or a teacher) will become overwhelmed trying to keep track, and your child may not enjoy (benefit from) the ones you pick.

Elementary school teachers work with 18-25 children, for most of each day; middle and high school teachers may have 4 or 5 different classes of 18-25 children each. In either case, your child will not be the only one with needs, any hour of any day. A teacher's ability to provide accommodations will be limited by the **laws of physics and math**, among others: an object (the teacher) cannot be in two places (or more) at one time, and 25 divided by 1 still leaves 25 students being watched by 1 teacher.

When I see a full page (or more) of accommodations in an IEP, they are almost always describing the features or components of **a more specialized (and smaller) class placement** even though the school doesn't call it that. If a child actually **needs** most of what is being listed, you're facing a problem similar to that of the shark hunters in the movie *Jaws*: "you're gonna need a bigger boat"—ie, a more comprehensive program.

In order for a child to receive benefits from a 504 Plan, the accommodations have to be available and provided as often as they are needed. This means the teacher or teachers must have the time and bandwidth to provide them. The effectiveness of these accommodations must be observed in improved performance at school and at home. Since there are no progress reports with this Plan, it will be up to (wait for it!) **parents** to ensure the accommodations are actually **put into place** and employed **consistently.** This can be an exhausting task, depending on the number of accommodations and the age of your child.

Since you can't follow your child around the school and observe each class, you will need to rely on a combination of a "white board", regular communication with teachers and specialists, and consistent monitoring of your child's work, attitude, and emotional state. I talk much more about monitoring in a later chapter, and discuss the "nuts and bolts" of how best to do it. For now, just know that **if** your child needed and got an accommodation plan, and **if** things are going well for him or her in terms of schoolwork, and **if** the school personnel can tell you what accommodations they are really using and it basically matches the plan, **then** you have some hope that this whole scheme is working.

As I said in an earlier chapter, the first few accommodations are the ones most likely to be implemented consistently. When I'm working with parents and the rest of the Team, I push for the ones that will **make the most difference** to a child's day. Here's a list of accommodations often provided in a 504 Plan, to give you some idea of the scope of what can be offered in the classroom to help your child understand the curriculum and meet standards for performance:

# Top Thirty-plus Accommodations in IEPs and 504 Plans

- Provide preferential seating near the point of instruction (often front of class)

- Allow extra time to process information and provide responses

- Provide verbal prompts or cues to aid retrieval of words or information

- Provide frequent check-ins to ensure comprehension of information

- Repeat and clarify directions

- Preview vocabulary and concepts for content classes

- Use test formats that provide cues, such as matching, multiple choice, or fill in the blank with a "word bank"

- Allow extended time to complete tests (this is a biggie for high school students)

- Allow use of a calculator, math chart, or other aid for arithmetic

- Check agenda book to ensure all assignments are entered completely and legibly

- Provide end of day check-in to organize materials and homework

- Allow child to work in a quiet area of classroom

- Provide "movement breaks", opportunities to run errands or hand out papers
- Use a visual or tactile signal by the teacher, such as a tap on the desk, to help student re-focus attention
- Provide extra set of textbooks for use at home
- Make use of sensory aids such as elastic bands, sit-n-move cushions, or a small object (a "fidget") to hold in the hand
- Provide an opportunity for "heavy pressure" tasks such as wall push-ups or carrying heavy items
- Connect new material being presented to previously-taught material
- break down" more complex verbal information into smaller "chunks" of simpler language
- Present material to be memorized in smaller, pre-organized groupings
- Use raised-line paper and/or pencil grips for improved legibility
- Read classroom materials to student as necessary
- Use graphic organizers, templates or outlines for written language tasks
- Provide a full set of classroom notes
- Provide an outline of course material to be covered, a syllabus, and a study guide for tests
- Allow use of a computer for written language tasks or for note-taking
- Provide a "scribe" (often an aide, sometimes the teacher) who will write what the student dictates, for any written work
- Provide concrete models or examples of completed projects
- Provide concrete demonstrations of tasks and skills
- Prepare student for transitions or changes to schedule
- Allow use of a brief "time out" to regain emotional self-control
- Provide opportunity to re-take tests with grade lower than C (lets inattentive kids or those with memory problems have a second chance)

Pretty overwhelming, isn't it? I have a great memory and I'm good at multi-tasking, and I wouldn't want to be responsible for using most of these accommodations in a substantially-separate class of 8 children, **much less a regular education class**. In my opinion, if your child needs many of the services I just listed **in order to manage classroom expectations**, then chances are he or she is not going to be doing very well.

The more significant the **changes** need to be, compared to the regular classroom procedures and processes, the more likely your child is going to be "out of step" with the rest of his classmates. He's more likely to be confused by what he hears, to be unable to remember what to do or how to do it, to be unable to start or complete work, and possibly unable to read what is given out.

These children often spend a lot of time "watching" other children to see what they should be doing. I've observed that from elementary through middle school. They may do better in some classes such as science, where the task is very "hands on" and often demonstrated first, or when working on projects in small groups where other children can pick up the slack. But in general, they won't be able to follow the instructions independently or produce an expected amount of finished work.

Being "a little behind" doesn't mean this type of plan isn't working, but some children have **no idea** what is going on in a class. They are not interacting with the material appropriately for real learning. They don't understand concepts or retain information. They can't process the language or read the board or read the instructions. They are not capable of "effective progress" or independent learning in any academic area, with this amount of support.

I worked with a family whose very bright 4th grader had a language-processing disability and retrieval problems as well as dyslexia. She got pull-out reading services several times per week. The reading teacher was certified but not skilled, in my opinion—not only did she choose incredibly outdated and uninspiring books without controlled vocabulary for the guided reading part of the tutorial, but she paired this shy, sensitive child with a very competitive one who had no retrieval problems and thus "jumped in" with the answers before this child could think of them, seriously reducing this child's learning and causing her to feel stupid.

As bad as that was, the classroom of 25 children was worse. This girl spent the rest of the day here, supposedly receiving a ton of accommodations as part of her IEP. There was an aide part-time. When I observed, it was clear she was always **at least** "a step behind", needing information to be repeated and rephrased. This did not happen for her on a consistent basis, which left her very anxious. When the teacher or aide **did** repeat, they drew attention to her by singling her out by name, producing even more emotional distress. The girl came home in tears most days, confused and embarrassed. She could not read any class material or homework on her own, and often they would not be modified as her plan said they would be. The amount of support that was listed meant she **needed** a more specialized class, and even what was listed was **not provided** on a regular basis.

Years ago, I observed a 6th grade boy in a middle school science class that was studying anatomy and physiology. This was a wealthy suburb, and the teacher seemed proud of the quantity and complexity of material he was presenting—with visuals, but **very rapidly**. The boy had several significant language-based learning disabilities and a communication disorder. His IEP included a full page of classroom accommodations, **most of which were not in evidence when I observed**. In fact, given the pace and complexity of the class, I did not think it could be sufficiently adapted for him to make "effective progress". This boy was so overwhelmed, he was showing physical stress symptoms, including disturbed sleep and depression.

The bottom line is that accommodations can be a good thing, if all your child needs is **a few specific changes or adjustments** in order to fully access the curriculum. Children with moderate ADD or executive functioning disorders, for example, can manage quite well **if** their **academic skills are close to grade level**, and the **right** accommodations are provided **every day to support their performance.**

My rule is: the **farther** a child's functioning is from grade-level expectations, the **less effective** accommodations in a regular classroom will be in helping that child make "effective progress" and access the curriculum. Once there is a significant learning disability—of whatever type—a child needs more specialized instruction in a smaller setting. This is true even if a child is bright, motivated, socially successful and well-behaved. Those are great assets, but they don't mean a child will learn without the right instruction.

**Learning** is what matters—making enough progress to ideally **get off an IEP** and function independently in an academic setting.

Remember—**you know your child best.** When you and your independent expert meet with the Team to discuss a plan, regardless of the type, you need to **bring a list** of the adjustments you both think your child needs to be successful. Prioritize, of course, so the most important ones are first, where they stand a better chance of being implemented. Be sure you as parents have a system in place to get regular feedback from the school to monitor compliance with the plan (they can't refuse to do this). Compare what you hear and see at home with the information you get from the school, and the papers and tests your child brings home. Note grades and your child's mood and self-confidence.

**Most of all**, do not lie to yourself or allow the school to lie to you, even if they seem sincere and you (or your child) want him to remain in regular education classes. The school **will not** be able to put "ten pounds" of accommodations in a "five pound" bag. They may tell you they can and will, with the best of intentions, but you must not believe them. If your child **needs** "ten pounds" of accommodations, then he or she needs a more intensive program.

# CHAPTER 10

# HOW TO TELL IF YOUR CHILD IS MAKING "EFFECTIVE PROGRESS"

*"In order that people may be happy in their work, these three things are needed: they must be fit for it. They must not do too much of it. And they must have a sense of success in it."*
*John Ruskin, educator and philosopher*

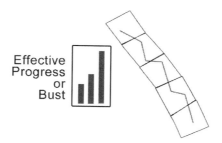

Most parents try really hard not to lie to their children. Rich or poor, black or white or polka-dotted, single parent household or multiple parents, there are unspoken rules: I will love you, take care of you, try to keep you safe—and not lie to you.

I'm not talking about Santa Claus or the tooth fairy. I'm talking about sending your child off to school each day. Children (at least until they become teenagers) think their parents know everything. If they are being sent to a certain school or class or program, they assume it must be "right", or their parents wouldn't have sent them. They tend to believe it when parents say, "this is the best program for you; it will help you learn." Children **want** to believe

155

there is help for them; even cynical teens mostly want to get help so they can do better. They bring a good attitude to their "special ed" services, and try to do their best.

That level of trust puts a burden on parents. What if the parents are wrong? What if this **isn't** the best program? What if their child **doesn't** make progress, read better, understand the teacher more often, make friends, feel safe? What if the services are incorrect or inadequate?

How can a parent **know**—and what can you do about it? My attitude is, as in other dealings with a school system, "Trust, but verify".

# Progress Reports

Once your child has an IEP, you will get progress reports as often as you get a report card (3-4 times per year). However, I have found these are often less than helpful in monitoring a child's performance.

Look at it from a "real world" perspective, not the overly-optimistic perspective that says "all the teachers can provide all the necessary services in the time that is available to all the eligible children, who are learning everything they should be learning". If that were true, I'd be out of a job.

In the real world, a special education teacher or other specialist will have a caseload of anywhere from 6 to 30 students, and will be writing these progress reports **in addition to** providing the direct and indirect services in each child's educational plan, going to meetings, consulting with teachers and other staff, and doing updated or initial testing—all in a day that is too short (in my opinion) and frequently interrupted by a huge number of possible changes to their schedule.

To me, it is not surprising that these progress reports often don't contain meaningful or measurable information about your child's progress. I'm surprised they get done at all.

That said, it is **not acceptable** for there to be so little accountability. It is not acceptable to read the same basic report each quarter, saying your child is "making progress towards his IEP goals", with nothing concrete to show that is true. It's certainly not acceptable when goals, objectives, and benchmarks don't change from one IEP to the next, because the child hasn't really progressed.

It's even less acceptable when I read in these progress reports that certain skills are supposedly being gained, but my own testing shows a complete lack of mastery of these same skills.

# Evaluating Progress

If school systems were committed to providing effective, accurate and frequent monitoring of a child's progress, it would be possible. They would need to use materials or technology that allowed ongoing evaluations of what a child had learned, and, more important, **retained.** There are software programs available to schools that provide this information, though public schools rarely use them.

For example, there is Lexia, a computer program designed for children with dyslexia. Based on well-designed research (yes, there is some!) that looked at the auditory processing skills of these children, it presents word sounds **much** more slowly, giving the child's brain a chance to identify the sounds. It is designed as repeated practice that will increase in difficulty, with a return to previous material to ensure the retention of skills (known as "mastery"). It is individualized for each child, allows practice at the child's current level of mastery, and moves through a sequential program to increase skills for accurate auditory analysis and automaticity. It provides a "floor" or foundation for further reading instruction.

There is Symphony Math, a program designed for children between kindergarten and 3rd grade, approximately. The focus is on basic "number sense", setting up and solving arithmetic operations (addition, subtraction, etc), analyzing and solving number sentences (8 + _ = 10), and understanding groups of number facts ("fact families"). These skills are essential for any success in math throughout school. The programs are completely individualized for each child, and provide constant review of previously-taught material ("spiraling"). A child will move through the levels at his or her own pace, moving back to any skill area for which they can't demonstrate mastery. The program displays colored graphs of a child's progress on a daily basis. Every child can look at his or her scores; they know what level they are working on, and what skills they are having difficulty with, and what they need to do to get to the next level.

For children with severe learning disabilities and lower cognitive skills, there are programs such as Edmark reading and TouchMath, that provide the same multi-sensory teaching, spiraling and review, and sequential presentation of basic material, at a slower pace and at a more concrete level. These programs also allow a teacher or parent to measure progress and mastery.

There are other computer-based remedial programs that are effective and well-regarded, including Fast ForWord and Earobics, that provide ongoing evaluation of mastery. In addition, a number of well-established non-computer programs provide measurable data about a child's progress. Significantly, these are also teaching methods that are very effective for use with children who have learning disabilities. They provide pre- and post-teaching tests that document a child's skill levels, and ensure that a child is retaining material that has been taught. Children progress at their own pace, with structure and support.

Some examples are the Lindamood Phonemic Sequencing Program (LiPS) that teaches the individual sounds and the mouth positions necessary to make those sounds. As with Lexia, the program exaggerates and lets a child practice the actual physical movements they will need for reading, using pictures, word labels ("lip poppers"), a mirror, and teacher demonstration. There is testing used before, during, and after the program, showing the skills that have been mastered. In addition, the Lindamood Auditory Conceptualization Test (LAC-3) tests a child's ability to accurately hear and manipulate individual sounds and sound sequences.

The Wilson Reading Program is a highly structured, sequential, phonetic reading program that is accompanied by a pre- and post-teaching test that shows how much a child has learned and **retained**. This test, the WADE, can be administered after completion of each level of instruction, or at the beginning and end of the school year. It is also useful for demonstrating **regression** after a vacation. Many children have trouble hanging on to skills in areas where their neurology is not working properly (resulting in a "learning disability"). They need a **lot** more practice and review than one would expect, in order to fully master these skills and use them over time. The Wilson program has this built-in evaluation feature that is helpful to both parents and teachers, **assuming it is used properly and regularly**.

There are other individualized special education reading programs, and math programs, that allow objective testing on a regular basis to monitor progress and assess mastery. Please don't think these are "fancy", "new" programs that schools cannot afford. The materials themselves are not expensive, and the programs have been around for many years (Orton-Gillingham remedial instruction for students with dyslexia has been used since the 1960s). Teacher training is required, and may take 9 months-2 years of weekly classes to complete, but school systems often pay for this training and increase a teacher's salary afterward.

In my opinion, most of the necessary methodology for effective teaching and evaluating progress **is already available to a school system,** including materials for children with no learning disabilities at all. McGraw-Hill, a large publisher of educational materials, sells a leveled, individualized reading program that includes phonics instruction, early reading fluency and vocabulary, and ongoing development of reading skills/comprehension. It is called SRA Reading, and I used it when I was in school (back when George Washington was a boy!). Children work individually, check their accuracy themselves, and move up through the color-coded levels at their own pace.

Obviously, it isn't "new", and it isn't considered "sexy" or "exciting", but it works, and that's good enough for me. Parents, teachers and children can monitor progress. Grade-level equivalents are included, which in my opinion puts this program ahead of others that are used in schools for screening or instruction that use letter-codes to indicate performance levels. You have to pry the grade-equivalents out of school personnel with a chisel, and the parents I talk with often have **no idea** at what grade level their children are actually reading.

If school personnel won't tell you where your child is performing in terms of a **grade-level equivalent,** they either **don't know** or they **don't want you to know.** It's one or the other, and neither is acceptable.

These are only a sampling of the special education or regular education teaching methods that include ongoing, objective evaluation of a child's progress. I include them because I consider each one to be well-designed, effective in teaching certain skills, and—equally important—able to provide hard data about your child's skills. While some of them do not seem to have significant research studies, based on the Institute for Educational Studies website, they **have** resulted in improved grade level performance as measured by independent testing.

When schools or specialists don't use these types of programs, you are less likely to get the kind of accurate monitoring you need to determine if your child is making "effective progress". In every specialty, there are tools for measuring whether the services are making a concrete difference. If schools are not using them, you won't be able to rely on the feedback you receive in a typical progress report.

Also, don't let school personnel tell you that the "grade level" of your child's performance isn't important. If that were true, children would simply "enter" school at age 5 and "leave" at age 18, and there would be no grade levels at all. School is meant to be a **sequential progression** in which later learning builds on earlier skill development. Schools break up this learning into chunks which they then distribute through grades K-12.

There is, in fact, a **list** of the set of skills that your child is expected to master at each grade level. It's called the curriculum, and it should be written down somewhere and **available for you to read**.

Bottom line: until schools move to a "mastery" model, in which children have individual learning plans based on their needs (all children have needs or they wouldn't need school) and move "on" or "up" when they can demonstrate mastery of skills, and leave when they've got them, schools will continue to move children through "grades". They will also be aware of whether the children are performing at "grade level" in different subjects, though there may be some reluctance to share this information.

# Using Performance Levels in the IEP

In some cases, the goals and performance levels (the first two parts of page 5 of the IEP) are duplicated wholly or in part from year to year. I have read IEPs in which the benchmarks and objectives did not change in any substantive way over several years, because the children **had not made any measurable progress.**

One recent case of mine involved a young teen girl with a nonverbal learning disability (NLD) whose math skills hadn't improved in 3 years. The school did not understand her disability or how to address it, and had grouped her with children with language-based learning problems and mild autism-spectrum disorders (**because those were the closest "peers" they had**). I do not consider this an acceptable strategy, by the way, but they'd gotten away with it for years.

The other children in her group were working on pre-algebra in the small, structured 7th grade math class, while this child was still struggling to understand basic arithmetic. She was not even fully accurate when using a calculator! Her math goals and objectives were worded in a way that attempted to "match" what was being taught, but **her performance levels never changed**. Clearly, she was not making any type of progress in math, and was also beginning to "top out" in English, as the literature became more abstract and used more figurative language. She needed a program designed for children with NLD, which adapted much more of the curriculum than just math.

In another case, a 10 year old girl had been diagnosed with a communication disorder and significant language-based learning disabilities in first grade. This was fine, but her services were completely inadequate and she made almost no progress. Her IEP goals and objectives were **almost identical from year to year,** even as the school moved her from program to program. To them, it made sense to keep the goals the same—she was still attempting to master basic reading, math, and written language skills.

By the time she was in 5th grade, her IEP listed her diagnosis as "low cognitive ability", because her skills were still so low and she wasn't making expected cognitive growth (Note to parents: this is often what happens when services are inadequate; a child can't access the curriculum or make expected gains in thinking and problem-solving. They don't get any less **intelligent**, but it **seems** that way because they aren't keeping up with peers in terms of learning).

This was so blatantly unfair that school personnel did not even argue when the parents and I told them, after my testing, that this child needed placement in a private program designed for children with significant learning disabilities. They knew they hadn't met her needs. Unfortunately, she's now in middle school, with elementary school skills.

In both cases, the school's progress reports always indicated that the child was cooperative, good-natured, a hard worker, and "making progress towards her goals". The first 3 didn't matter, and the last one wasn't true. When there isn't regular testing with **appropriate instruments** to demonstrate progress and mastery, parents have no way to be sure their children are in fact gaining skills or strategies.

# Monitoring by Parents

So, where does this leave you, the parents? Just because there is a signed IEP doesn't mean your job is done. Sorry!

In some cases, you will be able to **see** the progress. For example:

- Children receiving speech/language services should demonstrate improved articulation and pronunciation, more accurate grammar and syntax, improved vocabulary skills, and use of more complex language. Your child should display a better ability to follow directions and analyze spoken language accurately, or an improved memory span. If services are also provided in class, your child should show an increased ability to independently "make sense" of what is being said and taught, to follow directions and use strategies to cope with word retrieval difficulties.

- Children receiving occupational therapy services should demonstrate greater skill and accuracy in copying what they see, whether this is letters of the alphabet, notes off the board, or charts and diagrams for science class. Writing should become easier, more fluid—as well as more legible. Your child should show improved skills for following multi-step directions, putting a puzzle together, and sequencing a process such as a recipe, the story line in a book, or the steps needed to solve an arithmetic problem. The accuracy of their eye-hand coordination should improve, as well as hand and upper-body strength.

- Children receiving physical therapy, adaptive physical education or sensory integration services should display greater large-muscle strength and coordination—for throwing or kicking a ball, walking on a line, playing games that require following a set of rules and working with other children, and using their bodies effectively. Children with sensory deficits should be better able to tolerate input such as noise, crowded rooms, different textures of food or clothing, changes in routine, or expectations for flexibility in their behavior.

- Children with reading problems, phonetic weaknesses, lack of smoothness and accuracy, or poor comprehension should show improvements in these skills, which you will see if they read to you at home. Without the specialized tests, you won't be able to tell exactly **how much growth** your child is making in these areas, but you should see things becoming easier, more automatic, and less frustrating for your child as he or she reads. Parents can also observe **whether** a child is choosing to read more often, **what** they are choosing, and the **length of time** they read before becoming tired or frustrated. If reading is easier, a child will choose to pick up a book that is more challenging, such as a chapter book. If all they want to look at is comics, Lego instructions or video game manuals, or Anime (graphic novels), they are probably not yet able to follow a more complicated story line. Reading for a longer time builds "reading muscles", which are essential as a child moves into upper elementary grades (4th and 5th). Parents can also check the backs of many chapter books, where the level of difficulty may be marked (RL 4 means a 4th grade level of difficulty). Your observations will give you a good idea of whether your child is making progress, even without a re-evaluation.

- Children or adolescents who are getting help in a learning center or resource room should show evidence of better organizational skills and more completed work. They should be finishing a larger percentage of their homework and doing so with greater independence. They should be bringing home the necessary books and papers for homework each night, and their agenda book should contain clear and accurate assignments, including upcoming tests and long-term assignments. These should be broken down so your child can complete them in a step by step manner. Your child should have complete study guides for tests (in the subjects where they receive support) and copies of classroom notes, if appropriate. Most important, your child should be able to **explain** the assignments, and he or she should **not** be completing homework in school. School time is **learning time.** Homework is meant to be done **at home.**

Obviously, what you see, in terms of improvement, will depend on what **areas of need** your child demonstrated, what **skills** were not in place, what **goals and objectives** were listed in the IEP. But if you don't see changes in the areas that were listed as needing to improve—SAY SOMETHING.

Remember- **you know your child best**. The **whole point** of an IEP is to **get your child off an IEP**, to help him or her make "effective progress" so they can access a grade level curriculum **without** specially designed instruction. It really is that simple. If you don't see concrete changes, something isn't right—the services, the personnel, the placement. Don't let the school tell you everything is going well unless you see it with your own eyes.

If all your child has is a 504 Accommodation Plan, you will **not** get progress reports, which makes it even harder to "verify" that many of the accommodations are actually being done as often as they should be. Your child may be able to tell you about some, and you may see some if you look at assignments or see copies of class notes, but if a child's grades and confidence and independent work habits don't reassure you, then an observation by your independent evaluator or advocate may be the only way to tell what is really happening.

In my experience, a 504 plan is often poorly implemented by a school system. The accommodations are time-consuming for regular and special education teachers, and with many other students to attend to (a regular education teacher in high school may see 100 students each day), there is a good chance that the necessary accommodations will be done on an irregular basis, and sometimes not at all.

Parents complain to me that this type of plan is designed to "appease" them, to get them to **think** their child will be monitored and helped, when in fact they will often be left without the needed support and structure. Sadly, I have to agree with them. While I am sympathetic to the time constraints and multiple demands that impact a teacher or specialist's day, these accommodations are often **necessary** for a child to be successful in the regular education program. It's one reason I ask for the fewest, most important ones to be listed. It's why I ask bluntly whether it will be possible to provide these accommodations with **consistency, on a daily basis**. It's why parents need to find ways to ensure that the accommodations are in fact **being provided** for their children.

Another way to gauge progress is by noticing your child's social/emotional functioning. What is his mood at the end of the day? Is he exhausted, unhappy, frustrated, or angry? Does he whine or cry when it's time to do homework, or (if he's older) does he never quite get around to doing it? Does it take him all night, so there's no "down time" for him to relax and enjoy being with family? What's his social life like? Are kids calling him to get together? Does he have energy for outside interests?

What does your child **say** about his or her day? Children are often very honest. They will tell you what happened—and what did not. Did they receive their services or did the schedule get changed? If they were supposed to receive support from a specialist in the regular classroom, was this helpful or were they still confused? Did they get the notes/outline/templates they needed? Was their specialist there to work with them? Did their agenda book and backpack get checked?

It is important to believe what your child tells you. If what they say doesn't match what is supposed to happen according to the IEP—SAY SOMETHING.

This may prove to be a frustrating experience. Some teachers and specialists are readily available, while others are not. Some use email but many do not. Some have a phone in their classrooms, but others are much more difficult to reach. It may take several days to connect if you leave phone messages on their voicemail. Sometimes, you may need to write a note and wait for a reply. You may need to show up at school and ask to see a specialist or teacher (though it is good to leave a phone message saying when you will be there).

Just be sure to **do it**, for your child's sake. If you are frustrated, imagine how much worse it is for your child, who has **no power** in this situation.

For students in high school, one goal in the IEP will often involve self-advocacy. School personnel may tell you it is **your child's** responsibility to take care of certain things—but then make it impossible for him to do it.

One example would be a student who is expected to check in with teachers in his major subjects to see if he's up to date on all work, or to ask a question about lecture material, a homework assignment or an upcoming test. This is self-advocacy, and it is a good thing.

However, teachers are not chained to their desks or confined to their rooms. In a Team meeting, they will state that they are in their classrooms without fail, every afternoon, for at least 45 minutes—but won't be there the day **your** child shows up with his questions. Or they'll have 3 other students there already, and either your child will give up and leave, or won't get the attention he needs.

In that case, your child won't be able to do his part, and the school will say it is **his fault.** This is unfair.

Make sure, when you are in the Team meeting (or later, if your child is having a problem) that there is more than one way for your child to get information about notes, assignments, tests or homework—on line, in person, through your child's special education teacher or liaison. In my experience, teens **will try** to check in with teachers or go for extra help, but this is not always effective. Don't let your child be blamed when there's a game of "teacher tag", in which the teacher is there when your child is **not,** and **not there** when your child shows up.

# Outside Re-Evaluation

The other way to keep track of your child's progress is to have a re-evaluation done by the psychologist or other specialist who saw your child for an independent evaluation.

Schools re-test every three years, which in my opinion is **far too infrequently** for a child with a significant learning problem. The re-testing will also suffer from the same limitations I discussed in the chapter on Independent Evaluations. They may give standardized testing in one or more academic areas on a regular basis (which takes up an appalling amount of class time, but that's another issue). As I mentioned, these tests often do not provide enough concrete information about your child's **actual levels of performance,** in grade-level terms.

What does "proficient" mean? I'm sure it is described in some state or local document, but chances are you won't **have** that document to look at when you get just the scores, 5 months after the tests were given. How much of a grade-level math curriculum did your child understand and actually use? What grade level of difficulty can she actually read and understand?

Unless your child is being taught one of the remedial programs that includes pre- and post-testing, as described above, you simply don't have concrete information. In my opinion, you can't rely on the progress reports.

These reports will almost always say that a child is "making progress towards her goals". It's hard to believe, but I **very rarely** see a progress report in which the special education teacher or specialist writes that the child "is not making progress" and "won't reach the IEP goal" by the end of the IEP period. Unless the lack of progress can be "blamed" on emotional or behavioral problems, or something else outside the school's control, **it probably won't be noted**.

I did see one progress report in the past few years that honestly admitted the girl would not meet her IEP goals. She was significantly depressed, in addition to her learning disabilities. She was receiving services that were inadequate to support her impaired receptive and expressive language skills. She needed a **lot** more speech therapy. She was also receiving about **half** the level of remedial instruction in reading that she needed, and as a result couldn't read the class texts or extra books that were assigned. She needed more specialized help, **regardless of her depression**.

Rather than address her inadequate services, school personnel seemed to conclude that she wasn't **capable** of making expected progress—mostly because of her depression. This seemed to tell only a small part of the real story, and I disagreed strongly with the Team. The parents pursued and obtained a private placement.

If a teacher admits that a child is **not making progress,** this would suggest that what they are doing is not working. This means they would have to consider doing something **different**, which might well cost more or take additional time. In my experience, there is a strong tradition of not "rocking the boat" in public school systems. This may well interfere with getting the right services to meet your child's needs.

The only way for parents to be sure that their child is making progress, in addition to their own observations, is to monitor growth through a partial or full re-evaluation.

## Keeping Goals in Mind

"Man becomes that which he gazes upon," as George Harrison said. You might want to make a copy of the **goals and objectives** from your child's IEP and keep them in sight at your house. It's easy to forget, in the bustle of everyday life, what skills are supposed to be getting better. Charts, checklists and reminders have a long history of being effective in changing behavior.

Make a **big chart**. Write the goals on a big index card or a piece of poster board. Post them where you and your child will **see them** every day—on the refrigerator, on the table or desk where your child does homework, above the computer monitor. This allows you to refer to the specific goals and objectives and think about "effective progress".

If these are the goals your child is supposed to be working on, how's it going? Do you and your child see any improvement? This is not magic, folks—if the services are working, you should both be able to tell. It's not string theory or genetic mapping; chances are, you're as smart as the people working with your child. If you can't understand what they're supposed to be doing—and see the positive effects—it's likely they don't see them, either.

Be sure you and your child **know** what he or she should be getting out of this IEP. If **you** don't see it happening, and **your child** doesn't see it happening, and **updated testing** doesn't show improvement, then it's time to start objecting.

I recently read an article (Time, April 2010) about paying children to improve their academic performance. This was set up as real double-blind experiments, in several large cities and using different age groups and tasks. The part I found most interesting was the scientists' explanation of **why** some of the experiments **worked** (not all of them did). They found that the children who were asked to do simple, **concrete things** that they **already knew how to do** and that **they could control** made the most gains. The second graders who were paid each time they read a book and took a simple, computerized quiz afterward, read more books, and actually scored significantly higher on reading-comprehension tests at the end of the year. Plus, the gains seemed to continue the following year, **without payments**.

Bottom line—children **improve the most in any area** when they know **exactly** what to do and **how** to do it. The tasks need to be ones they understand and **can control**, such as practicing math facts or reading fluency, or coming home with an accurate assignment book or completing a homework paper. Put those goals up on the wall and **talk with your child** about how to meet them.

# When you think your child is not making progress

If parents are prepared and supported by an independent expert or advocate during the Team meeting (as I hope you were), then their child's IEP may contain all the easily-obtainable services that the school was willing to offer without too much argument. Even if it is clear to you that things are not going well, you may have problems getting more appropriate services.

As I mentioned in the chapter on the IEP, school administrators are very aware that services and skilled staff cost money. There is only so much to "go around", assuming they actually have within the system the services your child needs. The more they give to your child, the less there is for the rest of the students. Therefore, the school may well provide all sorts of rationalizations for why they want to limit services.

In my opinion, it is dishonest of them to tell you they want to limit your child's access to a service, placement, or program for **any reason** other than **financial**. I cannot think of a situation in which a school system could be accused of providing **more services** than a child needs. It simply isn't going to happen.

Remember, an independent evaluator or advocate **whom you have hired** does not have any reason to ask for more help than your child needs to be successful. That's one of the primary reasons you sought out this person, besides their skills as an evaluator. They are skilled, experienced, and (most important) **independent**. They have no "skin in the game", no hidden agenda, no concern other than your child's need to make "effective progress" and access the curriculum.

This is a situation where you can't skimp or "get away with" less remediation, instruction or support than your child needs to overcome their learning difficulties. If the destination is 100 miles away and your car gets 25 miles to the gallon, you **can't get there** with 2 gallons of gas. You won't make it.

If a cake needs to bake for an hour, no realistic person would say, "well, let's bake it for 30 minutes and hope that's enough." Yet this kind of "half-baked" reasoning is how decisions about services are often made.

If a child needs daily reinforcement and teaching of skills to master phonics, fluency or math concepts, then that's what they need. Giving them less just means they won't meet the goal. If they need a daily check-in to keep them organized and productive, or daily time in the learning center to make sure they know the vocabulary and concepts for science or social studies, then giving them less just sets them up for failure. If you are not seeing growth in skills and improvement in overall performance, there's a good chance it's due to insufficient services.

- Children who receive Wilson Reading instruction in a group of 4 or 5 children **will not** make as much progress as a child seen individually.

- Children who work with a certified reading specialist who is completely trained and has experience working with a given reading program (such as Wilson or Lindamood) will **make more progress** than kids seen by someone without full training or certification by the people who designed the method.

Last year, I sat in a Team meeting for a 5th grade boy with significant learning disabilities. He also learned more slowly overall due to low average cognitive ability. The school had placed him in a special education class for Language Arts, Reading, Math, and Phonics, where he spent the entire morning. He'd made almost no progress in two years, however, and his parents were concerned. The special education teacher stated in the meeting that she used many different remedial programs with him—all of which were appropriate—but then admitted that she was not certified to teach **any** of them. She'd taken weekend introductory classes or read the instructional materials, and if it sounded like a promising method, she simply "used it".

When I observed a phonics lesson for this boy and several other children, the teacher was slow, did not present an entire lesson, fumbled with materials, and provided much less instruction and practice during the session than I had observed with other, fully trained teachers. It was easy to imagine how the boy had made so little progress!

- Children who require language-based instruction in order to understand academic material **will not** do as well in a regular education class with a paraprofessional (or even a special education teacher) for part of the day. They will misunderstand key aspects of instruction, won't remember as much as they need to, and will often not be able to retrieve necessary information from memory.

- Children with communication problems who need speech/language therapy, or those with fine motor or visual-motor problems who need occupational therapy (or other specialist services) need these services **enough times per week** so the skills become automatized and can be transferred back to the regular education setting.

School administrators will tell you there is no research to "prove" the above assertions. In fact, the U.S. Education Department has a position paper written by a group of experts, describing what a well-designed research study should include, and **listing a number of interventions** that have been proven to increase academic skills—including individual tutorial services for children with reading disabilities. ([www.ies.ed.gov/wwc](www.ies.ed.gov/wwc))

Given the dubious quality of most "educational research", however, I am equally comfortable relying on my 30+ years of experience (several hundred years, if I add up the experience of the advocates and attorneys I work with) when discussing services. Without the right amount of services, your child may be wasting his time in special education.

Rather than arguing about whether there is "proof" of a need for increased service delivery, let's look at the private schools designed to meet the needs of children with significant language-based learning disabilities and dyslexia. These schools provide an educational experience that is often very different from the one provided in a public school. They are designed for children with significant learning difficulties, but they are able to serve only a fraction of the children who **could benefit** from their services, due to lack of space and high cost. The tuition is **up to six times** what a public school spends per pupil.

In the chapter on Placement, I listed the services and accommodations provided by this type of school. Even **with** such high tuition, these schools struggle to survive financially. Whatever remedial instruction they provide has got to be **the minimum** necessary for a child with language learning disabilities to make "effective progress" and be successful. **Because** they watch every penny, they aren't going to do **more** than is needed, but they aren't likely to do **less**, either. That's because they **have to ensure growth and mastery**. Otherwise, parents would not keep their children in these programs (which involve leaving one's friends and commuting up to an hour each way) and **public schools would refuse to pay for them**.

So, for children with substantial learning problems, the public school should **match** the most important services in terms of personnel, amount and frequency of service, and group size, in order to ensure "effective progress" for your child.

Remember—**the goal is to get your child off** an IEP. The **sooner** your child gains these needed skills, learns to compensate for his or her difficulties, and pulls his or her performance up to grade level—the **sooner** these special education services can be discontinued and your child can **stop** costing the system extra money.

Theoretically, you and the school system **have the same goal. Keep reminding them of this**, and keep pushing for the right services offered with the right frequency. The younger your child, the more **effective** a given service will be, and the **more often** they should have it.

It's just like exercise, as I said earlier. Daily is better than once a week. These skills are similar to muscles. Your child is trying to develop a new and different neurological pathway to use **instead of** the typical one that would be used for a given skill (such as reading). Establishing and strengthening this new pathway takes a great deal of time and effort, and daily practice increases your child's chances of success. It's just common sense.

Bottom line:

- Keep your "eyes on the prize" (your child's goals and objectives as listed in the IEP)

- Make sure that your child consistently receives the services you agreed to

- Monitor your child's growth in skills, emotional state, and ability to access the curriculum

- If you don't see growth, or services are not consistently provided—SAY SOMETHING. It is the **school's job** to improve your child's skills.

- You can re-convene the Team along with your advocate or expert, get updated achievement or psychological testing, ask for more frequent feedback about your child's performance, or ask your independent evaluator to observe your child's program, but know that it is **your responsibility** to monitor your child's progress and get changes where necessary.

- Your goal (and mine, as an independent evaluator) is for your child to get **up** to grade level and **off** an IEP.

# CHAPTER 11

# WHY IS A SCHOOL OBSERVATION IMPORTANT?

*"As long as one keeps searching, the answers come."*
*Joan Baez, singer*

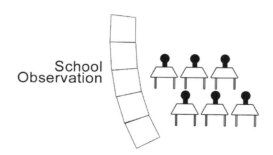

## Why parents should request an observation

Who would you rather have operate on you—a surgeon who'd actually performed hundreds of the same surgical procedure, or one who had read the medical texts and looked at pictures of the surgery? If you plan to take a trip, which is the more valuable experience—spending a week traveling through Italy, or just reading the guidebook? I'm sure you would agree that the first situation is more likely to be useful and informative, not to mention safer!

Unless we're talking about a blizzard or a ten-car pile-up on the highway, it's better to have actually **been there** and **seen the situation yourself,** rather than merely **hearing about it.** It's the same with a school observation.

As an independent evaluator, I am being paid to produce an accurate, detailed diagnostic picture of your child, along with focused, usable recommendations that will enable him or her to make "effective progress" and perform closer to grade level. Parents will tell me what they "think" is going on in school, but generally they haven't physically been there and aren't sure what to look for. School personnel will also tell me what they "think" is going on, but they are part of the situation. They have a strong vested interest in having things "go well", and therefore cannot always be **objective.**

It is **my job** to be objective. I have **nothing to gain** from reporting what I saw and heard with anything less than complete **accuracy. I get paid whether the school program is fabulous or shameful.** I do not need to "stretch out the work" by doing tasks that aren't important; there are other children who need my services. I don't get anything "extra" from either a parent or a school, based on my conclusions.

In spite of what some school's attorney may tell you, neither I nor other independent evaluators have a vendetta against the public schools. School is a hugely important part of a child's life. I want children to be well-educated, independent, capable thinkers and emotionally healthy, for the good of the country and for my own selfish reasons. Look at it realistically. Who's going to pay my social security or take care of the country when I'm an old lady, if today's children can't get well-paying jobs and think for themselves?

No, my interests here have nothing to do with "trashing" a public school for the sake of some warped power trip. I do what I do because the stakes are too high for me to remain silent. Without successful public schools, we are all in trouble. And **successful public school programs** will fulfill their purpose and **meet their goals.** They will provide the essential remedial or compensatory services so your child can make "effective progress" in the general education curriculum.

If the schools are doing their jobs, **I will be able to see it** during a school observation. If they aren't, I'm afraid I will be able to see that, too.

The real reason the attorneys roll their eyes when they see my name in a case file is because they **know** I will be honest. That's a scary thought, because honestly, the reason your child may be having difficulty making progress in school is due to the **programs and personnel** they work with every day. As I've said before, it's neither magic nor rocket science (with apologies to the wizards and rocket scientists out there!).

There must be a "goodness of fit" between your child's needs and the services being provided. I recently read an article about creativity, and one researcher said, "Suppose the person you hired to repave your driveway covered it with salami—that would be original, surely, but inappropriate." I laughed at the mental image, but the man had a good point.

In schools, I am looking for the parts of your child's day that are **effective.** Not the parts that seem creative or "new and exciting" or pleasing **to the teachers,** but the parts **that work to enhance a child's actual learning and mastery.** If I don't see enough solid "working parts" in a child's day, I know that child is not going to make "effective progress".

In order to be most effective in advocating for your child's needs, an independent evaluator must have three things: skill, data, and a backbone. He or she must have the skills to gather the necessary information during testing and put together an integrated "portrait" of your child. They must have all of the data they need for a complete picture of the child's learning needs and the services being provided. And they must have the willingness to say in a Team meeting (or other setting) what they believe to be true.

# Potential Problems

Part of the data an independent evaluator need comes from a school observation. This person needs to actually **sit** in the back of the room during classes, **observe** the teachers and the other students, **see** the printed materials and **listen** to the language being used, and **determine** how well this situation, as a whole, meets **your child's needs**.

In cases where there are likely to be disagreements with the school system, the psychologist needs to personally obtain this data, even though parents and educational advocates may have also observed classes. If events move beyond the Team meeting, to a mediation or hearing, this psychologist is going to be the one "on the spot" and asked to testify as an independent professional who is advocating for your child. It's the cake analogy again—he or she has to know what all of the ingredients are, and mix them personally, so he or she can be confident about what the cake will look like when it is done. It's a matter of maintaining professional integrity.

It doesn't matter what the school says is happening, or how well the other children in a class might be doing, or how qualified the personnel might be. It doesn't even matter if this program is better than what your child had before, or if he or she is "okay" with the placement. The **goal** is "effective progress" until the point where your child **no longer needs an IEP**.

Twenty years ago, I could call the school principal or the classroom teacher and set a date to observe. I would show up and the secretary would point me in the right direction, give me a school map, and say, "good luck" (in some big high schools, I worried about getting lost and starving to death; I wondered how long it would be before someone came looking for me!). I stayed as long as I needed to, saw what I needed to see, spoke with teachers briefly after class, asked questions, and left when I was done. If there was a class I did not need to see, I went to the library or the teacher's lounge and did paperwork. Those days, unfortunately, are gone.

School systems are increasingly worried about what I will see when I observe. They claim this is because observations "disrupt" classes and "upset" the students. They claim that observers have later said things that were untrue. As a result, scheduling an observation has become more difficult every year.

Some schools have wanted me to sign an agreement that I am not there to evaluate teachers or programs (this is nonsense, of course—what do they think I am there to evaluate, the cafeteria food?) They insist that I be accompanied by a "minder"—another member of the school staff—presumably so that I can't "make things up" that didn't really happen. For a short while several years ago, several systems asked for a copy of my notes when I finished.

Schools try to limit the **amount of time** I can observe. In some cases, I need to return for a second visit to see the necessary classes (in one awful case, I came back 6 times due to last-minute class cancellations or changes in the agenda, which meant I couldn't observe actual teaching when I arrived). I know they hope I will give up, but I can be more persistent than a toddler. I need to see what I need to see.

Schools also try to limit **what** I can see. I can't observe an individual tutorial unless it is for the child I am evaluating. If the child is not currently placed in the program I am observing, this makes it difficult to observe specialists to determine their effectiveness. School administrators warn me I can't ask questions of the teacher during class (again, this is non-sense; I have **never** interfered with a class by interrupting a teacher. I ask any questions after class is dismissed, when the teachers often approach me on their own, to see if I need any more information).

In fact, the only time I can remember involving myself in a class was the 2$^{nd}$ grade with 27 children that I described earlier. When they were divided into 3 math groups and sent to work independently, the group working near where I was sitting was confused and utterly clueless about how to do the exercise they'd been given (measuring in metric and standard units, a typically-unclear Everyday Math assignment). They asked me for help, since I was an adult, which I thought was a sensible thing for them to do. The teacher was busy with another group. I could either have let them sit and do nothing productive for the next 20 minutes, or answered their questions so they would understand what to do. I answered the questions.

Given the hassles involved, I try to observe only when I have substantial concerns about whether a particular program is adequate to meet one child's specific needs. In many cases, **some** of the services being provided are appropriate. **Some** of the time, the child understands what is being taught, and is learning. **Some** of the accommodations are being provided consistently. It is the whole picture that does not add up.

Years ago, I evaluated a child at the end of 2$^{nd}$ grade, who had already repeated one year. There was a family history of dyslexia, and this girl was one of the most severely dyslexic children I'd ever evaluated. She was receiving a daily individual reading tutorial from a certified specialist, but her progress was very slow. I might have accepted that, given her learning disability, until I observed her in school. In the regular classroom, she was almost totally detached from the flow of instruction and work. She couldn't read **anything**. She struggled to write much more than her name since she had no spelling skills or memory for words, and often she did not seem to understand what the teacher was saying. She mostly appeared to be in "her own world". She sat in circle, but did not participate. At recess, she wandered without talking to other children, though she participated nonverbally on the climbing equipment.

In addition to her dyslexia, her receptive and expressive language skills were so impaired that she could not participate in a meaningful way in the curriculum or even with her peers.

My testing documented her good intelligence, but also a great deal of underlying sadness. This child had "no voice" in her regular education setting, and needed a **much** more adapted placement, in which the language of instruction and the task expectations would be modified enough to allow her to participate and learn. Since the school did not have a language-based program at the elementary level, she needed an out-of-district placement.

If I had looked only at this girl's IEP, I might have thought she was receiving appropriate services. She got speech/language and occupational therapies, several times per week, as well as her reading services, and there was an aide in the classroom on a part-time basis. **It still wasn't enough.** When I observed for a full morning, it was clear that every single day there were 3 or 4 **hours** when she might as well have been in a foreign country.

# What an observer is looking for

So what do you, as a parent, get for your money when your independent evaluator does a school observation? In my practice, I only observe for children whom I have tested. Otherwise, I lack a crucial piece of the puzzle when I advocate for services and programs. How do I really **know** what this child needs if I haven't worked with him directly? If I don't have **my own** testing data, how can I say **which services or programs** can best address his problems with learning, attention, social interaction, or sensory integration? The answer is, I can't.

These are some of the areas an independent evaluator should focus on when observing:

- The size and composition of the class where the child spends most of his day. In a regular classroom, this includes the size and layout of the room, the level of background noise, and whether the room has areas for quiet work. It includes the total number of children and their needs, and how often the teacher is interrupted (and by what). What other adults are in the class, and what are they doing? What types of distractions are there?

- The style and effectiveness of the teacher. This includes how the teacher gains and holds attention. How structured is this person's style, and how well-organized is his or her classroom? Does the teacher use his or her voice effectively to support instruction? What specific teaching techniques are being used to introduce and review information, how multi-sensory is the teaching style, and what instructional programs (for reading or math, say) are being used. The younger the grade, the more multi-sensory the presentation should be. Ideally, children are **doing** while they are **listening**, especially when concepts are being introduced.

- The particular methods being used to teach reading and math. These will vary between school districts, and an observer will always want to see the materials and texts, ask about the scope of what is being taught throughout the year, ask how progress is measured, and how it is individualized for different children.

It is important to note the approximate grade level of textbooks once these are in use, whether they are well organized or too "wordy" and dense, how much review is provided at the end of sections or chapters, how new vocabulary is explained, and how often certain visual elements such as time lines, charts and graphs, and relevant illustrations are used in the text. There are some excellent textbooks in use, but I find a large percentage of them to be grim. Many texts are either poorly organized or above grade level in complexity, which makes them challenging for children with learning difficulties. Teachers often seem "proud" of having texts that are advanced, though I am not sure it benefits the majority of the class in terms of effective learning.

In early grades, it is important to look at the reading program to see whether it is "whole language" based or more phonetic and structural. How controlled is the vocabulary, what is the phonics component like, and what do the books at the beginning and end of the grade look like in terms of difficulty? What are the general expectations for reading at this grade level? Can the child being observed "make sense" of the level of reading, or will he struggle with decoding and comprehension?

In my experience, math programs in regular education are just as likely as reading programs to be inappropriate for children with learning problems. They are often too abstract, provide too little drill of basic concepts and facts, rely heavily on linguistic skills, and try to cover too many areas in too brief a time, leading to confusion and lack of mastery. There is too little focus on developing solid basic skills, and too much of an attempt to be "interesting" or "relevant" (mostly to the teacher, I believe). Your observer will be looking at the overall scope of the instruction for the year, and how well organized it seems to be.

- The extent to which the teacher is providing accommodations for individual students. Often, an observer won't be told how many children are on IEPs, but an experienced professional will be able to pick them out in a few minutes. What kinds of help are these children receiving, how much and how often?

- The language being used in the classroom. I have described what I consider to be important components of a "language-based class" in the chapter on placement. While an observer wouldn't expect to see this in regular education, at an elementary level they are looking for a certain clear, simple, and mostly concrete linguistic style. Teachers in early grades can't just "chat" on and on, without pausing to give children a chance to process what they've said. One instruction at a time works best. The questions and answers need to be part of a logical, structured format so children know what is expected. Consistent verbal feedback should be given.

With regard to the "format", some teachers readily "give" students the answers, so they never have to think for themselves. This isn't ideal, but I'm even less happy when they use the "guessing game" format (in which questions are presented in such a vague way, without appropriate parameters or lead-ins, that the answer could literally be **anything** and the children have to "read the teacher's mind" to get the answer). I am astonished at how often I see this happening. It does not, in my opinion, enable any meaningful learning and results in confusion every time.

- The extent to which notes, handouts, and other printed materials support learning for students. Here, one is looking for accommodations for children with learning difficulties—skeleton notes that they "add to", outlines of class instruction, lab report outlines, a review sheet or study guide, etc. What is the level of reading difficulty for these materials?

- If there is a special education teacher in the room, what does this person add to the effectiveness of instruction? You might think this is a dumb question, but if I had a nickel for every special education teacher who **did nothing** during a co-taught class period, I could retire right now. Most often, they stand or sit at the back of the room, listening. Sometimes, they take notes, and sometimes they "check in" with certain students during the class, but not always. In general, they **do not co-teach**, no matter what the Special Education administrator has said or what the class is called. They do not provide any part of the instruction during the class itself, other than answering a specific question from a student. They **do not say,** in front of the class, "let me explain this a different way" or "let's talk about some of this vocabulary". Occasionally, they will take a group of students to the back of the room to work, but this usually happens after the teacher is done teaching and the class is working in groups anyway (often on homework). If your child is present, how does this professional work with the child?

- If there is a paraprofessional in the room, what is this person doing (in general, and with your child)? In elementary classes, he or she may be working with one particular child (often one with developmental, emotional or behavioral problems) or may be there to assist a group of children who have IEPs. The role and effectiveness of these aides will vary depending on their training, experience, skill, and the needs of the children they are helping. Some are talented and essential for a given child's functioning. Others make little difference to the learning process. They tend to be used less often at a middle and high school level.

- If another specialist is in the room, who is she working with (including your child) and what is she doing?

- How do the children interact with one another and the teacher? Are there any behavioral issues that interfere with teaching? I'm always looking for examples of peer learning and support, and opportunities for children to use different ways of learning that are more helpful to them. Does the child who was evaluated seem to have relationships with other children in the class? What is his or her comfort level?

- What's it like when the bell rings and it's time to change class? How is the homework displayed and given to students? Is there a posted agenda? It now seems to be "trendy" to list the "major objective" of a class on the board, but I must confess I don't consistently see it being emphasized or taught.

- Your observer will often observe a specialist session or a tutorial, especially if your child receives these services. Here, they should be looking for the same elements as in a classroom—skill and experience, effectiveness of the teaching, composition of the group, whether the child is well-involved and seems to be making progress. They should also note whether there seems to be enough time in a session to present and review **enough material** for the child to make "effective progress", adding up the number of sessions he or she receives per cycle. One good session per week is not enough, if the child needs 3 or 5 to make measurable gains.

Ideally, your observer should try to see about half of a child's program, including one or more specialists and time in the regular classroom. If several subjects are taught within a learning center or substantially separate class (such as a language-based English class), these need to be seen as well. Most observations will take 3-4 hours.

# Public vs. Private Schools

What about **private school programs?** Is it ever necessary or appropriate to observe those, and how do they compare with public programs? The first answer is yes, I often observe private programs. There are a number of schools that serve children with learning disabilities, developmental issues, or behavioral/emotional problems within a few hours' drive of my office. Some are privately-run, some are public "charter" schools, and some are collaboratives or consortiums run by a group of public schools to serve a special population. There are also numerous regular education private schools (religious and secular), and I sometimes test children in these schools who are having difficulty.

Together, they number in the dozens, and I believe I have visited most of them. My appointment books show that I generally observe several times a year at the schools for children with learning disabilities. This population of children forms the majority of my testing referrals. Since I tend to see children who are "at the end of their rope" in terms of coping with their learning difficulties, there are times when I child I have evaluated needs this type of specialized, individualized program to make "effective progress". Sometimes they are already attending such a program, and I am testing and observing to monitor their progress and determine if this is still the best placement.

The issue of placement in a substantially-separate program was discussed in the previous chapter. It is obviously a big step for a family to make this decision, and is not easily accomplished. However, once the child is placed in an out-of-district school, for whatever reason, there is still a need for monitoring. Parents want to know that their child is receiving the necessary services in this setting to allow "effective progress" and the type of mastery the child will need to access the grade level curriculum—and hopefully return to a less-specialized setting.

So, I am often asked to observe possible programs **other than** the local public school, for **reasons** that are often quite similar. Once parents know their child's performance profile and areas of difficulty, they want to be sure the setting is the best possible "fit" for his or her individual needs. This would obviously include children with difficulties in other areas besides a specific learning disability, such as emotional and social functioning, cognitive or developmental performance, and attention deficits. Some parents choose a private school for other reasons, including special programs or an accelerated curriculum. They also need and want to know what is being taught in these programs.

At these schools, an observer will be looking at the same aspects of setting, instruction, personnel and peer group that are noted in a public school. He or she is looking for an appropriate setting where a child is actively learning, developing necessary skills and mastery, feeling comfortable and confident, and getting any needed service or help to support his or her growth. It doesn't matter where they spend their day, it has to be **an effective learning environment** where one can **see the learning** taking place.

Obviously, there will be huge differences in the **level** of instruction, and **how** the material is being taught, depending on the school's "mission". Most private schools will have a more homogeneous population, because they can "choose" whom they accept. For some children, this is an asset—for others, it is **essential**. There may be many differences in the **services or extracurricular activities** available, which are often chosen to meet the needs of the particular population (schools that serve dyslexics will have specialized reading tutorials; "prep" schools will emphasize sports; charter schools may have a focus on science and math, the arts, or accelerated academic pace; religious schools often emphasize a second language, etc.).

These differences are important only **to the extent** that they have an impact on the learning of a particular child. Parents can expect an **objective evaluation** of a school's program, and how well their child "fits" in this program.

One area of difference that I appreciate is the **ease** with which I can schedule an observation at a private school. The process could not be simpler. I call, I come just about whenever I want, I stay for as long as I want, and I see whatever classes I want. They sign me in and answer my questions, but no one follows me around as though I might steal the furniture.

When parents are involved in a dispute with a public school system about services or placement, it sometimes takes me months to schedule and complete my observation. In contrast, I can often do a full observation of a private program a few days after my initial call.

As to the second question—how do these programs compare to a public school program? I would say that **private schools** that parents pay for out of pocket tend to vary over a wide range. Some provide exactly what parents are looking for, whether that be smaller classes, a religious foundation, or superb sports opportunities. Others offer little appropriate structure or support for any students, a less-rigorous curriculum, and less attention than parents probably expected.

In many cases, the academic instruction is quite good, but this is not a given. I have observed some mediocre-to-useless private school academic classes, while (just as true) I see many public school classes where effective teaching and learning are taking place. No one program has a monopoly on excellent teaching, and I am sometimes excited and satisfied by what I see in both public and private settings.

Private schools that provide specialized behavioral, emotional, or developmental services also vary, in my experience. Some are comprehensive and superb, providing the consistent structure and feedback necessary to help children make healthy, age-appropriate behavioral changes. They "spell out" the desired behaviors and performance levels (both in classes and in social situations), and help children reach their individual goals through clear behavioral programs. The therapy, modeling and group services available are well-designed and effective. Other programs in this group are deficient in one or more areas, and don't support best growth.

School collaboratives or consortium programs are considered part of the public education system. They range from vocational schools, to programs for children with autism or spectrum disorders, to substantially separate programs for children with a wide range of problems, including low cognitive ability, behavioral and emotional problems, and learning disabilities. Public schools offer these as a lower-cost alternative to private special education programs. Again, I have found them to vary.

I have observed **vocational** programs that provided many appropriate support services for children with learning problems, but little in the way of remedial services. They seemed designed to "put a floor" under the teens, and "get them through" the program, but not to actually improve their skills in reading, written language or math. Having a good IEP may not help in this case, if the services are simply not available but the teen wants the vocational experience.

With programs designed for children with autism, spectrum disorders, or low cognitive functioning, the critical elements are the **peer group** and the **quality of instruction**, both **teacher** and **materials.** I have observed a number of these consortium classes, in a number of school systems, and have found the services to vary.

When I visited one collaborative (public) program several different times, to observe for an 11-year old boy with low cognitive ability and learning disabilities, there were many areas of concern. There was not enough individualized, supervised academic instruction using technology, even though the computer programs were available. Most of the children were much less verbal than this boy, leaving him without an appropriate peer group (this had been a problem in his public school program as well). They lacked his emotional range or ability to connect interpersonally. Overall, there was not enough direct academic instruction, even taking the students' cognitive limitations into account.

The social modeling, group sessions, and behavioral aspects of the program were handled by the regular education school psychologist, who did not have the experience to provide critical services to this group. When my client acted out in a minor way, he was disciplined as if he were a regular middle school student, which was completely inappropriate. He was asked to leave, and remained at home for several months before a place opened up in a private program with a group of children like himself, and a wonderful teacher. The only sad part was that it was too far away to commute, and he was very attached to his parents and siblings. He became a residential student, but I wished the closer program had been a better "fit" for him.

Schools designed to meet the needs of children with **specific learning disabilities** tend to provide the most consistently high levels of accommodation, remedial service, adapted instructional styles, and quality teaching, in my opinion. While not perfect, these schools **must** provide the highest standards of service if they are to survive. Remember, they cost a **great deal more** per child than a public program. They are vetted by school systems before a publicly-funded child is placed there, and they are scrutinized by these systems after placement—at least partly in the hope that the program won't produce sufficient progress and the child can be brought back to the public school.

Some of the finest examples of remedial services and adapted, language-based instruction have been at these private school programs. In each academic class and tutorial session, there was an emphasis on helping a child achieve mastery and automaticity, to develop effective thinking skills and strategies, to use a variety of templates and visual aids to enhance learning, and to provide crystal-clear explanations of concepts and facts.

So, there is no one "perfect program" out there, in either the public or private sector. But you knew that, didn't you? Parents live in the "real world" of jobs and services. What is a good fit for one child may not be enough for another, just as one job might suit you very well, but might not suit your neighbor.

You know you want the best program you can get to meet your child's needs, and **now you know** it takes monitoring to be sure those services are the **right ones** and are being **provided consistently**. In my opinion, the **only way** to be sure is to have an independent observation. If you are still debating the best placement for your child, this observation is even more important. The more questions you have, the more helpful this service will be.

The **primary objective** in any school observation is to ensure that the placement meets your child's needs **to the best possible extent.**

# What a public school may say

A public school system may try to cast doubt on what your observer has seen during an observation. Since he or she represents an outside, independent observer who may have concerns about the offered services, or who may not be satisfied with a given program, it is natural for school personnel to try to minimize the significance of their findings. Any experienced psychologist or advocate you work with should know **not only** how to gather the necessary information, but how to **present it** in an organized, clear, and credible manner.

School administrators will say that what is obtained is "a snapshot", with the implication that one should not be able to draw any conclusions from the observations. Over 30 years, I have not found this to be true, and my observations and conclusions are accepted as valid by hearing officers.

A few years ago, I testified at a hearing where the school's attorney tried to get me to agree that the school personnel **knew this child better** than I did, since they spent all day with her, and I had seen her only for an evaluation that lasted less than 5 hours (I'd also observed her in classes, several times). I disagreed, strongly. I heard the gasps of disbelief from the teachers sitting in the room. The attorney seemed a bit startled, and asked skeptically how I could say this.

I replied that I knew the child better than any of her teachers **because that was my job.** My professional training, the numerous tests I had administered, my reading of her records, and my own observations constituted a **far more detailed and reliable picture** of this child than any of her teachers possessed. As I pointed out, classroom teachers have to teach a large group, from 8-25 children depending on the class. The amount of attention they can give to an individual child is limited, often ranging from 0-5 minutes per class. I have documented this in observations for many years, often using my wristwatch. **Of course** I know the child better. If that were not true, **parents would not seek out my services**.

I'm not saying there haven't been problems. By now, everything that **could** go wrong, **has** gone wrong. I've been snowed out, of course, and snowed **on,** such as when I observed during a blizzard at a private school in Connecticut (I'd already driven 3+ hours and stayed overnight, so if they were holding classes, I was going to observe). I've shown up to find absent teachers, absent students, school assemblies, lengthy fire drills, power outages, student teachers taking over for the day, and classes where a test was scheduled (not much to see there) or a movie was being shown. It goes without saying that those occasions are not used as part of my evaluation of a given program.

No matter **what day** I show up, I'm going to see the important things, as long as I've arranged to see the proper classes (which is part of my job). Parents often worry and ask whether the school will "make the program look good" because I'm there. Don't I wish! If they could do that when I visited, they could do it every day!

In fact, I am not worried about discussing in detail what I am looking for. If schools read this and say, "oh, we should make sure this is part of our program", or "we need our teachers/specialists to be really competent in this area", or "the language-based program needs to include all four core academic classes", I would be **thrilled**. It would mean more children would receive the services they actually need in order to make "effective progress". My job would be so much easier.

I tell parents that schools **can't** make the program "look good" for the observation, because they often don't even know what I'm looking for. They can't "pretend" the services exist or put them in just for the day, like a "staged set" in Hollywood. In my experience, what I see is what's actually happening.

I don't care if the classroom is neat or if the teacher has chosen to do a fun project that day. The school can make sure a child has his or her services **that day**, but they can't make a teacher or specialist or aide look competent if that person is **not**. Language-based instruction won't suddenly "appear" in the child's class on the day I visit, if it isn't being used on a regular basis. They may sit the child at a computer, but I can tell if the technology is familiar and is being used on a regular basis. Unless they are gifted actors, teachers will not provide accommodations to a student on the day I visit, if they are not already doing so. If things are generally poorly organized or out of control, if no one checks in with a student or even talks to them on a regular basis, **I will see it** for at least part of the observation.

So, since I don't believe they can "stack the deck", and I'm pretty sure they won't read this and start doing all the things I think they need to do, in this chapter I'm focused on helping you understand **what** a skilled observer can get out of this experience, and **how** an observation can help you get the best services for your child.

Based on my experience, the teaching style of each teacher, such as the level of organization, modification of language, and use of visual aids, is going to be the same from day to day. The same texts and other concrete materials and the same ways of **presenting** materials will be used on a daily basis. The interactions between teachers and students, and those between the students themselves, are going to be the same. Kids don't suddenly "make friends" or "listen attentively" because an observer is there. It is easy to evaluate the quality of interaction between adults and children, because this is so hard to "fake". The skill and experience of a tutor or specialist will be evident, no matter which day the visit takes place. Even if a child is usually seen in a group and they show your expert an individual session, he or she is evaluating the skills of the **adult**. The overall quality of a separate class or an entire program will be seen at **many different points** during an observation.

School personnel may claim that children will not be their usual selves because there is an observer in the room. I can tell you one thing **for sure**—schools make my job more difficult by insisting I be accompanied by a staff member. Sometimes, this is the special education director, whom the children do not know, but at other times it is the school psychologist or even the vice principal, whom they **definitely do know. Those people** make them anxious, not me. Several times, schools have tried to give me **two** "minders", for some reason, but I refuse to proceed. It is impossible to **not** have an impact when there are **three** people observing—especially in a special education class with 7 or 8 children, or some tiny service delivery room with barely enough space for the child and the specialist. I tell them it's inappropriate, and they back down.

For years, I observed on my own. I would slink into a classroom like a ghost, sit in a corner or the back of the room, avoid eye contact or conversation with anyone, and attempt to be "wallpaper". I did my best to keep my head down, so the teacher wouldn't call attention to me or (even worse) introduce me. If she did, I would nod and go back to trying to be invisible. For the most part, it was very effective.

Most children ignore me, to be honest. Younger ones, 2nd grade or below, will sometimes come up to me and ask why I'm there. Good question. I tell them I'm there to observe the teacher, and they nod and go back to work. Sometimes they ask for help. If I can direct them to the teacher, I do, but there have been a few times when I simply answered the question because it was quicker.

Children with emotional or behavior issues will often act out more because my presence upsets the balance in the "system", but usually this settles after a few minutes. If it doesn't, that is diagnostic, telling me the child or children are vulnerable in ways that need to be addressed as part of their class and program. I'm then looking harder to see that the thera-peutic component is being employed during the rest of the observation.

With older children, in middle or high school, it's kind of like a startle response—it fades over time. They will often notice me and "look me over" in the first class, maybe even the second. After awhile, however, they get tired of reacting. They adjust to seeing me there and go back to doing whatever it is that they usually do. Most kids that age are more concerned with themselves and their peers than with adults, for the most part. I've actually seen some pretty **astonishing behaviors** in all types of classes, so I know the kids are ignoring me most of the time.

What about your child, if he or she is present? Well, they either recognize the observer or they don't. Your expert may be observing before testing (which is rare) or the testing may have been done months ago, and they only vaguely remember him or her. This is best. If they do remember the observer—and particularly if a child has been told this person is coming—it may take a few minutes longer before they forget he or she is there.

It is best not to say anything to your child about an observation, unless he or she is extremely anxious or reactive, and needs time to adjust to the idea that a different person will be in class. Unfortunately, teachers often "warn" a child that there will be an observer, possibly so they will "behave better" or "try harder". This is a waste of time, of course, but it does make a child more anxious.

In any event, the focus is on the adult(s) in the room, and the overall "experience" of the class itself. Your expert will not be staring at your child as though trying to read his mind. She won't be staring at **anyone,** or looking over anyone's shoulder, or inserting herself into the class in any way. She is merely wallpaper. A skilled professional will not **do** anything notable, and will not draw attention to herself.

The same cannot always be said for the school personnel who accompany your expert. Some of them are quiet and discrete, but others "make a point" of chatting up the teacher as they enter the room, introducing themselves and the expert (or at least the expert) with drama, and greeting any students they may know in the class. During my observations, these people have gotten up and walked around during class, asked for handouts or texts (I wait until they are offered, or the end of the class), and even offered help to one or more children. All of this draws attention to us, which I am trying to avoid.

This is one reason why it is important to schedule several hours of observation. Your expert needs enough data points, and may need additional time for things to "settle down" so the observation is valid, especially if a co-observer has a "look at me" problem.

When the observation is complete, your expert will have many pages of notes, since it is likely they've practically been counting breaths or noting the brands of sneakers being worn. The goal, to state it again, is to miss nothing. The information will be **factual**, as much as possible, and the expert will not be writing general impressions or conclusions (unless some-thing is just so wonderful or awful that they can't resist).

There's a reason I believe this is important. While schools in my area are not asking for copies anymore before I leave, the notes may be subpoenaed by the school's attorney if the case goes to a special education hearing. This is a service **you as a parent** have **paid for**, and my conclusions, my professional judgments, are therefore **yours.** I will certainly offer those to you when we speak after the observation.

If a school wants the benefit of my expertise, in my opinion, they can **pay for it.** Since they have not, I'm not going to give them ways of possibly making the program "just enough better" to interfere with our ability to get a more appropriate program for your child. This sounds harsh, but I've seen it happen. Schools can drag things out for years by offering new IEPs with some additional service that I've recommended or noted to be missing, while the overall program remains inadequate. Meanwhile, your child is unable to make "effective progress" and develop the skills he or she needs to access the curriculum.

In general, I do not type my notes up into a report unless your attorney asks me to do so. A written report will take several hours to compose, and I will need to charge for my time. Often, it isn't necessary.

The notes are available to you or any other independent professionals we may work with. If I am asked to attend a Team meeting or mediation afterward, I will provide a verbal summary of what I saw. If I am asked to testify in a hearing, then I will be asked by your attorney to not only describe what I saw in detail, but also to offer my professional evaluation of whether the program is appropriate. Your attorney may also ask for my observations and conclusions in written form to submit to a hearing officer before the actual hearing, in an attempt to settle the case. This is common practice and I will always do so.

These have been my experiences during many years of practice. Your expert may work in a somewhat different manner, and your attorney may request different things, depending on the circumstances.

The benefits to you of having an independent observation are that you have a detailed, unbiased, professional assessment of your child's program, and further insights into what needs to be added or changed to support your child's growth and learning. This information can also be used to provide real and concrete benefits to your child, if it is used effectively.

# CHAPTER 12

# WHAT IF THINGS DON'T GO WELL? WHAT ARE YOUR OPTIONS?

*"Education is a critical national security issue for our future, and politics must stop at the schoolhouse door."*
*William J. Clinton, former U.S. president, 1997 State of the Union address*

It's late at night, and you're sitting at your kitchen table staring at piles of papers. Teacher reports, school testing reports, private evaluations, IEPs, progress reports, samples of your child's homework and classwork, standardized test results—you may have more information than you can keep track of. Some of it you may not even understand. But one thing is clear, as you sit and think about your child: you are still worried. You have too many questions and not enough answers. You and your child are not on a path that will ensure success.

He is not growing and learning as well as you think he should, based on his intelligence. She is not performing at grade level, and can't do some (or many) of the things her peers can do. He has no friends. She is anxious, discouraged, and often difficult to live with.

What should you do?

What you do next depends on how far you have already traveled on the Education game board.

Perhaps you are only at the **beginning**, observing areas of difficulty and talking with your child's teacher(s). In that case, it might be time to request testing by the school or to find an independent evaluator. Deciding which to do first may be a financial decision, or it may depend on what types of testing you think your child needs.

If you are concerned about a specific learning disability, attention deficit, or emotional problem, then a neuropsychologist (one with training and experience in neuropsychological assessments as well as cognitive and personality testing) is who you are going to want eventually. Most public schools will not diagnose those conditions, so even if you let them do the testing initially, a more in-depth or specialized evaluation will be needed.

**Remember the rule: younger is better.** You want to know about any learning disabilities or other disorders when your child has a young enough nervous system to make best use of remedial instruction. The **younger** the child, the more you need a **comprehensive evaluation** that will look at all the possible causes or contributing factors affecting growth, and provide **the most accurate and useful recommendations** to ensure "effective progress".

Whether you have testing done by the school (for financial reasons) or independently, get the most comprehensive assessments that are available. When you fill out the school form to ask for testing, request evaluations from **every specialist** in the system. Cover as many bases as possible.

Perhaps you have already had **testing by the school**, but there are still unanswered questions. This can happen even if there appears to be a problem only in a specific area, such as articulation, speech and language skills, or fine motor/visual motor skills. If the evaluation is done and **you still have questions or concerns**, don't stop there. Get an outside evaluation in this area, which may well find difficulties missed by the school. The outside evaluator will also make recommendations based on **your child's needs**, not what services the school has available. This may be especially relevant with children who have sensory integration disorders, or fine and visual motor deficits. In my experience, I have found that school evaluators both under-diagnose and under-treat these conditions.

Perhaps you have had school testing and a Team meeting, and there was a finding of "no special needs". You may not agree with this decision. It is your right to request an independent evaluation. In Massachusetts, such an evaluation will generally be partially paid for by the school. I say "partially" because the state rate of reimbursement may be lower than any independent private-practice psychologist charges, because it "allows" fewer hours for testing and does not include all the tests an experienced evaluator needs to give. As a result, only some of the testing you want and your child needs will be covered (this is true for insurance companies as well). The evaluator may specify which tests will be included in a given battery, and which are not.

As I said in an earlier chapter, using an independent psychologist has advantages over a hospital or clinic, since you can work with one who will provide any needed follow-up service. The rules, fees, and exceptions may be different in your state, so consulting the state's department of education is advised.

Some school systems may try to limit what testing can be done, by saying that a psychologist can't charge more than the allowed state rate. This is true—**for the tests that are included in the bill sent to the school system.** However, you are free to contract with a psychologist for additional tests, if these are needed. Payment for a neuropsychological evaluation does not include academic tests, which you certainly want, or projective testing, which you may want. The important thing is to be sure that **your child is given all the necessary tests** to make a diagnosis.

If the independent evaluator finds a learning disability or other problem that is interfering with your child's ability to make "effective progress", you can give the report to the school and request that the Team re-convene to consider this new information. School systems are obligated to do this within 10 school days, and they generally try to comply.

There will be one of three results from this Team meeting: another finding of "no special needs", a decision to write a 504 Accommodation Plan, or a decision to write an Individualized Education Program. Whatever the Team decides, **be sure you agree** with the decision. Yes, you are part of the Team, and yes, you will hopefully have your independent evaluator or an advocate with you. That does **not ensure** you will get the result you believe is right for your child.

If you are **not in agreement**, and your child currently **does not** have an IEP, you have a limited set of options. You cannot **reject** something (thus moving to the next level of meeting) that your child doesn't have. You can legally challenge the denial of eligibility in a due process hearing, but this is a very expensive option. In most cases, you will have to "wait out" the school system until your child's difficulties increase, to the point where they are willing to write an IEP or a 504 Plan and provide services. This is often stressful for parents and children, and may waste years of a child's education.

Some parents hire an outside tutor or specialist to work with their child, making a decision to provide services even though the school does not agree that they are needed.

It's important for parents to understand the **limitations** of this choice. One potential problem is that the outside services may support a child "just enough" to allow some degree of progress. In most cases, this will not be enough for "effective progress", for a variety of reasons. Most children with a specific learning disability will also need support **in their classes**, which obviously won't be happening. They will need accommodations that won't be in place. When they are in school, working on different subjects with different teaching methods, or dealing with peers, or trying to access the grade-level curriculum—**they are on their own.** In most cases, the outside tutorial will not give them the range of skills they need to handle the entire day. Plus, few parents will be able to schedule services **as often** as their child needs. What may happen is that your child makes just enough progress to keep from failing, but not enough for effective learning or mastery. Meanwhile, the school system is "off the hook".

I would never presume to tell you what to do in this case. **You know your child best.** Some children are too anxious or vulnerable to wait; they need to see progress in their skills right away. Some **parents** aren't able to wait, or they make a choice **not to wait.** I just want you to understand the consequences of that choice—both good and not-so-good.

Unfortunately, many parents don't have even this choice, because they can't afford to purchase the services their children need. It is unfair, but the education system in this country is **rationed**, and children do not always get the services they need. Some parents are able to purchase some or all of the services or programs their children need, and thus "get around" the rationing.

I believe this is not only unfair, but it represents a moral failing on the part of school personnel and administrators, superintendents, school boards, elected officials in every state and in the federal government, and **all of us as individuals.** I believe we all have a part in this unequal system, unless we speak out against it. All across the country, children are being denied the services they need because of financial decisions made by all of us—by school personnel **and** ordinary citizens. I believe we face a catastrophe in the future, unless we find a more just and effective way to educate our children.

Perhaps the result of your **second** Team meeting is that the school agrees to provide a 504 Accommodation Plan or an IEP for your child. If so, then you and your independent evaluator will have input into the services the school provides to your child, as described in previous chapters. Once a plan is written, you can accept it or reject it, fully or in part.

The services may appear to be appropriate and sufficient to allow "effective progress", and you accept the plan. If **some** services are appropriate, but you believe your child needs more, you can accept the plan **in part,** and reject the failure to provide additional services. If you and your advocate or evaluator believe the placement or services **will not** allow your child to be successful, you can reject the entire plan.

Sometimes, parents accept a plan in good faith, thinking their child will begin to make progress and compensate for his or her learning problems. Then, at a later time, they sit at the kitchen table looking at progress reports, wondering why their child is still struggling or failing. They realize their child needs different services in order to be successful. When parents have reached that point, it is time to re-examine and possibly reject the IEP.

I realize it sounds as though **most of the time** you will be choosing to reject what the school system offers. It's a depressing thought. In my experience, many children are **not** offered the services that will allow them to make "effective progress" towards getting off an IEP. I'm sure that plenty of other children are getting what they need, but those children (and their parents) do not tend to be the ones walking through my door.

Once your child **has** an IEP or a 504 Plan, you as parents have a few more options. You now, at least, have **something concrete** to bargain over.

If your testing is complete and you are confident of the diagnosis and recommendations, but the school offers too little or inadequate services, and you've already had more than one Team meeting to discuss your concerns, then you can mark the "response" section on the last page of the IEP where it says "I reject the IEP as developed". This kicks things up to the next level.

Please note that I am not an attorney. I am not advising you to use my remarks as legal advice. I have worked with attorneys on cases for the past 30 years, and we have a deal—they don't test children and I don't offer legal information. I will tell you when I think it is time to consult an attorney. The next two sections, dealing with mediations and hearings, are designed to give you a sense of the "flow" of events, what some of your choices are, and what the consequences of those choices may be.

There is a third option, which involves a parent filing a complaint against the district for noncompliance with some part of an IEP, or another violation of the laws pertaining to your child's education. This is done through the state department of education, using whatever office deals with "problem resolution" or "quality assurance". I have not been involved in these complaints very often, although there have been cases where the family's attorney filed a complaint during the time I was working with them. I would recommend getting legal advice before filing a complaint.

By law, the school system needs to forward your child's rejected IEP to the Bureau of Special Education Appeals. It is a good idea for you to check that this has been done in a timely manner. The Bureau then sends you a letter, asking whether you would like to request a mediation or a hearing. These are **very** different paths, and in fact some parents pursue both. A hearing requires an attorney and can take many months to even be scheduled. A mediation can be handled by a parent plus an independent evaluator and/or an advocate (at least, I hope you will have one or both working with you), and is often scheduled within a month or two of the request. Some parents figure it is worthwhile trying mediation while also setting in motion the work needed to prepare for a hearing. Then, if mediation is unsuccessful, they are already several months closer to the hearing date.

A **mediation** is a meeting between the school and parents, using the services of a trained professional mediator to try to resolve disputes about services or placement for a child. Parents can bring with them anyone they choose, including professionals, an advocate, or a friend or family member. The school is generally represented by the special education director, and possibly others from the school Team. The mediator is an impartial 3rd party who listens to both sides and tries to facilitate an agreement.

Mediations take place in an agreed-upon location, often a school administration office or conference room. They generally last about two hours. The mediator may choose to meet only with the entire group, or may speak with each side privately, once or several times during the session, trying to help both parties find a middle ground that is acceptable. Mediations are confidential, and thus anything discussed should not be repeated outside the session.

This means, for example, that if an agreement is reached, parents are expected to keep the details to themselves, so that school officials won't find themselves swamped by similar requests from other parents. I know, and I agree with you—every child **should** be entitled to these same services if they are needed, but schools want to deal with each family **individually**, figuring many families won't make this level of effort.

If no agreement is reached, then the notes of everyone present are thrown away. Nothing said in the mediation can be used (in terms of a direct quote) in a hearing.

Again, this tends to serve the needs of the school system, since any offer they might make during the mediation can't then be used to "prove" that the school was willing to offer more than the initial IEP contained. For example, during discussion of options with the mediator in private, the school may offer to increase the frequency of a service, or even to provide an additional service (such as individual tutoring over the summer, instead of the standard generic "summer school" group). The mediator will then present this offer to the parents. It might be **part** of whatever service or program that parents believe their child needs, but not enough.

In that case, with no agreement, the case **may** go to a hearing, if parents pursue the matter. But the services **in dispute** at the hearing will be those **in the rejected IEP,** not anything more that might have been offered in mediation. A hearing uses the IEP as the starting point, which of course means that parents have to "climb the entire hill" from the bottom, regardless of what else might have been offered in the meantime.

In my experience, mediations have been most useful when the school system has already agreed to give the parents a car, and the disagreements are over how "loaded" it will be. If you aren't already **close to an agreement**, it is not likely you will succeed with mediation.

It makes sense, if you think about it. The mediator has no real "clout" with either side; he or she has no authority to force anyone to do anything. If you and the school are haggling over one or more details in your child's IEP or 504 Plan that don't have a huge impact on the school's "bottom line", the school may very well give in to avoid the much greater expense and hassle of a hearing.

Remember, this is all about **money.** As in, what is the **bottom line** in terms of finances? How much money are they going to be spending on your child, and how do they keep that sum as low as possible? In my professional opinion, this is the most honest explanation I can offer for a school's decisions. It is **not really about your child**.

Parents don't want their child pulled out of class any more often than necessary. They certainly don't want to send their child to a different school, possibly in a different town, and take them away from any friends they might have. They don't want to sacrifice a child's summer vacation if it isn't important. **No parent brags** about how many services their child receives!

If services and programs were free, or if a school could provide as much service as a child truly needed to make "effective progress" for the same amount of money as they were spending on a child with **no** special needs, **there would be no disagreements.** It is not ideology or research results or concern for your child that motivates a school—it is money. I would stake my professional reputation on this being true.

Over the past 30 years, it has become much harder to reach agreement through mediation. There seems to be less "good will" and more of a "hard line" attitude on the part of school administrators. I feel this is because of ever-increasing financial scrutiny of school expenses—especially for special education services. These services are getting more expensive, certainly, but there are also **more children** being identified as needing special education or adapted programs.

This is not the school's fault. In fact, I believe it is due to the failure of a **"one size fits all"** education system, that is **unwilling** to adopt the proper policies and technology to be able to individualize instruction for students, while at the same time **increasing** the breadth of what children are expected to learn. It is also not the school's fault that everyone looking at the bottom line is having a heart attack over the **cost** of these special education services. It **is** their fault, in my opinion, that school administrators don't **speak up**, and point out the fact that they can't be expected to "do more with less" forever. I'm all in favor of a "can do" attitude, but even the Marines aren't magicians.

What this means for your family is that schools everywhere are making every effort to provide services in the least expensive ways—mostly in classrooms—whether this is best for the child or not, because there is an urgent attempt by every school system to control costs.

As a result, I have found school systems less willing to negotiate "in good faith" through mediation. They are calculating that the next step in "pushing this boulder up the hill" is so costly and difficult that few parents will be able to manage it. They assume most parents will "settle" for what they've gotten for their child and supplement with outside services if they can.

Some of the incremental improvements to a child's IEP or 504 Plan that I've been able to achieve through mediation during the past few years include:

- An increase in specialist sessions, such as speech or occupational therapy, often from one to three, or from two to four, per cycle.

- An increase in individual tutorial sessions per cycle, for services such as reading or phonics

- Sensory integration therapy provided by the school, including classroom consultation

- A paraprofessional or instructional aide in the regular classroom, usually for part of the academic day, to support understanding of the curriculum and the child's ability to produce work

- An increase in time in the learning center or resource room, to provide support for one or more academic classes

- Commitment to provide specific accommodations that I believe will support a child's "effective progress" in the regular classroom

- Designing and implementing a behavior program to support a child with emotional difficulties, along with regular monitoring of the program

- Individual remedial services during the summer, often for 4-6 weeks, several times per week, to continue a specific reading or phonics program

- Payment for an independent evaluation

This is a far cry from 10 or 15 years ago, when I obtained (through mediation) outside placements in private special education schools for a number of children I had tested. I helped parents negotiate agreements for individual reading tutorials during the school year and throughout the summer, sometimes provided by professionals or centers that were not part of the public school. I also helped get several children placed in private thera-peutic day programs. Today, we would need to go through a hearing to obtain this level of service.

Parents need to be aware of the limitations of mediation, but there will be times when the process is helpful, and allows a child to receive enough services so that he or she **may,** with luck, achieve "effective progress". However, when a child has **substantial unmet needs**, and is making **limited or no progress,** or **is displaying signs of decreased function-ing (academic or emotional),** it may be necessary to consider the final option, a Bureau of Special Education Appeals hearing.

At this point, I tell parents that it is time to consult an attorney. I have worked with many of the best in the Boston area over the past 30 years, and I can provide a list of attorneys whom I feel are particularly skilled and effective. If you are working with an independent evaluator or educational advocate, they will almost certainly have such a list to share with you.

It is not against the law for parents to file a hearing request themselves. They can repre-sent themselves at the actual hearing, and argue for their child's needs, call witnesses, cross-examine, etc. It is not unheard of, but it is almost always unsuccessful. Even with my experi-ence as a psychologist and as someone who has testified at hearings, I would not attempt this on my own. There are too many legal requirements and complexities. A school system will be much less likely to negotiate a settlement, figuring that parents must have a weak case or they'd be working with an attorney.

You may in fact have an excellent case, and the real reason may be financial. Doing it yourself may be the only way you think you can get services for your child. However, I would urge you to contact an agency that helps people find low-cost legal services, and in the worst case wait until an attorney who will take your case pro bono or on a sliding fee scale is avail-able. You could also consult with a special education attorney and use him or her as a consult-ant, if the attorney you are working with does not have a lot of special education experience.

I do a certain amount of pro bono or reduced-fee work, as I think any person in a helping profession should (and as the attorneys I work with do). Unfortunately, the need is greater than the supply, in both disciplines. There are **many** children who need services whom I am not able to help, **even after testing**, because parents can't afford to continue, but I have to give you my honest opinion here, and that is that **using a professional significantly improves your chances of success**.

There are times when parents will decide to file for a hearing without trying mediation first (generally because we've agreed that it won't be helpful). As I said, sometimes the child I've tested needs such a significant change in services or placement that we are unlikely to persuade the public school with just my data and observations. The child may **need** this placement, and everyone may **know it** (even some school personnel) but the cost is too much for the school to agree during this "first round".

Parents need to realize that they are choosing to embark on a very different game, at this point. We are no longer playing Candyland or Life. It's much more like **high stakes Poker** with a very high opening bid (or whatever the term is for the money you put down just to sit at the table). The process of initiating and following through with a hearing can take up to a year and cost up to $25,000. This does not include any private school tuition or other costs that parents may have to pay up-front, if they choose to have their child begin in the new placement while the hearing proceeds.

The first "bluff" is therefore from the school system, which gambles that most parents won't be able to afford to sit at the table. Some parents have high incomes or wealthy grandparents or home equity to borrow against, and a few even pay for the tuition themselves and avoid the hearing process altogether.

I have mixed feelings about that last choice. In one case, I discovered that 3 children with severe dyslexia who were classmates of my youngest child had each been placed in a private special education school, with parents picking up the tab in each case. Part of me was grateful, as a taxpayer, but a larger part was outraged. These were children with well-documented, significant learning disabilities (they were essentially non-readers going in to 3rd grade, although they had received some out-of-class remedial services). In my opinion, the school system had **failed** to educate them and should have paid for the private placements.

However, as both the parents and I knew, nothing was guaranteed if they went to a hearing, even with cases that seemed this clear-cut. The school system was "playing the game", offering a language-based class in another school for part of each morning, which the school said would "meet their needs". It wouldn't, based on my testing and experience, but a hearing officer **might** agree with the school, since they were offering a change in placement.

The scenario could well have played out this way: the parents would be stuck **trying** this next step, **waiting** half a year, **watching** the children make inadequate progress, **going back** to the table to argue for more services, being given another "incremental increase" and having to play this out again, possibly going to hearing in a year or two, while the curriculum demands increased and each child's self-esteem was shredded.

The parents each told me they couldn't do it. Their children needed comprehensive services **now,** not two years from now. They did what they were able to do, and paid for the schools themselves.

I have a mental "data base" that I've compiled over the years, of the outcomes for more than a thousand children I've seen for testing and then followed, sometimes until they are in college. I am particularly interested in **outcomes**: how these children did over time. I don't have "double blind" data, since I can't take the same child and put him in **both** the school-recommended program and the program I think is best for his learning or development. However, with enough individual "data points", I can arrive at some conclusions. More important, I have seen the patterns shown by these 3 children throughout my career, in terms of placement and results.

One child attended the private program (a school designed for children with dyslexia and language-based learning disabilities) for 3 years, and then returned to public school and was (reasonably) successful with an IEP through high school. A second child had more persistent learning disabilities along with attention deficit disorder. He absolutely needed the small, structured, language-based classes in order to make "effective progress". His parents paid for the first 3 years, then went to hearing to obtain funding for middle and high school.

The third child also attended the private program for 3 years. Both he and his parents wanted him to return to public school, which he did in 6th grade. He received support outside his classes in a learning center, but no language-based classes were available. For 3 years, he and his mother worked at home for many hours each night, essentially re-doing the entire day's work so the child would understand what had been taught. Just for the record, this child had superior intelligence and a very strong work ethic. When I saw him for re-evaluation in the spring of 8th grade, he had not only made essentially **no progress** in reading and written language, but he'd lost 22 IQ points on the nonverbal scale, and was almost too depressed to get out of bed in the morning. The system had essentially "broken" him.

Needless to say, I **begged** the parents to get him out of the public school. They rejected the IEP and obtained funding for high school, in a special education program designed to support him and teach the remedial skills he needed. For the next 4 years, he struggled to regain his emotional health and level of motivation, as well as the necessary skills to allow him to move past high school.

So, the public school would say that the first child would probably have been "fine", if he'd stayed in public school. They would tell you the second child might have made "more progress" in the "more challenging" public curriculum. I would disagree with both statements. In the third case, I had as close as I ever hope to come to a "double blind" experiment, as the child went from an ineffective public program (3 years) to a highly adapted language-based program (3 years), back to a public program that did not support him (3 years), and finally back to an appropriate private setting (4 years). The emotional damage, wasted academic time, reduced skill levels, and impaired potential were **so evident** in his test results, it nearly brought me to tears.

This is not a game. It is your child's **life** and **future.** The thought of what these children go through as they struggle to get through school brings out an intense level of passion in me. I think of this boy, and many others, and I feel angry. My only goal is to be so persuasive, organized, persistent and knowledgeable that I will convince a hearing officer of a child's absolute **right** to a certain program. Over the years, I have often been successful, but I know it depends on having **a certain weight of data**, and being **very well prepared**.

Never forget that for school systems, this is a matter not of love, but of **money**—yours and theirs. It's basically a game of "chicken". Even when the parents have an excellent case, schools know only a few **will be able** to follow through, so it is to their advantage to be difficult. Who knows, you might go away! What's in your hand (the merit of your case) doesn't matter if you don't have the money to go "all in".

Of course, the school system can't play this game for free, either. It costs them as much as it costs you, in terms of attorneys and preparation. That is somewhat useful for bargaining. However, they don't have to pay any of their staff to testify or observe, since their salaries are already paid. Parents **do** need to pay for their experts, in addition to the initial testing and attendance at Team meetings. It is easy to see how this becomes a very expensive negotiation between a school and parents.

Filing a **hearing request** can be done by an attorney for the parents, or by a school system. In either case, my role as an independent evaluator would be to argue for **the best interests of the child**, who is my client. This would be true even if I were hired by the school system (which has happened many times for evaluations and even program assessments, but not for a hearing). A school system might file if they have offered what they believe is the best program to meet a child's needs, and the parents have rejected it, and they thus feel unable to provide an adequate education and help a child make "effective progress".

I can imagine circumstances where this might happen. A school system might offer a very strict behavioral program for a child with more complex emotional problems, possibly because that is the best they have available. The child may be too difficult to manage in the regular classroom. Parents might want to try an aide in the regular classroom, or might be unhappy with some aspects of the therapeutic program, and reject the school's offer, causing the school system to file for a hearing.

A school system might want a child to remain in a substantially separate class for the entire day, due to acting-out behaviors, autism or cognitive limitations. Parents might want more mainstreaming in the regular classroom, with a specialized aide assigned to assist their child. This would result in a higher cost to the school, which might insist that the child needed to be in the separate class all the time, and file for a hearing.

I can think of other possibilities, but I believe it is rare for a school system to be the one to file. In my experience, parents are usually the ones who file for a hearing when they cannot get appropriate services to meet their child's needs **in any other way**.

The law states that a hearing request can be filed if there is a dispute between parents and school system regarding: eligibility; evaluation; the IEP; placement issues; whether the school system followed the law in providing services; technical or procedural errors; and/or failure to provide a Free and Appropriate Public Education (FAPE) under section 504 of the Rehabilitation Act of 1973 (this would include a child's 504 Accommodation Plan).

In practice, the dispute often centers around **placement issues** arising from **an IEP** that does not provide sufficient services to allow a child to make "effective progress" to meet his or her "educational potential".

When parents first consult an attorney, he or she will review the case as it currently stands, noting the services that are being provided, ones that were offered and rejected, the child's relevant history, testing done by the school and by outside experts, progress reports, etc. This initial step allows the attorney to decide whether there is sufficient evidence to proceed. Sufficient evidence includes procedural violations; lack of academic progress; a significant "gap" between current grade level and the child's academic performance, or between cognitive functioning and academic performance; significant emotional or behavioral problems that are not addressed by the child's program; or a program that denies FAPE.

This initial consultation may be free, charged on an hourly basis, or paid for up-front by a lump sum fee called a retainer. I may have some idea of which method is used by which attorney, just as I know which outside specialists take insurance for partial payment and which do not. I will tell parents what I know, if they ask. Not all attorneys charge the same fees, of course. I try to match the family's needs with the right professionals, considering cost as one factor.

The issue of my fee, of course, is discussed with parents right from the beginning, when they call me to schedule an evaluation. I have some idea of parents' financial resources, and I am honest about what each step in the game is likely to cost, whether it is an outside specialist who doesn't take insurance, or the choice between continuing to argue with the school or just buying tutorial services to meet a child's needs.

Unless parents are printing money in the basement (which I can't really recommend), I need to be aware of what they can afford. I will need to consider **how best** to use their resources to get the **most services** for their child. I can't be emotional and say "this **should** be covered by the school system, or by insurance"; that doesn't help the child. **Results** are what matter, even if I have to hold my nose when telling parents the way the system **really** works.

Usually, I send parents to an attorney for his or her unbiased legal assessment of the merits of the case. Lawyers don't like losing any more than I do. The ones I recommend would never tell a parent their case "looked good" when it did not. I trust their judgment, and their knowledge of the law. They know what's been "settled" by previous decisions and what is still being debated. I recommend attorneys whom I feel are talented and experienced professionals. Ones who have been to hearings, and who know how to evaluate a potential case because they've done so on many occasions. I also know their track record, which **includes** how often they've been able to get a "good settlement" that avoids a hearing, but still serves most of a child's needs. As I will explain, this may be the best outcome, even though it may not provide 100% of what a parent wanted.

I trust these attorneys to be **objective** with regard to the legal merits, as I am objective about the test results. I may have **feelings** about the unfairness of a child's current situation, but this is not enough. Many things in life are unfair, but that doesn't mean they will all be corrected. I need information, facts, and a legal justification to proceed.

If you are not yet working with an independent evaluator or an experienced advocate, for some reason, but still want to consult an attorney, then I would recommend one of two things.

You could contact an organization such as the Federation for Children with Special Needs (or a similar organization in your state), the Children's Defense Fund, or the Disability Law Foundation, to see if they have a list of attorneys **who specialize in working with parents of children with special needs, such as learning disabilities.**

It is **very important** to work with an experienced attorney who has a track record of working **only** with parents on these matters. I do not recommend psychologists who have the reputation of working "for" school systems, in the sense of "telling them what they want to hear". There are a number of those in the Boston area; I call them "bought psychologists" and don't trust their objectivity. In the same way, I don't believe an attorney can objectively represent both school systems **and** parents. They have to come down on one side of the fence or the other. You are looking for an attorney who has made the decision to **represent parents and children** and fight for their rights.

You may have a friend, work colleague, fellow PTA or PAC member, or neighbor who has a child with special needs. These people may have worked with an attorney and can give you a recommendation, which is the second method of finding a good professional. In that case, I would urge you to discuss certain things before making a decision to hire this person. I would want to know the **amount of relevant experience** the attorney has, and **whether he or she represents only parents and children.** It's the same as when you are hiring an independent evaluator—you **really don't want** to have to do this a second time, because your professional wasn't up to the job. Better to ask questions first, and find the best person for your needs.

The attorney you hire will discuss the strength of the current case with you. He or she may think that a case is not "strong enough" to risk a hearing (and be clear on this: **there is always a risk in any hearing, no matter how solid a case the parents appear to have).** He or she may advise going back to try to negotiate further with the school, waiting longer, asking for mediation, or getting **or stopping** outside, supplemental services. He or she may want additional or updated testing, in one or more areas, or an observation of the school's proposed program by your expert before making a decision.

If the facts in hand strongly support the parents' case, the attorney will generally proceed to the next step. He or she will talk with me, to get my candid professional "take" on the child's needs and current functioning. The attorneys I recommend know my work and my willingness to testify, so that is not a concern for them. If parents are working with an attorney I do not know, things may proceed somewhat differently.

Recently, this situation occurred, and the attorney insisted on extensive preparation with me, to ensure I was going to be able to do what he needed me to do. We met 3 times in person, and had several lengthy phone conversations, as he laid out how he would present the case, the details of my testimony, how I might respond to certain cross-examination questions, and where the "tough spots" were likely to be. We had not worked together before, but by the day of the hearing we were an extremely effective team, able to read each other and provide the best possible case for this child. I was gratified when we won, and I will be happy to work with him in the future.

Filing a request for a hearing involves putting together a very detailed and compelling document. It will be read and considered not only by the Bureau, but also by the opposite side (in your case, the school system). The strength of this document can influence the attitude of the school system, and their willingness to negotiate to reach a **settlement agreement** before the hearing takes place.

The **timing** of a filing can be significant in deciding whether parents can see this through to the end. As I discussed in the chapter on placements, most private programs that are well-regarded for their services and success (regardless of the area of special need that they address) have many more applicants than they can take. **It is a waste of time to win a hearing if you don't have an appropriate placement for your child**.

Prevailing in a hearing does not mean your child automatically receives the services he or she needs. It means the hearing officer has concluded that the child is entitled to, and should be provided with, a certain set of services designed to ensure the child will make "effective progress" in accessing the curriculum. **The decision does not magically make these services available**.

If parents were seeking additional services within the public school system, such as individual tutorials or language-based classes, a therapeutic program or an aide during the school day, then the school will need to give the child these services, even if it means hiring personnel. However, many hearings deal with the need for a specialized private placement. There is no guarantee that such a program will have a space available for your child once the hearing officer reaches a decision.

Most parents and attorneys try to anticipate this problem, by finding and getting a child accepted into an appropriate program before or during the hearing process. This can result in another problem, having to do with money. Once your child is accepted, usually (but not always) in the spring, the school will want a deposit of several thousand dollars to hold the place. By early summer, the first part of tuition is due, often 1/3 to 1/2 of the total. This begins getting into serious money.

What if there hasn't been a decision? Parents can't be assured of winning, and could find themselves responsible for a bill they can't pay. Not all hearings happen in early spring. What if the decision comes down in August, or November? How can parents plan?

In many cases, they can't. I try to help parents work out a reasonable time-line to the best possible outcome. If I see a child for testing between July and December, we can try to get our "ducks in a row" so that the application and the hearing request are coordinated. Fortunately, I know most cases will settle, or I'd be in big trouble come March.

But many children are seen in the spring, when, as I say, "everyone's glue begins to melt". The spring is when many children begin really falling apart, and parents become aware that the current situation (whatever that is) isn't working. So, I often see children after the "window" of best opportunity for finding a placement has passed.

Each child's situation will be unique, however, and will have many more variables than I could possibly take into account. I've seen children for testing in May, found them a placement, and had the school system agree to pay for it, so the child could start in September. I've had an opening "show up" in the summer or fall, when the program had been full in the spring. In one case, with the public school's cooperation, a child was placed in November. Another time, I needed to do a re-evaluation at the very end of December and get the report out in 5 days, so a child could transfer to a more appropriate program that would take her mid-year. Such openings happen on a regular basis, but I can't count on it.

Some parents will pay the deposit and even the first tuition payment to secure a place and allow their child to begin the school year. If they prevail in the hearing, that money would be repaid by the school system. It's a gamble, but I already explained this game. Parents need strong nerves in addition to everything else.

At a hearing, we need to be able to show that the current program is not sufficient to allow "effective progress". If a school has offered a major change to the child's IEP, which the parents rejected, the parents' attorney will sometimes decide that the child still needs to be placed in this new program for a period of time, to demonstrate that it isn't adequate.

This can cause problems with the whole "timing" issue, if it means there is no longer a place available in the more appropriate private program once we are ready to move the child. It's not always possible to time it "right". Sometimes, there is no place available in a suitable private program, and we need to find an "intermediate" placement that doesn't have the full range of services, even though the school has agreed to pay for more. Sometimes, parents won't have the down payment and the hearing is not for several months. As a result, the child may need to stay in an inadequate program for another year. All these factors, and more, influence the decisions about **when** and even **if** a hearing request should be filed.

This next part is important, and should be reassuring to parents: In my experience over the past 30 years, **most cases** where I have significant concerns about a child's special needs and the program(s) he or she needs, in order to make "effective progress", **will be settled without a hearing**.

Because of my reputation and experience, a high percentage of the children I see are struggling significantly or failing, due to the severity of their special needs. Children are often referred directly to me; I rarely see a child "off the street" who is doing well (no need for an independent evaluation) or who is having only minor difficulties (parents and schools can generally deal with these). I see the ones who are on "life support": in crisis, giving up, losing ground on a daily basis. I see the children who **can't** access the curriculum, who **don't** have the necessary skills, and whose **learning disabilities** prevent them from making any kind of "effective progress".

Given that this type of child represents the bulk of my caseload, I've had school attorneys accuse me of spending all my time going to hearings to get outside placements. In that case, I'd have died long before now, of exhaustion! Of the roughly 65 cases I see each year, probably 20-25% need a substantially separate placement, either within the school system or at a private school—but fewer than ONE CASE actually goes to hearing.

School attorneys also accuse me of being "always on the side of the parents". I take significant exception to this accusation. I am **always on the side on the child**, and since I've built my practice on that ideal for 30 years, I obviously think it's a good thing. Often, it means I disagree with school systems, but not always.

A few years ago, I tested a child who had been placed in a private program for children with learning disabilities and dyslexia. The child had a difficult temperament, which seemed to be tolerated and even encouraged by his parents. As a result, he argued with staff and challenged them constantly. He resisted learning or using the specialized techniques being taught in classes and in his tutorial. After 3 years, he still hadn't "bought into the system", and his progress had been limited. He wanted to return to public school, where he thought things would be "easier". The public school program lacked some individual services (ones that this boy had actually not made good use of) but was otherwise appropriate. I told the parents I couldn't support going to hearing to continue the placement. This meant I agreed with the public school, though I'm not sure they ever knew of my honesty in the case.

**No one** involved in these cases wants to go to hearing any more often than absolutely necessary. Hearings are time-consuming, highly stressful, exacting, expensive and **risky**. There are no guarantees of a certain outcome for **anyone**. They are like the most experimental treatments or surgeries—a last resort.

So, if there is a strong case for more or better services (based on testing, observations, the child's independent class work, parent reports), we may well have been able to get them through a Team meeting (or two). We may have been able to use progress reports or re-evaluations to show lack of "effective progress" over time, and thus prod the school into providing more services. We may have been successful in mediation. And if not, we may still be able to negotiate a better program for this child **before the hearing date**.

Attorneys for both sides often talk on the phone, to discuss details of the case, or to follow up on certain documents they have requested. Both attorneys know how strong a case the parents have, who the major witnesses will be, who the hearing officer is. They can "figure the odds" of winning. They also will discuss possible offers from the school, and the parents' responses.

This process is not something that is publicized; I often know nothing until I get a call that the case "has settled", and even then I don't get all the details. They are supposed to be kept private—again, for the school's benefit. If they see themselves as "giving in" this one time, they don't want the whole system to know the details. Parents are instructed to keep the details to themselves.

Sometimes, there will be numerous offers sent back and forth, each one edging closer to what parents can "live with" without going beyond what a school can be persuaded to "give". It is nerve-wracking for parents. If they have some "wiggle room" in what they can accept, their attorney will use this to influence the final offer. This is high stakes poker, remember— but without the free booze and waitresses in skimpy outfits.

For example, some parents can afford to pay **some** of the expenses to send a child to a private special education program. Since the costs vary from around $35,000. (for a day placement, not counting transportation) to over $100,000. per year (for a residential therapeutic placement), this is obviously not an option for many parents. However, an offer to pay 25% of the tuition can sometimes result in a multi-year settlement at a school with the services and type of classes that will enable a child to make better than "effective progress". A parent who can provide transportation to a school may be more likely to get a settlement deal on tuition, though in many cases the district already has other children going to the same school in a private van, and the savings are not enough to produce a deal.

There are many variations on the themes of "shared cost" or "limited number of years" or other compromises, and a good school attorney will try to get the district to offer these, since they ultimately save the school district money, too. This game of "chicken" does not **always** result in a settlement. School districts sometimes get stubborn and decide to "make a point", or they feel they have the stronger case and will win at a hearing. You would think this would be decided rationally, but it doesn't seem to work that way.

While these negotiations are happening, there may also be a **pre-hearing conference**. This can be requested by either party, or by the hearing officer. It is basically another mediation-type meeting, with the attorneys present. The hearing officer will explain to the parents the risks of a hearing (as if they weren't already worried enough!) and make sure the school knows they will be liable for the parents' legal fees if the parents prevail at a hearing. He or she will try to resolve the dispute and reach an agreement, though there is little negotiating. In my experience, it rarely works during the meeting, but there is still time before the hearing, and both attorneys will keep trying.

In case you aren't already confused enough, there is **one other option**. When a hearing date has been set, the parents can agree to a **settlement conference**, which is run by a specialist at the Bureau who has both legal and negotiating skills. This person does not currently serve as a hearing officer or mediator, though he or she may have been both. Basically, if it works, it's similar to locking both parties in a room together and not letting them go to the bathroom until they reach an agreement.

The settlement officer has read the entire case. She (in Boston, this person is a talented, tough, smart woman with a great sense of humor) begins with both sides in the room together (parents, school officials, experts, and attorneys), and allows them to make their main points. Then she meets separately with each side, and tells them bluntly how she sees things—who she thinks has the stronger case and why, what she thinks the hearing officer will decide and why, what are the main risks each side is taking. It's "reality 101", and it's often difficult to hear when you have a lot of emotion invested in a certain outcome.

She also shuttles back and forth with offers and counter-offers, sometimes for hours. Everyone knows this is the last option before a hearing, and there is often more flexibility here, acknowledging the "realities" and trying to get the best possible deal.

So, once my testing is completed, there will be a certain number of meetings, observations, and negotiations with a school system. In all but a **very small minority** of cases (many fewer than one per year), the result will be an acceptable plan for the child, or some combination of a partial plan plus outside services and careful monitoring. If the final plan on offer is inappropriate or too limited to allow a child to make "adequate progress" in accessing the general curriculum, **then we will proceed with the hearing.**

Hearings generally take 3 full days, with the side that filed going first. The hearing officer moderates and guides the flow of this process. All testimony is tape-recorded, and the hearing officer also takes extensive notes. Each side has binders containing the documents that have been entered as evidence, by both the school system and the parents. These documents can be referred to at any time by any witness or by the attorneys, but one must testify from **memory,** not by reading from a report.

The hearing officer begins by discussing the ground rules, and "sets the stage" for how the hearing will proceed. He or she then begins taping and enters the official data into the record—the BSEA hearing number, the two parties involved, the date. This is a legal situation, not like the courtroom dramas on TV, but still conducted in a very professional manner. You should know that all hearings become part of the public record, and can be viewed on-line.

The parents' attorney begins with an opening statement, outlining the child's relevant history in terms of schooling, testing, medical issues, and attempts to meet his or her needs. He or she will summarize the parents' concerns, the steps they took to try to obtain appropriate services for their child, and some information about the child's current placement and performance.

At that point, the attorney will begin calling witnesses. Since I am usually the primary expert who will make a case for the child's needs, I am called either first or second, after the parents. Obviously, if you as parents have gotten to this point, you understand the importance of working with a psychologist who is willing **and able** to testify on your child's behalf.

A skilled, experienced neuropsychologist has the credentials, the relevant data from testing and observations, the expertise, and hopefully the ability to present a clear picture of your child's needs. He or she must also be able to maintain focus and composure, and "think flexibly". After testifying and answering the questions of your attorney, he or she will be cross-examined by the school's attorney. This can and does get nasty at times. It is this attorney's job to cast doubt on your witness' credibility, memory, credentials, and objectivity. It is his or her job to poke holes in the testing or observations, as well as the witness' conclusions.

As the primary witness, I know I will receive the full force of the attorney's attempts to discredit me. I need to stay calm and listen carefully, since there are limits on the ways I can respond and defend my positions.

My testimony generally runs 4-7 hours, which is another reason you want someone experienced, who won't wilt and who can roll with whatever happens. I've only had one instance where, after I'd spoken for two hours straight, the hearing officer realized the tape recorder had not been turned on. I was much less experienced then, and the parents' attorney looked at me with dismay. I took a deep breath, nodded to the hearing officer, and spoke for **another two hours,** repeating **everything** I had just said. It wasn't fun, but it **did** have the advantage of giving me a **second opportunity** to present my findings and conclusions.

The quality of testimony can and does affect the outcome. The burden of proof is on **parents** to show that the program on offer from the school system denies their child a "free and appropriate public education", and that a "more restrictive" setting is in fact the only one that will allow "effective progress". It is a high bar to begin with, and the views of a hearing officer can move that bar slightly higher or lower. There are lots of ways for a case to fail to "get over the bar".

Years ago, I testified for a high school student placed in a private school for children with dyslexia. This program was out of state, and there was another program in-state that served the same population. Obviously, the public school preferred the in-state program, which cost approximately half as much.

The parents believed that the specific remedial reading program used by the out-of-state school (Orton-Gillingham) was the best hope for helping their son, who was severely dyslexic. I was in a somewhat uncomfortable position, since I regarded the in-state program highly. In preparing to testify, I spent time thinking about why this teen might need **that particular program,** and not the one nearby.

When I observed the out-of-state school, I focused on the specific differences between the programs, as well as the ways in which the Orton-Gillingham philosophy was consistently employed throughout the school day. I was **so focused,** in fact, that the English teacher later told me he'd thought I **hated** his class, since I hadn't smiled at any of his jokes or reacted to what anyone said; I just scribbled fiercely during the entire class. I was startled, but assured him his class had been one of the most outstanding classes of any type that I'd ever observed. I just couldn't afford to miss **anything.**

After my observation, I agreed with the parents. Based on my knowledge of dyslexia and reading disorders, and my understanding of the different remedial methods used to help people compensate for specific types of reading disabilities, this teen absolutely needed this approach. There were also social and emotional reasons why this was the best placement for him.

We went to hearing, and I was on the stand for 7 hours, a record for me. I was the only witness that day, which was Friday. On the Monday, the hearing officer called the two attorneys into a private meeting and told them they needed to "settle the case". Amazingly, my testimony had convinced him that he would decide in favor of the parents, and he didn't see the sense in dragging this out any further.

I am not always so fortunate in cutting a hearing short, but I know how important my testimony will be. If I don't convince the hearing officer of the parents' case, it is not likely that they will prevail. That's not bragging, but it is what I have experienced over many years. I need to set out such a clear and convincing case, with enough **factual data** from testing and enough weight to my **professional observations**, that my **conclusions** are accepted as being valid. If I can do that, I will have served this child's needs to the best of my ability.

There will usually be other witnesses called by the parents' attorney, followed by the school district's witnesses. Each side is allowed a closing statement, and then the hearing is adjourned. The hearing officer must issue his or her written decision within 45 days, which must seem like an eternity to waiting parents.

If you've gone "all in", I wish you the best of luck. I know for a fact that **you know your child best,** and you **would not** have sat down at the table unless you truly believed your child needed **the services and programs** you've been fighting for. I hope the information I've provided has helped you play your best hand, and that your child will soon be on his or her way to making "effective progress" in learning and development.

# CHAPTER 13

# KEEPING FAITH- MONITORING, FOLLOW UP, AND OTHER PROFESSIONALS IN THE MIX

*"The people who get on in this world are the people who get up and look for the circumstances they want—and if they can't find them, they make them."*
George Bernard Shaw, playwright

*"It is better to light one little candle than to curse the darkness."*
Eleanor Roosevelt

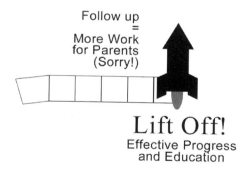

It must be incredibly satisfying for parents to know—possibly for the first time since their child began in preschool—that he or she is in a "good place", receiving the support, accommodations and services needed for appropriate learning. I know how good it makes **me** feel, and I'm just the psychologist.

However, as the Navy SEALs say, "the only easy day was yesterday". Yep, your work isn't done. As long as your child is in school (from age 3 to age 22, on average) you will need to **monitor** the programs and your child's progress. You will need to be **involved** in helping your child make that progress.

It's the same as when you **weren't sure** that the services or types of instruction were the right ones. In order to ensure that the current services will enable your child to make **progress** towards **grade-level functioning** and the ability to **get off an IEP,** someone's got to be "minding the store".

Programs change. Personnel and peers change. Your own child changes. This last one is actually the most important, most **positive** reason for your continued vigilance. If your child is improving, the **goal posts** need to keep moving as well, so growth can be maintained.

School personnel (both public and private) are often overworked. They are frequently asked to take on more duties or attend more meetings. Their attention spans are vulnerable. Their schedules are often less under their control than they would like. Even the best teachers and specialists can lose sight of your child's unique needs, or decide to teach a skill in a way that doesn't "work" for your child.

Remember the **triangle** graphic, that represents the flow of communication necessary for your child's effective progress? The sides have arrows at each end, to highlight the **dynamic flow** of communication between you as parents, your child, and the school. It is essential that the flow be maintained in **all six directions.**

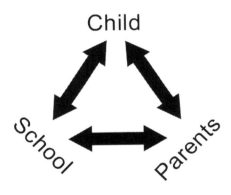

Flow of Communication
and Responsibility

Let me give an example of how poor communication interfered with a child's learning. Years ago, I observed several classes for an 8th grade child with severe learning disabilities whom I had evaluated. The girl was in an out-of-district placement, a school I considered best suited to meet her substantial learning needs. However, in one of the classes, the teacher had clearly gone "off-message". She was not using language-based instruction appropriately. She was presenting a huge amount of complex material without sufficient organization or visual aids, and was expecting the children to memorize this material. The children struggled with the quantity of information, the multi-syllabic vocabulary, the lack of cueing, and the expectations for memory. The child I had tested was near the bottom of this special education class in terms of skills, and was seriously overwhelmed.

As luck would have it, the public school paying for this placement **also** observed this class. The special education administrator came to the review meeting and was furious—in my opinion, with complete justification. I had planned to raise my own concerns during this meeting, but clearly I should have done so sooner. The meeting was a disaster, and the value of the entire program came under question by the public school. Yes, they wanted the child back, to lower their costs, but they did have a valid complaint. Fortunately, the department head at the private school addressed the issue, immediately and effectively, but for me the situation just reinforced my belief in the importance of monitoring.

This child's parents had also been "asleep at the wheel", which didn't help. Since the child's placement in the private program, they had given over all responsibility to her teachers, and did not even monitor homework, much less reinforce what was being taught. The child lost crucial opportunities to improve her skills while she was in this program, because she needed more practice to help those skills "stick" in memory and become fully usable.

Bottom line: the buyer (you) must always beware. Communication in all directions is key to maintaining the best rate of growth for your child. There is **no program**—public or private, to be honest—so perfect that it can't be messed up. **You know your child best. No one will be as consistently concerned with your child's learning and development as you are.**

If everyone who worked with your child **did what needed to be done**, you wouldn't be reading this book. Part of your job is to keep everyone focused and honest. Your child will not **magically** improve, no matter **where** he or she is placed.

Just as you probably mentally run through what's in the refrigerator on your way home from work, or who's got what sport after school, or any of a dozen other daily lists, you will need to keep "on top" of what is happening for your child, because of their learning disabilities or other special need.

- Make sure you know what is being worked on, in the major academic classes, tutorial sessions, and work with specialists. What topics are being taught and discussed in science or social studies, what are they learning in math and English, what longer-term assignments are coming down the road, what specific skills are being worked on with the reading specialist or occupational therapist?

- Do you see progress?

- Is your child happy? No matter where they are placed, they should not arrive home exhausted, cranky, worried, "used up", or confused.

- How's the social life going? Does your child have energy for this, are they making calls to peers, are other children calling them?

- Can your child tell you what is happening in class? What they are learning? Even a 6 year old can tell a parent **something** they learned in class, or demonstrate what they are working on in sessions with their specialist.

- What does the homework look like? There had better **be some**, or else something is seriously missing from this program.

Depending on your child's needs, you are probably working with other professionals outside the school system. It is rare for me to test a child who does not currently have contact with specialists in other disciplines. These professionals have busy lives, too. They need to be "stirred" regularly to keep them active and "in the mix" in ways that are most helpful to your child. Sometimes, this may feel as though you are herding cats, but the best results for your child are obtained when a team of professionals work well together, monitored by parents.

**Pediatricians** need to be kept informed of your child's growth and progress in all areas, not just his or her physical health. If yours doesn't want to know this information, find another who does. In my experience, most pediatricians want to be "in the loop" regarding a child's academic, social, and emotional progress. They are often the first to notice an area of difficulty or delay, in fact. They will notice developmental delays and problems with early academic or pre-academic skills (letter recognition, number sense and ideas of "quantity", hand dominance, attention span and activity level, coordination, etc.). They make referrals to other specialists and want to receive reports of any testing.

I especially like working with pediatricians who are pro-active and encourage parents to seek an independent opinion if there are concerns. Parents, in turn, need to ask questions of the pediatrician and **listen to the answers**, schedule follow-up visits, ask for referrals, and **share any ongoing concerns**, to make best use of the pediatrician's skills.

**Therapists** whom you or your child see privately (psychologists, social workers, nurse practitioners, and sometimes psychiatrists) are often a lot more helpful than counseling personnel in schools. This is because you, as a parent, can choose a therapist based on something other than availability. Doing therapy is not like making donuts, and different therapists have personal strengths, experience, techniques and areas of expertise that can be "matched" to your needs or the needs of your child. When therapy is provided by the school, your child works with the person who is **available** in his or her school.

If you are looking for a private therapist, you can ask for referrals from your child's doctor or other specialists, or from friends or parents whose children have similar needs. You can "shop around" until you feel comfortable and understood. As therapy progresses, you can expect regular updates, and you will be involved in discussing or changing the goals. Most important, you will be able to insist on seeing **positive progress** towards meeting those goals. In most cases, therapy is not meant to maintain the current level of functioning, but to lead to some improvements in emotional health or social behaviors. If there isn't any sign of improvement, then you as the consumer should discuss changing **goals**, changing **who** actually works with the therapist, or changing **therapists**.

**Psychiatrists** are medical doctors, and generally are the prescribers when a child takes medication for a neurological condition. There are times when the pediatrician, a neurologist, or a nurse practitioner will prescribe medication, or even a psychologist who has been certified in this area. Regardless of their degree, he or she is a **crucial part of the treatment team**, if a child needs medication.

In many cases, there is not one particular medication that would immediately come to mind as the "best choice" for a given condition. This is not like giving insulin for diabetes, or an antibiotic for a bacterial infection. Learning disabilities, anxiety disorders, depression, attention deficits, problems with behavior or self-control, social skills deficits—all of these originate in the brain. As I said in an earlier chapter, we don't yet understand **what causes** these problems, or how best to **relieve them** with medication. The odds of success are better than random, but in some cases not by much. There may be interactions between one or more brain-based problems, such as anxiety **and** depression, or reduced social awareness **and** attention deficit. In fact, if you consider the possible combinations of just the 6 problem areas I listed above, you end up with hundreds of possibilities.

Most children will display difficulty in more than one area. There will be several possible medications to treat each condition (not all of which are fully tested on and approved for children), and obviously a range of dosages. Individual children will respond better or worse to each medication or combination that is tried. There are lots of possible side effects. I'm sure you can see how complicated this becomes.

Parents often discuss with me whether it is "worth it" to even try medication, given all the reasons it may not work. This depends on the types and severity of a child's problems, but I try to give them a "reality baseline" to start from.

First, **medication** is almost **never** a substitute for remedial services or appropriate class design. Even if medication could **perfectly eliminate** a child's attention deficit or anxiety, the learning or language or motor problems are going to remain. Even a diabetic needs to adjust his or her diet, exercise, and stress levels to manage the disease adequately, and your child's neurological problems may be much more complex than diabetes.

**Never let a school convince you that all your child needs is medication in order to be successful.**

That said, I see many children who arouse my sympathy during the testing session, because they suffer as a consequence of their neurology. When I find myself **wishing** someone would give this poor child some medication so he or she could **feel better and learn better**, I always discuss the option with parents. I present it as the child being "out of balance", which is a different way of thinking about their child, but one that parents usually have noticed and agree with. I'm not hoping for a "cure" as much as "improved control" and better ability to cope with daily expectations.

A child who cannot stay focused, who is too anxious or sad to put energy into learning, who is bothered or upset by everything around them because of sensory problems—this child will have a smaller "window of opportunity" for learning each day. He or she will be **less**

**available** to absorb any adapted instruction, due to the "static interference" from their neurology. These children are often helped by medication, if the right type and dose can be found.

Second, even **if** the need is significant enough, it takes **time and effort** to find the right medication. Parents and school personnel must be willing and able to provide **feedback** to a prescribing professional, sometimes for months at a time.

In my experience, psychiatrists and neurologists are less likely to be active members of a child's treatment team, unless parents are very persistent in scheduling follow-up meetings and insisting that the prescriber "keep trying" until a child shows a positive and noticeable response to a given medication and dosage. These specialists are often considered the "best experts" in dealing with medication issues, but they may be too busy or too often unavailable to provide the necessary follow-up. In the Boston area, it can take **months** just to get an initial appointment, and many practices are full. I've also heard of physicians who prescribe one certain medication most of the time, but aren't likely to try different combinations and doses.

Since our knowledge of **what works and why** is still rather limited, it can be tempting to accept a small improvement as the best that can be done. However, I am not going to make excuses for these practitioners. In most cases, they are responsible for the size of their practice, and I expect the same responsiveness, flexibility, and high standards that I expect of myself, or any other professional.

If parents want to try medication, I will suggest several possible ways to proceed, and there are a few professionals whom I can recommend, if the parents' location and budget allow. We talk about the importance of **follow-up** and **monitoring**, and why they might decide the medication is not enough of a help. On average, half of the children I see are either taking medication or begin doing so after the evaluation.

Many parents hire **outside specialists** to work with their child. Often, this is because the school is not willing to offer a specific service for **the necessary number of sessions** per week. In some cases, the service may **not be available** at all, or the **quality will not be adequate** to address a child's needs. These services could include an individual reading tutorial by a reading specialist, speech and language therapy, occupational or sensory integration therapy, or a "process tutor" for a teen with executive functioning problems.

As a general rule, private specialists, even those working at a hospital or a private tutoring center, **have to be competent and effective** or they risk losing their jobs. School personnel have no such worries, once they achieve tenure. They may be skilled, dedicated and effective, or they may be none of these things, but **you as parents do not control the quality of service your child is scheduled to receive in school.** When you hire a service outside, in contrast, you can make sure your child is not wasting his or her time.

No matter who works with your child, or where they are located, **you want frequent feedback about your child's performance.** I am not talking about those wimpy progress reports, either.

- You should plan to talk or exchange emails with the specialist **at least once a month.** There should be an opportunity to discuss the goals your child needs to work on, to ask whether he or she is actually working on those goals, what type of progress they are making, and—wait for it—**what you can do at home to support the outside services**

- Make and post a **chart** at home, with the specific goals your child needs to achieve, who is working on which ones, and when the next check-in is scheduled. A "white board" is inexpensive and allows for changes as goals are met or changed. Be sure to include specific activities you are doing at home. Your child should be able to see and consult this chart as often as you do. After all, it is **your child's education.** Your job is to **help** him or her along the road.

Let's look at specific therapies that are most often offered to children with special needs. **What can you do at home** to reinforce what is being taught during time with the specialist? Whether **in school** or **privately**, the **one thing I know is that there won't be enough time in these sessions to ensure mastery.** Even a daily tutorial will not be enough to **fully remediate** a significant learning disability, unless parents supplement with extra help at home.

I know; this isn't really what you wanted to hear. Sorry, folks. One of my friends has a dish towel with a 50's-era ultra-perky smiling housewife on it, and the caption, "I'll sleep when I'm dead". It made me roll my eyes, even though I could relate. You don't have to wait that long, just until your kids are finished with school.

- A **private tutorial session**—this will generally be provided by a private tutor who works independently or at a private learning center. Parents often use these services to "top up" early remedial instruction in phonics, reading, or math, when the public school either doesn't have the particular program a child needs, or isn't willing to provide services as often as needed for "effective progress", in the opinion of parents or an independent evaluator. For older children, it is a way to get individual tutoring in specific areas of weakness, when the school's "resource room" or "learning center" may offer only group "support" that doesn't give your child what he needs. **In both cases,** the skills being taught or reinforced will need to be practiced at home. Use the "white board" to keep track of specific tasks (letter sounds, spelling rules, math facts) and how often your child practices. Make use of car travel time and flashcards, if necessary. For young children, using the same materials is a good idea. For older children and teens, the skills will be used in actual school assignments, which you will observe and monitor while your child does homework.

**Remember**—one of the few types of remedial instruction that the Institute for Educational Studies lists as being both **well researched** and **effective** is daily, individual reading instruction for young children with a reading disability. If your child is in this group, **make sure** he or she has this daily reinforcement, no matter what you have to do.

- **Speech and Language**—many parents will supplement what is offered in school, since schools rarely offer more than two, 30-minute small group sessions, which results in about 10 minutes each time of practice that is focused on your child (based on my observations). Privately, a child can have a focused hour of individual work. Some specialists are fully certified in one or more of the Lindamood therapies, that include remedial programs for phonemic awareness, auditory training, vocabulary or language comprehension. These are excellent if your child has a language-based learning disability (choosing the right program, of course) and may not be available in a school, on an individual basis. In addition, a focused block of time to work on articulation, vocabulary, word retrieval strategies, grammar, expressive language organization, or pragmatic language "scripts" is more effective than sitting and waiting most of the time in a group setting.

- **At home**, parents will want to reinforce and practice these skills, at least a few minutes each day. Play a game that allows your child to practice skills for auditory discrimination, auditory sequential memory, or language fluency, such as "20 Questions" or "I'm going on a trip and packing..." (an increasing number of items). Pick one vocabulary word a day and see who can use it the most times. Work on one spelling rule per week. Tell stories in sequence, taking turns adding the next event. Banish the word "whatever" from your house; when your child gets stuck, give him or her the time and encouragement to find the word they are looking for, and talk about the strategies they can use. What you do will be guided by what your child needs to work on, and I'd keep it simple, with one task per week.

- **Occupational Therapy**—here is one of my pet peeves with the public school system, the quality of service offered in this crucial area. Most school-based OTs are concerned **only** with whether a child can produce letters that are legible to any degree. As I tell parents, if a child has two hands, many Occupational Therapist will say he or she "is fine", even when that is **so not the case.** Their testing disagrees with mine so often (with their results almost always falling in "the average range"), I wonder if we have seen the same child! I am constantly arguing for more appropriate OT services in schools, often without success. School personnel think I'm nuts, but after 30 years of observation and testing, I believe there is a **clear correlation** between visual-motor and fine motor skills and the ability to access the curriculum. In many cases, letter formation is the least of my concerns.

- **I frequently see children who can't make sense of what they see, can't break down or re-integrate visual images or patterns, don't understand the idea of working sequentially on a task, are not accurate in visual scanning, and can't copy what they see with a pencil. All of these skills** have an impact on learning—by interfering with smooth scanning of print, or the ability to know where to start a task, what sequence of steps to use, and how to know when one is finished, or the ability to analyze patterns in math or maps in geography, to name just a few. Hand strength, trunk control, upper body coordination, eye-hand coordination, and basic drawing skills are also important. Yet many Occupational Therapists look at me as though I'm from Mars when I suggest these skills be worked on in sessions. If a child can hold a pencil (an extremely low "bar", in my opinion), the OT's work here is "done".

- Recently, I tested a child with exactly this type of problem. His skills for visual analysis and visual-spatial integration were impaired. He often "missed" visual details, mis-sequenced letters when reading words, and did not work in the proper sequence or direction on tasks. This resulted in problems with learning across the curriculum. His mother brought in a social studies test, in which he answered the multiple choice questions correctly, but was **completely incorrect** in answering questions that involved analyzing a map. By report, he had been studying the U.S. states and capitals, but his labeling of a second map was again **completely incorrect.** This child's difficulties were noted **in the school's testing** during first grade, but were not addressed. At the end of fourth grade, his academic skills were shaky and extremely uneven, causing him to dislike school and consider himself "dumb".

- **If I fight hard enough,** and basically tell the Occupational Therapist what needs to be done, I can sometimes get some appropriate service in school. However, I almost always want more, and if parents can afford it, I suggest outside services. An occupational therapist working in the private sector will **not only** understand my concerns, he or she will have **specific tools** and **exercises** designed to strengthen these important skills to support academic understanding and learning. An hour a week, individually, beginning **at the earliest possible age**—with follow up at home, of course.

- **Even without private Occupational Therapy sessions,** parents can reinforce these critical skills. Often, after an evaluation, when I am discussing recommendations with parents, I will give them a number of suggestions for improving motor planning and visual or fine motor skills. Children with problems in this area tend to avoid **certain types of activities** (no surprise here!) and parents may not even be aware of how "out of balance" their child's skills are. I suggest visual-spatial tasks such as solving mazes, doing word searches, Where's Waldo or I Spy books, hidden pictures, games such as Rush Hour (Junior) or tangrams, even the old Tetris video game. Start out with the simplest jigsaw puzzles and move up as skills increase; do them **with** your child, but let them do most of the work and **talk about** why it's good to work in a certain way. Children can practice visual-motor skills by tracing, copying, and drawing. The Ed Emberly books (look in the library) provide step-by-step pictures and produce neat results. Find a simple woodworking or other craft project that requires fine motor dexterity and sequential processing. Basically, **make your child use his eyes and his hands in a coordinated way to produce a product or solve a problem.** Oh, and he's got to use **a tool** much of the time; Legos alone or video games don't seem to do the trick.

- I am sure you can think of more games and activities. Just remember, if it isn't done on a **regular basis**, the skill is **not** going to improve. These skills may seem simple or even unrelated to schoolwork, but my experience has shown they are in fact very helpful.

- **Physical Therapy**—These services may be offered as actual physical therapy sessions, or as adaptive physical education if the difficulties are less severe. In both cases, school services tend to be provided in a skillful way, but you will need to be in regular contact with the provider to know what to practice at home. In general, these are gross motor coordination and motor planning skills, the ones needed for throwing, kicking, running, balance, and performing a sequence of motor movements. Depending on the degree of motor system involvement, services will be provided 1-4 times per week. Obviously, a child who has a degree of cerebral palsy or other paralysis will need more service than one who is awkward or "clumsy" on the playground.

- **Reinforcing** skills can often be done with low-key but regular practice, such as jogging around the block with your child, tossing a ball at a target (beanbags or a Velcro game might work), or going to a playground with a variety of equipment if they are young enough. Many children benefit from being enrolled in one or more **individual** activities that develop skills **at the child's own pace.** These include swimming, yoga, martial arts, tennis, track, non-competitive gymnastics, figure skating or hockey (if your child can tolerate falling down a lot at first), or a small, supportive dance class that doesn't care if your child ever auditions for the Nutcracker. The idea is to allow your child to practice and repeat certain gross motor actions and sequences, to improve neurological functioning, and to gain confidence, working at his or her own pace. Remember—**you know your child best.** Find the sports that suit your child's interests, and make sure they are not judged in a competitive manner. You want to see improved skills, and in fact I've seen cases in which an awkward child became a better-than-average athlete over the years, as a result of determination and practice. Also, for a child with motor weaknesses, **being involved in at least one athletic activity should not be an option**, but a part of their educational program. It's **the same as** working with a reading specialist if a child has a reading disability.

- **Sensory Integration Therapy**—Your child may be diagnosed with a sensory integration disorder, which you as parents were probably aware of in early childhood. Problems with absorbing and filtering sensory input will affect all parts of a child's day, both at home and in school. I've briefly outlined the signs of sensory integration disorder in earlier chapters, but I would recommend a book in the appendix for more detailed information. Once a school recognizes this issue, they may or may not offer sensory integration services. Many school systems do not have the necessary specialized equipment, which is expensive. The service providers are usually occupational therapists, who, as I have noted, are generally over-scheduled and **inclined to under-treat** a child's difficulties. Also, recognizing and diagnosing these problems has increased in recent years, so schools are still "catching up" in terms of even having appropriately-trained personnel. Although a sensory disorder will affect your child across the school day, in nearly every area, the services offered will often not be enough to **re-organize or "re-teach" the nervous system so it is less reactive**.

- I almost always recommend **outside services** if at all possible, even when school services are offered. I have seen much better results with private therapy, though I must add that **consistent follow-through** and reinforcement at home is **required** for growth. Unless your child is seen for SI services **every day**, you will need to ensure this level of practice. It's like "going to the gym" for your child's brain, and he or she needs the stimulation every day, especially if they are under age 10.

- Whatever the sensory integration therapist is working on, that's what you need to work on at home. Deep-pressure, skin brushing, weight-bearing tasks, vestibular system stimulators such as swinging, and other physical actions often need to be done daily. Specific cognitive strategies to improve tolerance of noise, smells, bright lights, or tastes can be practiced at home.

- The **cognitive strategies** are particularly important, to teach your child to **recognize** when he or she is becoming overwhelmed, and then to use a **spoken request or concrete strategy** to reduce stimulation **in socially acceptable ways**. In many cases, children with sensory integration problems are seen as "inflexible", which affects their relationships with peers, teachers, and parents. You can play "what if" games with your child, and explore his or her possible reactions when feeling overwhelmed (you could run away, you could hit the other child- not such good options; you could ask a teacher for a time out or move to a quiet part of the classroom- better options). This is a weakness that your child will need to deal with forever; the sooner he or she develops effective strategies to manage the condition, the better overall "quality of life" and social success he or she will have.

- **Attention Deficit Disorder, with or without Hyperactivity**—This, as much as any neurological condition, will need to be managed throughout your child's life. Like Type-1 Diabetes, it does not go away, and it affects every part of your child's day. School systems tend to have limited options to help children with ADD or ADHD, since a typical day revolves around group instruction, being able to tolerate waiting (in line or for a teacher's attention) or tolerate being bored, being able to persist with tasks that may not be particularly interesting, "tuning in" to listen when something important is being said (without advance warning), and "paying attention" to stuff a teacher thinks is important (even if the child doesn't). Schools need children to tolerate and be successful under these conditions, since they can't offer individual instruction. The format of school is not the best environment for a child with reduced attention, which is why school systems recommend medication. In many cases, I agree, but only as **one** of a list of interventions.

- **Accommodations** to help students with ADD/ADHD deal with academic expectations have been discussed in an earlier chapter. Assuming your child does not have another type of learning disability, these accommodations will enhance learning and success in school. **It is extremely important for parents to have regular contact with a teacher or other liaison who sees your child every day, to monitor your child's performance.** I recommend a weekly check-in, by phone or email or a short written summary. You want to know **what was expected, what got done and what did not, and what's coming up soon.** Parents need a **list of accommodations** the school has agreed to provide, posted in a visible place. Refer to the list when exchanging feedback with your child's teacher. If there was a problem with your child's perform-ance, was a certain accommodation used, or not? If not, why not? What can be done to correct the problem next week? Get this stuff **in writing,** possibly in a communication book. Add to it each week, so you have an ongoing record.

- It is **the school's job** to provide appropriate supports and help to your child with ADD, so that he or she can be more consistently successful. It is **your job** to check on **how well** this is being done, week after week. It's not quite like scrubbing the bath-room with a toothbrush, but it's close, which is why schools and parents may try to "wiggle out" of doing it consistently. **Try to hang in there**—it won't last forever, and your child **will** get better over time. Adult **consistency** and child **self-awareness** are your goals.

- In terms of following up at home, you probably already have books about helping your child with ADD or ADHD. I've listed several in the appendix, and they all have more lists of things that parents can do than there are minutes in a day. The most helpful ways of adapting your household to meet your child's needs, in my experience, are increased consistency, advance planning, lots of visual reminders and check lists, set-ting time limits, having very clear expectations, and helping your child learn cognitive strategies to increase self-awareness and planning skills.

- This last one is probably the most important, because **this is your child's life and your child's problem.** Eventually, children move out and live on their own as adults, and will have to manage their ADD symptoms in college, work, and relationships. By then, it often appears as an "executive functioning disorder". There are excellent coaches and "process tutors" who can work with your child in this area beginning in the early teens, developing compensatory skills and strategies. I highly recommend them because they put the responsibility where it **needs to be**, and offer **concrete, usable ways** of coping with the effects of this neurological condition.

- One last note for parents—follow-through for ADD and ADHD includes monitoring your child's diet, sleep, physical exercise and social relationships, all of which suffer with this condition. While they are young, you will do it, but teach them to be self-aware and to take responsibility as soon as you can (teenagers **won't** do what you tell them, but they **will often** make good choices if they're already in the habit and notice that they feel better as a result). To put it simply, in my experience these children need to eat protein every few hours, to minimize sugar, to get tons of sleep, and to do some kind of aerobic exercise as many days as possible. Some parents I know shut down all electronics in the house at a certain time, and carry cheese sticks and a jump rope in their cars at all times (really!).

This is not an exhaustive list, though it may seem overwhelming. No **single child** will have all these areas of difficulty or need all these outside services. The ideas are meant to guide your thinking as you work with a specialist to reinforce your child's learning. The spe-cialist may have other suggestions or ideas that better fit with your child's needs. Be creative and think outside the box, but **please** make supporting the specialist services part of your schedule.

What about the **specialized academic services** your child receives **in school**? What should a parent be doing to reinforce and increase the effectiveness of **remedial or tutorial services**? Does it matter whether the services seem adequate or not? Should a parent let the school handle the special education part of a child's education?

Answering the last question is easy—no. School is short. One hundred eighty days is approximately **half the year**. A public school day is approximately 6 ½ hours. If you subtract time to get settled between subjects, mealtime, recess, assemblies, specials such as art and gym, and "waiting around time", the **actual instructional time per school day in elementary school averages 4 hours,** which could be considered as **2 hours per day over the course of an entire year.** Based on my observations, that's an upper limit. In middle and high school, it may be slightly more, if you assume 5 academic subjects per day and continuous instruction during each of those classes (a pretty rosy assumption). It's not enough time for children who have no learning difficulties (just look at the international test scores). For children **with** learning disabilities, it's **a completely inadequate amount of time.**

One of these days, we adults will realize that children wake up each and every morning ready to learn, eager to learn, and needing to learn. We will acknowledge that for children, school is their **job.** We will give them the amount of instruction they need on a yearly basis to master a demanding academic curriculum and to develop the skills necessary for the jobs they will want to do as adults. If adults were only productive an average of 2 hours per day, what would become of us? Why do we keep assuming that children can do what we could not—that they can master all the needed skills in ¼ of a working day, with too little adapted instruction and "no say" in what they even work on? Does it really "make sense" for a gifted reader to have to sit through a grade-level reading group, when what she needs to work on is her social skills or her coordination? When that 2 hours per day is pitched to the "average learner", **many children** are left behind.

If your child receives **specialized instruction** in one or more academic areas, designed to help them make "effective progress" and "access the curriculum" to the extent of their "cognitive potential", **you had better be prepared to help.** In this, as with specialist services, parents need to consistently review, practice and help a child develop automaticity in skills.

Time to add some more items to the "white board". What **exactly** is your child working on in her out-of-class remedial sessions or her special education class? What are the **goals** for each session? Based on the previous chapter on monitoring, you may already have this list of goals and objectives to measure progress. Now, where is your child getting **stuck**? What doesn't he **understand**?

You will find this out by **asking the person** providing these academic services, using whatever method of getting **regular feedback** works best for both of you. Phone, email, and a communication book are all good. There may be one person, or half a dozen, but you **must** have direct contact on a monthly basis with **each person who works with your child**, not just a "he's doing fine" provided by a liaison.

If your child attends a special education private placement, the progress reports will be far more detailed and quantitative. You **still** need to know what to be working on. If your child is able to tell you, that's great, but confirm what he or she says by communicating with the special education teacher or tutor. If they **don't agree,** have them meet and talk until they do. You need a clear answer to the question, "what can I do to help?", to make the best use of your time at home with your child.

Through 8th grade, the majority of homework should consist of review and practice, in my opinion. If it doesn't, why not? If regular homework isn't coming home, why not? There should be **something** concrete to review every night, and a certain amount of time being spent on this review. Given the limited teaching that occurs in most classes, teachers should be **making use** of home hours to the fullest extent possible.

I don't have a problem with homework that consists of reading a book or a text and answering questions, or working on a report or a longer-term project. I do expect to see more of this in grades 5 through 8, **in addition to** reviewing basic skills. In the earlier grades, there should be much more practice of foundation skills, so that these basics are firmly established. If your child receives **special education instruction or tutoring** (some type of pull-out service) in one of the basic skill areas (phonics or decoding, reading fluency and accuracy, comprehension, spelling, writing, arithmetic, math problem solving, or memorization), I expect some type of review task to be done each night to help solidify what is being taught.

The more a skill is **practiced,** the more likely it is to become automatic. The more **automatic** a skill becomes, the more it can be used to support learning complex, grade level material. The higher the grade, the more complex material will be presented. So, you help your child best by helping them **practice.**

Please note, I believe that flexible thinking, independent problem solving, and creativity in all disciplines are **essential** to produce a **fully educated** young adult. However, I also believe that unless there is true **mastery** in reading, math, and written language, most of those higher-level skills will not be developed or expressed. There's got to be a foundation, or the upper stories will collapse.

What do you need to do with your child, five or six times per week?

- Elementary age (kindergarten through grade 3): 15-30 minutes of something that looks like "school work". Practice phonics or word recognition or math facts using flashcards (yes, it works, and no, your child's creativity will not be stunted). Work on their goals, whatever they are. Review what they've done in their tutorial, using the same materials if possible. Have them read to you if that's an area of need (perhaps while you make dinner)—and always talk about **what** they've read. Play a game or do an activity (or some writing) to work on fine motor, visual motor, or sensory integration skills. If there is a social or emotional goal, figure out how to practice this with an adult or another child (siblings can be used as "helpers" with your supervision, and a treat for the helper). Organize what came home from school, and what needs to go back. Show your child this organization. Set a timer if you like, and then **use the white board to record what your child practiced.** Children **love** to see their progress, and signs of their **effort.** Use different colors and make it look snazzy!

- One parent I know uses simple round colored magnets (available from Target or Staples) and labels each color with a task to be completed (R for reading, M for math, S for sports, Sh for taking a shower, P for piano, etc) and puts them on one side of a tape strip on the refrigerator. There are a certain number of each, depending on how often the tasks are to be done each week. The child moves the magnet to the other side of the tape after the task is completed. If the child needs to read 5 times per week, for example, there are 5 magnets labeled R. The plus here is that your child can immediately see what **needs** to be done and what **has** been done on a weekly basis. If something is skipped one night, your child can see that it's Wednesday and there are still 4 R magnets left, helping them plan their time. It also helps your child to take "ownership" of the home tasks that are needed to solidify their skills, which is just as important as the skills themselves.

- Upper elementary (grades 4 and 5): 30-45 minutes of practice and review, some of which can be done independently if that is consistent with your child's goals. For example, "reading muscles" are developed by reading silently; better concentration skills are developed by sticking with a practice drill for an increasing amount of time without constant monitoring or reminders. You can use a timer, but **you must be sitting in the same room with your child.** At this age, a child with a learning disability still needs structure and direct supervision—not to mention the emotional support—from a parent while working. Your child will likely have more skills to practice now: spelling rules, decoding rules, fluency, proofreading written work, remembering more math facts and how to do more complex arithmetic. Keep your child's **goals** in mind (both for academic growth and for extra services such as speech or OT) and make sure you are getting the appropriate materials to practice each night.

If your elementary age child is substantially behind grade level, don't be tempted to work longer than an hour. You can break your practice up into "chunks" of time, if necessary, but be sure your child is **fully engaged** and **knows what he or she is working on. If it never seems as though you're doing enough, your child probably needs more individualized instruction than he or she is receiving.**

**Consistency** matters a lot. A productive 20 minutes each night is better than struggling for 2 hours one night, then skipping the next 3. This practice should not "take over" your life, but if you are reading this book, then your child's education is clearly one of your priorities. Helping him or her make "effective progress" by working on the special education goals is the best way to help.

Often, a child in elementary school will receive services outside the classroom while the rest of the class is doing some other academic work. It may not be possible to schedule services so your child misses only art or library, for example. However, your child should not generally be responsible for doing work that was assigned or taught while he or she was out of the room. This leads to confusion, overload, and a very unhappy child. Be sure the specialist and the classroom teacher have **agreed** on what work your child is responsible for.

If your child's special education services **overlap most of** or **replace** an entire subject, such as language arts, reading, or math, then the special educator should be responsible for instruction, homework, and progress **in that subject.** The work coming home for you to practice and review **should come from this specialist.** Keep it clear in your own mind, or sure as anything your child will be confused.

- Be sure to **continue using a chart** or white board to monitor your child's efforts and growth on a daily basis. Children in upper elementary are **much more aware** of their areas of deficiency. They are more sensitive and may get negative feedback from peers. Academic and classroom expectations are increasing, and they may feel they will never "catch up". They need you to point out all the areas in which they are making progress—and these will surely be visible if your child is practicing each night. Encourage your child to mark the board himself, to celebrate his efforts and achievements, even if all he did was sit beside another child at lunch and make conversation. Remember, if it's listed as a **goal,** your child should **know what it is** and be **working on it**.

- Children in middle school (6th through 8th grades) will have a much more diverse set of assignments, which makes it **even more important** for you to use **a concrete organizer**. The same principle rules apply. You will need to know what your child is working on (**goals**) in the major academic subjects, regardless of the type of class he or she is placed in (special education and/or regular education). You will also need **goals** for any specialist services. You will need **materials** to review and practice with your child. You will need **regular feedback** from your child's teachers and specialists. You and your child will want to **keep track** of the time you spend and note the signs of improvement.

- By now, you may notice that your child will be able to do some or even most of his or her assignments independently. Your regular practice will have helped them develop increased focus and persistence. Even children with ADD/ADHD will improve with practice. That is great news, and a necessary skill for high school and beyond. **However,** you will still need to know **what** they are working on, and be sure it **relates** to one of their **goals.**

- And **whenever possible**, you should still be **in sight**, and doing something that seems like **work**. Many parents use this time to pay bills or do their own paperwork. It doesn't matter if you read a book, answer work emails or do a crossword puzzle, but **don't** chat on the phone or play a computer game—save that for later. Your child should feel you are "sharing" this "work time", and are available to answer questions or discuss ideas. Obviously, if there's a test coming up, you will be helping your child review and prepare.

- If your child wants to work in his room, take it one step at a time. Let him complete one assignment and show it to you. Track the time it takes and make him aware if he seems to work less efficiently in his room. **Ownership** of his learning style (along with any tendencies to be distracted) is essential, so he can figure out what to do about it. If he can't get the work done in a timely manner on his own, he should work with you nearby for another few days, then try it again. **Talk about** how he will stay on-task, about **how long** he thinks an assignment will take, about being able to have some "down time" **once the work is done.** This important skill is often developed little by little in middle school, with practice and **explicit monitoring.** Even children with significant learning disabilities need to learn to work more independently. Your child needs you to help.

- For this age group, one major difference in the work coming home is that there will often be many more assignments to be completed **over time.** Even in a resource room/learning center or a substantially-separate class, the teachers will be introducing reports or other assignments that are due one week to several weeks later. They will be trying to parallel the regular education curriculum. **They should also be providing explicit instruction and templates or organizers so children know what is expected and how to produce it.** If this does not happen, you as parents need to intervene. It is not your job to **teach** your child how to handle these longer assignments, only to **supervise and practice** the skills that have been taught. Accountability is key; make sure school personnel are doing their jobs.

Direct remedial services to develop specific skills may be a smaller part of your child's IEP by this time, with any luck. If the **services** provided in the past have been **adequate to ensure "effective progress",** your child will have more of the necessary **foundation skills.** With **your help** these skills will have become as automatic as possible, given your child's special needs and learning ability. If these basic skills are **not** automatic by now, I refer you back to an earlier chapter so you can begin the process of getting more and better services to correct the problem.

- By high school, teens are expected to have **fully usable** basic academic skills, **executive functioning** skills to manage their workload, **abstract reasoning, analytic, and independent problem solving** skills, and a **sustained attention span.** For your child with special needs, any or all of these skills may be impaired and not at grade level. The IEP or 504 Accommodation Plan in place should provide the necessary "floor" to allow your child to access the general education curriculum and **be successful.**

- If one of these plans is **not in place** and your child is struggling (or worse), you know what to do. Head back to an earlier chapter and figure out where to begin and what steps to follow to get the necessary services and supports.

- Even with appropriate services, it's still a case of "trust, but verify". No one in the school is going to care about your child's progress the way you do. Regardless of what they may tell you, there are too many students with too many needs, and too few specialists with too few hours to provide services. The equation does not balance.

- Often, your child's **desire for independence** will interfere with getting consistent, adequate help. He or she may want to get through the school day without help from a learning center, or may want to move back to a regular class rather than a smaller, more specialized one. You may be told that homework has been done "in school", or that they can do it on their own, in their rooms. Your alarm bell should be clanging by now. Tell your teen that **the same rules** apply to them as to school personnel (that should amuse your child, at least!). They need to "show you the money" on a consistent basis—assignment books **with assignments**, completed homework, tests and quizzes, and evidence that they are using appropriate organizational aids and executive functioning skills.

- Some teachers use the internet and post a student's current standing, grades, missing assignments, etc, as well as a list of class assignments. This is great where it exists, but in my experience this information will not be available from all your child's teachers.

- You should still arrange to receive regular feedback about your child's services and performance. I prefer some kind of **weekly check-in,** since in high school a student can get **very behind very quickly.** This should be arranged between **you and the teacher.** In an earlier chapter I discussed the problems with asking your teen to get a weekly update from teachers. Avoid making your teen play "tag" with his teachers. If at all possible, set up a system of email or phone messages to get the necessary information.

- Is your child making good use of the services offered? Since these services are almost certainly provided in a group setting, it may be difficult to determine how much **usable help** your child actually receives. If skills don't seem to be improving, if assignments are done poorly or are "falling between the cracks", if tests are being failed or papers are getting poor grades, **speak up.**

- **Someone** in the school will be responsible for monitoring your child's progress. You need to **hold this person responsible** if your teen is having trouble making "effective progress". He or she may need more or different services, more individual help, more monitoring in school. Remember, this is a partnership, and the school needs to do its part. You may have to attend a number of meetings, with your advocate or independent evaluator if possible, to put in place a plan that actually **works.**

- Expectations will vary from course to course and from year to year. The sooner your teen has a plan that meets his needs, the better. It can be adapted over time, but in my experience the difficult part is getting the school to agree to put **appropriate levels of service** in place and then **monitor** the effects of those services. The second part of this contract often feels like I'm pushing water uphill, but it is essential. Without **effective monitoring**, there will probably be no "effective progress".

- Even if your teen is in an out-of-district placement, you should put a system in place to receive the necessary feedback. Progress can sometimes stall, for a variety of reasons. If you "plan backwards" from where you hope your teen will be functioning at the end of 12th grade, you can provide support, ask questions, and help optimize your teen's growth.

- Consider supplementing any school district standardized testing with an independent evaluation, so you know **precisely** what your teen's academic skill levels are. School systems **do not require** 12th grade skills in order to grant a high school diploma. Better to know sooner, rather than later, what your teen can actually do on his or her own. Remember—**you are your child's best advocate,** but you can't help if you don't have the facts.

I've discussed how the expectations and challenges will change as your child with special needs moves from early elementary to upper elementary, from there to middle school, and from middle to high school. There's one more transition, of course, which holds great significance for parents and students alike—going off to college.

One note: Some of you may have children who are biologically related to Frank Sinatra and are determined to do things "My Way". By now, you probably realize that this is your child's personal style (I have 3 of them like this, and I still haven't fully recovered). This is not meant to be a book about child-rearing techniques, so I will make only one point. If your child is determined to follow his or her own path and **resist or refuse** the help that is offered, there is only so much you can do. We are raising human beings here, not training dogs. For this type of child, you need to make the **consequences** of their **choices** extremely clear.

As my husband used to tell our kids, "when you've missed the bus, you've missed the bus." In other words, your teen's performance increasingly becomes his or her responsibility. You can write down on the white board what work is due and when it is due, but it is **your child's responsibility** to do the work and ask for help if needed. If the work is not completed or not handed in, their grades will suffer. If they have poor grades as a result of their choices, you as parents may decide that **they are not ready** for certain privileges or responsibilities. This may include deciding that they are not ready to attend college, even if they get admitted, as long as you are expected to foot the bill.

This may sound harsh, but it is the way the **real world** works, and these discussions with your child should be handled with great love. When your child is ready, **he will be ready**.

This rite of passage will test all the skills—academic, cognitive, social, emotional, and organizational—that your child has been able to acquire over the past 13 years. If the total "package" is enough to get him or her "over the hump", there will be an appropriate transition, an effective ability to learn and manage one's life, and thus **successful performance.** If not, there will be trouble.

If your child is in the process of applying to schools (early senior year), you should be looking objectively at his or her skills, possibly getting an independent evaluation, and possibly hiring outside tutorial services to bring your child up to speed in the areas of need. It is too late to get the public school to improve your child's skills; it needs to be done intensively, individually, and in most cases by a private specialist.

You and your child should do research to find out exactly what support services are available at the colleges they are considering. Many good schools these days offer some level of support or even remediation, since they have discovered that desirable applicants may lack grade level skills or are still struggling with a learning disability. Finding a "good fit" is not a sign of failure on the part of you or your child; it is a sign of good planning for success.

I often see students for independent evaluations in the time period between late junior year and late senior year. The testing and the report are designed to document areas of strength and weakness, academic performance levels, the presence and type of learning disability (if any), and the necessary services that will support learning and success. I strongly encourage parents to send these reports in with an application, or at least to make them available once a student has been accepted.

Colleges have been **very receptive** to these reports. Often, someone from the learning support center will contact me for additional details and recommendations. I evaluate students from public schools as often as ones from private, special education placements. They end up attending a wide range of colleges, some of them quite competitive.

Whether these students succeed depends on several key factors. The most important ones, in my experience, have to do with **personal maturity** and **organizational skills**. Colleges will help students to understand the material and show what they know on tests, through learning center support and test accommodations. They **can't help**, however, if the student doesn't show up for class, doesn't do assignments or turn them in reliably, and doesn't know how to manage his or her time.

The bottom line is that **parents can best help their children** by making sure they have the best organizational skills and are as emotionally ready as possible. No one is perfect, and **few students** are perfectly ready for such a huge **increase** in personal responsibility coupled with a huge **decrease** in structure or supervision. As I said earlier, parents need to be as honest as possible about their teen's level of readiness. Waiting until one is ready to go, while nerve-wracking and even embarrassing, is **much better** for a teen's self-esteem than flunking out, and costs a **great deal less money.**


## A Few Words about Support


Many parents traveling along the Game of Education Life will feel confused, overwhelmed, and discouraged at times. If your child has a significant problem with learning or behavior, you may wonder how you will make it through years of helping, monitoring, and advocating for your child's needs. I have tried to provide answers and a roadmap in this book, but it isn't the same as having someone who will listen patiently and without criticism, and offer support at times.

A "real" person is best—a spouse, family member, good friend, clergy person, or small support group. You will probably also collect some books that you find helpful. You may find a blog with good information or a Parent Advisory Council in your town. Remember—it's good to have more than one support person to turn to. Your support person won't always be available. When a child has significant learning needs, these don't "go away" after a certain amount of time. Spouses have work deadlines, difficult bosses, new jobs to master. Family members and friends may not always be sympathetic or have enough time to listen to your worries and concerns, year after year.

Believe me, I know this from experience. When I was struggling to get my daughter the help she needed, my husband was as concerned and involved as I was, and even so it was often a very lonely road.

In addition, I hope you will make time to take care of your own physical, emotional, and social needs. Happy parents don't guarantee happy children, but a parent who tries to "keep the tank half full" will have more energy and patience to offer a struggling child. As the airlines say, put on your own oxygen mask before helping the child beside you.

# A Closing Thought

So, with your support and active involvement, your child has progressed from preschool to college. It is my hope that he or she has received the necessary services and accommodations to meet their special needs. I hope their learning disabilities or other difficulties were identified early and addressed effectively. I hope they made "effective progress", mastered the necessary skills at each grade level, and are able to access their full potential. I wish them joy and success.

Most important, I hope the information in this book has helped you to be an effective advocate for your child. If I did this right, you were able to get the evaluations and services your child needed for growth and learning. You knew how to monitor progress and get changes made when things weren't working out. You made sure the system met your child's needs. As a result, there is now (or there will be) a well-prepared, emotionally healthy, independent young adult who can make a meaningful contribution to the future of the world.

We need every single one of them, and all they can contribute. I am proud to have helped you on this journey, and happy to have shared what little I know. Most of all, I hope you truly believe what I know for sure:

**You are still, and always will be, the one who knows your child best.**

Good luck to you and your family!

# DECISION TREE FOR DETERMINING ELIGIBILITY FOR SPECIAL EDUCATION SERVICES

Seeee http://www.doe.mass.edu/sped/iep/eng_toc.html and select "Special Education Eligibility Determination".

# INDIVIDUALIZED EDUCATION PROGRAM- BLANK FORM

See http://www.doe.mass.edu/sped/iep/eng_toc.html and select "Administrative Data Sheet: and "Individualized Education Program".

# APPENDIX 3

# BOOK LIST

Amen, Daniel G., M.D. – Change Your Brain, Change Your Life. Three Rivers Press, New York, 1998.

Ayers, A. Jean – Sensory Integration and the Child: 25th Anniversary Edition, Western Psychological Services, 2005.

Bausell, R. Barker – Too Simple to Fail: A Case for Educational Change. Oxford University Press, New York, 2010.

Braaten, Ellen and Gretchen Felopulos – Smart Talk about Psychological Testing for Kids. Guilford Press, New York, 2003.

Brazelton, T. Berry, M.D. – Infants and Mothers: Differences in Development (revised edition). Dell Publishers, New York, 1983.

Brazelton, T. Berry, M.D. and Joshua Sparrow – Touchpoints: Birth to Three. Da Capo Press, 2006 (second edition).

Dawson, Peg – Smart But Scattered: The Revolutionary "Executive Skills" Approach to Helping Kids Reach Their Potential. Guilford Press, New York, 2009.

Eisenberg, Arlene – What to Expect: The Toddler Years. (second edition) Workman Publishing,

Kranowitz, Carol – The Out-of-Sync Child: Recognizing and Coping with Sensory Processing Disorder. Perigree Trade, 2006.

Leach, Penelope – Your Baby and Child. Knopf Publishing, New York, 2010.

Levine, Melvin D., M.D. – Keeping a Head in School: A Student's Book about Learning Abilities and Learning Disorders. Educators Publishing Service, Inc., Cambridge, MA, 1990.

Levine, Melvin D., M.D. – All Kinds of Minds: A young Student's Book About Learning Abilities and Learning Disorders. Educator's Publishing Service, Inc., Cambridge, MA, 1992.

Levine, Melvin D., M.D. – Educational Care: A System for Understanding and Helping Children with Learning Problems at Home and in School. Educator's Publishing Service, Inc., Cambridge, MA, 1994.

Levine, Melvin D., M.D. – A Mind at a Time. Simon and Schuster, New York, 2003.

Meltzer, Lynn – Promoting Executive Functioning in the Classroom: What Works for Special Needs Learners. Guilford Press, New York, 2010.

Rief, Sandra F. – How to Reach and Teach Children with ADD/ADHD: Practical Techniques, Strategies and Interventions. Jossey-Bass, Indianapolis, IN, 2005.

Rubenstein, Marcia Brown – Raising NLD Superstars: What Families with Nonverbal Learning Disabilities Need to Know About Nurturing Confident, Competent Kids. Jessica Kingsley Publications, 2005.

Shaywitz, Sally, M.D. – Overcoming Dyslexia. Vantage Books, 2005.

Siegel, Lawrence M. – The Complete IEP Guide: How to Advocate for Your Special Ed Child. Nolo Publications, Berkeley, CA, 2007 (fifth edition).

Stacey, Roberta – Thinking About Language: Helping Students Say What They Mean and Mean What They Say. Landmark School Outreach Program, Prides Crossing, MA., 2003.

Tough, Paul – Whatever it Takes: Geoffrey Canada's Quest to Change Harlem and America. Mariner Books, New York, 2009.

Tomlinson, Carol Ann – The Differentiated Classroom. The Association for Supervision and Curriculum Development, Alexandria, VA, 1999.

Turecki, Stanley (author) and Leslie Tonner (co-author) – The Difficult Child: Expanded and Revised Edition. Bantam Publishers, New York, 2000.

Wright, Pam and Pete Wright – From Emotions to Advocacy (second edition): The Special Education Survival Guide. Harbor House Law Press, Inc., Hartfield, VA, 2007.

# APPENDIX 4

# FEDERAL LAW

Here is the URL to find the Federal Special Education Law, known as the Individuals with Disabilities Education Improvement Act of 2004. It is over 100 pages in length, and not designed for "casual reading". I include it here for convenience, but I am hoping parents will be working with an advocate, attorney, or skilled evaluator (preferably a psychologist) who will be familiar with the federal law and relevant state laws. This person will help you understand how the laws relate to your child and his or her needs.

www.idea.ed.gov

In addition, here is the website for the Massachusetts Department of Education's Special Education site, which also has links to both the federal and state laws. At this site, you can also find helpful booklets such as "Hearing Rules for Special Education Appeals" and "Parents Notice of Procedural Safeguards". These will have relevant material for parents in any state.

http://www.doe.mass.edu/sped/laws.html

# STATE DEPARTMENT OF EDUCATION WEBSITES

The Department of Education in each state is the place to go to find information about state and federal law, curriculum materials, available programs in cities and towns as well as the state itself, and contact information so you can ask questions.

Please note: these addresses were correct as of the time of publication.

Alabama: www.alsde.edu

Alaska: www.eed.state.ak.us

Arizona: www.ade.state.az.us

Arkansas: www.arkansased.org

California: www.cde.ca.gov

Colorado: www.cde.state.co.us

Connecticut: www.state.ct.us/sde

Delaware: www.doe.state.de.us

District of Columbia: www.k12.dc.us

Florida: www.fldoe.org

Georgia: www.doe.k12.ga.us

Hawaii: www.doe.k12.hi.us

Idaho: www.sde.state.id.us

Illinois: www.isbe.state.il.us

Indiana: www.doe.state.in.us

Iowa: www.state.ia.us/educate

Kansas: www.ksde.org

Kentucky: www.kde.state.ky.us

Louisiana: www.doe.state.la.us

Maine: www.state.me.us/education

Maryland: www.marylandpublicschools.org

Massachusetts: www.doe.mass.edu

Michigan: www.michigan.gov/mde

Minnesota: http://cfl.state.mn.us

Mississippi: www.mde.k12.ms.us

Missouri: www.dese.mo.us

Montana: www.opi.state.mt.us

Nebraska: www.nde.state.ne.us

Nevada: www.doe.nv.gov

New Hampshire: www.ed.state.nh.us

New Jersey: www.state.nj.us/education

New Mexico: www.ped.state.nm.us

New York: www.nysed.gov

North Carolina: www.ncpublicschools.org

North Dakota: www.dpi.state.nd.us

Ohio: www.ode.state.oh.us

Oklahoma: www.sde.state.ok.us

Oregon: www.ode.state.or.us

Pennsylvania: www.pde.state.pa.us

Rhode Island: www.ridoe.net

South Carolina: www.myscschools.com

South Dakota: http://doe.sd.gov

Tennessee: www.state.tn.us/education

Texas: www.tea.state.tx.us

Utah: www.usoe.k12.ut.us

Vermont: www.education.vermont.gov

Virginia: www.doe.virginia.gov

Washington: www.k12.wa.us

West Virginia: http://wvde.state.wv.us

Wisconsin: www.dpi.state.wi.us

Wyoming: www.k12.wy.us

# APPENDIX 6

# SPECIAL EDUCATION ORGANIZATIONS

While this is not intended as an exhaustive list, the following organizations are well-regarded and will have a variety of reference materials, including information about support groups, summer or respite services, curriculum materials, educational or remedial services for children with special needs, special academic programs, legal services, advocacy services, and articles on topics of interest. I hope some of these will prove useful to parents looking for additional information to help their children.

Educators Publishing Service
http://eps.schoolspecialty.com
a source for Primary Phonics workbooks, controlled readers, and other educational materials that can be used in school or at home to reinforce skills and mastery in all curriculum areas

Federation for Children with Special Needs, Boston, MA
www.fcsn.org
publishes "A Parent's Guide to Special Education"; provides information for parents about special education laws and programs; trains parents to advocate more effectively for their children. Provides a training course for special education advocates. A wealth of resources.

Federal Resource Center for Special Education, Washington, DC
www.rrfcnetwork.org

Family Education Network, Boston, MA
http://familyeducation.com
information on learning disabilities and children with special needs

Lindamood-Bell
www.lindamoodbell.com
products designed to help children with specific learning disabilities develop specific skills for reading, spelling, comprehension, language understanding, and math, as well as training and workshops for special education teachers

McGraw-Hill Publishers
https://www.mheonline.com
publishes SRA and other leveled, controlled vocabulary reading programs, many of which have proven track records for helping children develop reading mastery

Children's Defense Fund, Washington, DC
www.childrensdefense.org

American Bar Association Commission on Mental and Physical Disability Law
Washington, DC
www.abanet.org/disability

The International Dyslexia Association, Baltimore, MD
www.interdys.org
publishes articles about dyslexia and remedial programs for these students, including Orton-Gillingham reading

LD Online
www.ldonline.com
provides articles for parents, teachers, and children about learning disabilities, methodologies, laws, and educational programs

Learning Disabilities Association of America, Pittsburgh, PA
www.ldaamerica.org

Children and Adults with Attention Deficit Disorder (CHADD), Landover, MD
www.chadd.org
information and opportunities to network for parents of children with ADD/ADHD, as well as professionals working with this population, and adults with ADD

Internet Resources for Special Children
www.irsc.org

National Association for Professional Special Education Advocates (NAPSEA)
www.napsea.co
resources and training for educational advocates, as well as information for parents about how to find and work with an advocate